Book reviews/press comments for the first edition (2007)

". . . is very timely . . . a good analysis . . . a highly readable and incisive book . . . provides a clear guide to industry insiders . . . and a detailed understanding for those who read research".
Geoff de Freitas, *Shanghai Business Review*, May 2008

". . . sharp, readable and timely book . . ."
The Correspondent, the magazine of the Foreign Correspondents' Club of Hong Kong, Sept/Oct 2007 issue

". . . definitive best-practice guide . . . a very readable and engaging book filled with sound advice and workable recommendations".
Keith Hall, *China Daily*, April 13, 2007

". . . excellent book".
R. Sivanithy, *Singapore Business Times*, April 2, 2007

". . . an essential textbook for securities professionals around the world".
Johannes Ridu, *Malaysian Business/New Straits Times*, April 1, 2007

"It ought to be mandatory reading for courses focused on securities research".
MoneyLife, India, July 5, 2007

"Extensive case studies are also well-used and interesting. This is a sound and generally useful piece of work for all investment market professionals and, indeed, investors everywhere".
James Rose, *Corporate Governance Asia*

". . . plenty of practical examples".
CPA Australia, June 2007

Endorsements of the first edition (2007)

There is a strong need for this book . . . This book is relevant in any setting. It will equip analysts with many useful tools to help them achieve success.

Mark Mobius, *President of Templeton Emerging Markets Fund*

This guide to doing it properly is an obvious selection for the bookshelf of anyone who aspires to offer investment advice and a fine reference for anyone who receives such advice.

Jake van der Kamp, *Financial Columnist of* South China Morning Post

At last, here's a comprehensive yet easy-to-read guide explaining all the best practice principles involved in writing securities research. It is full of useful information . . . I highly recommend it.

Anthony Espina, *Chairman of Hong Kong Stockbrokers Association*

. . . essential reading for all people involved in writing securities research.

Andrew Leeming, *author of* The Super Analysts

Writing Securities Research

A Best Practice Guide

Second Edition

Writing Securities Research

A Best Practice Guide

Second Edition

Jeremy Bolland

WILEY

John Wiley & Sons (Asia) Pte. Ltd.

Other Wiley Editorial Offices

John Wiley & Sons, 111 River Street, Hoboken, NJ 07030, USA
John Wiley & Sons, The Atrium, Southern Gate, Chichester, West Sussex, P019 8SQ,
    United Kingdom
John Wiley & Sons (Canada) Ltd., 5353 Dundas Street West, Suite 400, Toronto, Ontario,
    M9B 6HB, Canada
John Wiley & Sons Australia Ltd., 42 McDougall Street, Milton, Queensland 4064,
    Australia
Wiley-VCH, Boschstrasse 12, D-69469 Weinheim, Germany

Library of Congress Cataloging-in-Publication Data

ISBN 978-0-470-82602-7

Typeset in 10/12pt Cheltenham by MPS Limited, A Macmillan Company, Chennai, India
Printed in Singapore by Toppan Security Printing Pte. Ltd.
10 9 8 7 6 5 4 3 2 1

Contents

To James

Not that you need any incentive to do well at school and not that a career in compliance is to be sniffed at, but sometimes I wish my father had alerted me to the consequences of not concentrating in class . . .

Foreword

Since Jeremy Bolland's first 2007 guide to writing securities research, there has been a remarkable change in the global financial system. Markets have had the most severe crisis in recent history with major companies failing and many investors suffering substantial losses. These events have underlined the critical importance of high-level securities research and the effective communication of the research. More and more investors now realize the need to understand the risks associated with their investments.

This need to better understand the risks associated with investing is answered by this second edition of *Writing Securities Research*. In this edition, Mr. Bolland greatly expands the section on investment risk. He includes many new case studies drawn from the financial crisis on various aspects of risk, including—crucially—a whole range of corporate governance issues.

In bull markets, some investors may not be so concerned about corporate governance issues. However, in bear or volatile markets, analysts need to be more specific in explaining the differentiating factors related to their recommendations. A good understanding of how well or badly companies are being managed is becoming increasingly important for both institutional and retail investors. The book therefore examines corporate governance issues such as social responsibility, executive compensation, equal treatment of shareholders, related-party transactions, independent non-executive directors and risk management. As usual Mr. Bolland uses real-life case studies to demonstrate each of these aspects. He rightly concludes that an analyst's job is not just about analyzing numbers; it's about assessing people too. More and more securities analysts need to understand this essential requirement.

Whereas the first edition of *Writing Securities Research* probably appealed more to sell-side equity analysts working in global investment banks and brokerages, this second edition more clearly distinguishes between such analysts and those working on the buy-side such as those working for mutual fund and hedge fund management companies. It also examines analysts' roles with respect to credit rating agencies, independent research output and sovereign wealth fund investment programs as well as specialized areas such as credit default swaps and investments complying with *Shari'ah* law.

The book is thus a comprehensive guide for securities research analysts around the world. Analysts who want to write research that is clear, concise and actionable should carefully read and digest the contents of this book.

I would say that it should also be compulsory reading for research managers, compliance officers, editors, securities lawyers, securities regulators and students of investment and finance.

Let's look at a summary of each chapter. The first chapter starts with key best-practice principles related to writing securities research such as fairness, honesty, integrity, transparency, accountability and consistency. An important theme emphasized in the first chapter is the use of publicly available information to avoid accusations of insider trading, rumor-spreading and defamation. Mr. Bolland also defines what would be considered securities research and thus what would fall under securities regulations. As a result of the financial crisis, the regulators' purview has evidently widened and now encompasses all types of derivatives such as credit default swaps. Mr. Bolland delves into the legal requirements and the correct interpretation of regulations issued by the SEC and other regulatory organizations around the world.

In the second chapter, topics include the proper methodology for disclosing the reasons for valuations, reporting changes in valuations and properly disclosing risks including any perceived corporate governance issues.

The third chapter looks into key issues relating to research independence. Here Mr. Bolland covers the potential conflicts of interest that analysts face. These don't just include the well-documented conflicts between analysts and their investment banking colleagues, but also potential conflicts between analysts and their sales and trading colleagues, their clients, and the companies they write about.

This is followed in the fourth chapter by a number of important activities surrounding research, such as e-mails, blogs and other communications. Most important here is the discussion regarding how seemingly innocent e-mails can end up in the public domain and, if their content is in conflict with the published research, give rise to potential liabilities.

The final chapter deals with a number of cogent and helpful suggestions on how best to communicate with readers in the securities industry, including tips regarding the careful use of words to prevent misunderstandings. Again, a number of interesting and often comical case studies are used to illustrate the concepts.

While new rules and regulations will inevitably be introduced around the world covering a wide range of topics impacting banks' capital adequacy, proprietary trading, hedge funds, derivatives, credit rating agencies and executive compensation, Mr. Bolland argues that securities research analysts are already subject to enough regulation. Rather than more regulation for analysts, he advocates the need for more education.

The world of securities research is very dynamic with analysts confronted with new challenges. One key challenge is the need for transparency in the way research is compensated. The shifting resource pool of analyst talent away from the high-cost and highly taxed developed markets to lower-cost emerging markets is another.

One thing is clear: analysts who are able to generate original investment ideas, and satisfy the information and analytical requirements of their client or clients while, at the same time, adhering to the highest ethical standards and stringent compliance rules will be very well placed to meet any new challenges facing them.

Jeremy Bolland's book helps to equip analysts with many useful tools to help them achieve securities research success.

Dr. Mark Mobius
Executive Chairman
Templeton Asset Management Ltd.
Author of *Equities: An Introduction to the Core Concepts*

Preface

Summary points and recommendations

- Sell-side securities analysts operating in the major markets around the world have to jump through hoops of fire to get their research published. There are research-specific procedures to follow, such as making sure they have the appropriate registrations and licenses, providing the necessary disclosures of interests and relationships, and ensuring their research is distributed to clients fairly.
- Then there are market rules concerning the illegal use of inside information and the spreading of rumors to manipulate prices. There are also other society-wide laws to adhere to, covering for example misrepresentation, defamation and intellectual property rights.
- Brokers, financial advisers, sales, marketers and traders should also appreciate that their own communications with clients might constitute research, and be subject to the same disclosure and distribution standards.
- Even buy-side analysts who prepare research for use only by internal fund managers need to avoid breaching market rules concerning the illegal use of inside information and the manipulation of prices.
- Indeed all investors are subject to the same rules and regulations. Press commentators and independent bloggers are not immune either. It remains to be seen how effectively regulators will be able to police the spreading of rumors by citizen-journalists and twitterers.
- Whatever new regulations are in store for banks, credit rating agencies or hedge funds, and whatever changes are made to accounting standards or executive remuneration practices, I would argue that equity analysts in developed markets don't need more layers of regulation; but more education and explanation of the underlying principles are evidently needed.
- In terms of research, securities regulators have traditionally been more concerned with equities research. However, they are increasingly turning their attention to research of other asset classes such as bonds. Even credit default swaps (CDSs) and contracts for difference (CFDs) are encroaching into the world of securities from a regulatory perspective.

- Analysts and other securities professionals are the focus of regulators' surveillance. Those who inadvertently breach regulations should not dig deeper holes for themselves by covering up their mistakes—they should alert their supervisors or compliance officers immediately.
- Analysts who follow the proper procedures and secure the appropriate approvals should have their employers' support in any investigation by regulators. If they go out on a limb and bypass the approval processes, they'll be on their own.
- Without the support of the employer, it will be even easier for a regulator to pressure an analyst suspected of wrongdoing into making a settlement.
- Penalties are serious nowadays. They are serious enough for improper conduct, but are even more serious for actual market abuse where illicit trading occurs. Where insufficient evidence is available for a criminal case, a regulator can always bring a civil action.
- It's not necessarily the published product that represents the greatest risk for analysts and other securities professionals. What they put in e-mails and say on the phone to clients and colleagues may also expose them to risks.
- Regulators and courts don't even need to understand the complexities in the arguments of analysts' research or in the products being sold; they merely need to catch inconsistencies in the way they are being brokered or promoted.
- By being the first to identify an M&A target, an analyst would probably be presumed by a regulator or court to be either trading on inside information or spreading false rumors to manipulate the security's price.
- There is a third possibility—that the analyst might just have arrived at his (or her) conclusions through some good research. Because the analyst runs an especially high risk of attracting the regulator's attention by putting a company into play, he must be even more meticulous than usual in demonstrating that his research is based on publicly available (and verifiable) facts and reasonable assumptions, and must make sure he has his employer's full support.
- Potential conflicts of interest abound. A good research report or credit rating has the power to move the market. All sorts of people will be trying to persuade the analyst to write favorably or unfavorably on a particular security. Analysts need to stick to their guns, and give their own honest and independent views.
- Analysts should not rely totally on what a company's management tells them, or what the press, regulators, auditors and credit rating agencies publish about the company; they need to do some investigative digging for themselves. Even though it may be difficult to identify fraud, ana-

lysts should at least be able to determine whether a company is devoting sufficient resources to risk management, and should have a good feel as to how pervasive the ethical culture is throughout the firm.

- In other words, it's not just about analyzing the numbers; it's about assessing people too. Analysts should dig deeper if they spot anything suspicious, for example, irregular accounting, inconsistent disclosures or unfair treatment of any particular class of stakeholder.

- Analysts not only need to justify their views and recommendations but they also need to highlight the risks to their investment case. Investors always want to know about risks, corporate governance issues and dividend yield, but they probably focus on these aspects even more during bear markets and periods of volatility.

- If a covered company loses, or is at risk of losing, a lawsuit in one country, the analyst would need to gauge the likelihood of the company losing similar cases in other countries. The analyst would need to advise clients as to what the financial and reputational implications may be, not just for the company in question but also for other covered companies within the sector or market. Might the company be exposed to potential damages claims and class-action suits?

- Analysts may need to satisfy specific criteria for sets of clients who have special investment needs, such as socially responsible investors or *Shari'ah*-compliant investors. Analysts could screen their universes to find stocks that satisfy these requirements.

- Many investors would not entertain the notion of buying into a company with a poor corporate governance record. Some activist hedge funds, however, might only be interested in investing in such companies, since that's where they see potential for change and potential value.

- Analysts need to give clients what they want, which means actionable ideas based on good research rather than a regurgitation of news. If analysts don't give investors what they want, someone else will.

- In order to be user-friendly for clients, analysts need to reverse their way of thinking. From initially being immersed in numbers, analysis and details, they need to emerge with a clear message or story in words.

- The title of the report must be especially meaningful and eye-catching, since this may be the only part of an analyst's report that some clients may see. Other headlines, subtitles and bullet points should help tell the story succinctly.

- As in any business, clients will only deal with analysts who can not only demonstrate that they make a good product (that is, good research and good investment calls) and provide good after-sales service, but who are transparent, trustworthy and fair too.

- However the business end of securities research develops, for example in terms of how sell-side research is paid for, one thing seems certain—that there'll always be a demand for good research and good investment ideas as well as for M&A advice. Analysts just need to make sure that they avoid the traps along the way. Hopefully this book will help them do that.
- As a final note, the global financial crisis of 2007–2009 has evidently put to rest the myth that there's such a thing as a risk-free investment. The terms "as safe as houses" and "as liquid as cash" will surely never hold the same level of conviction again, at least not until the next asset bubble . . .

Background

Background to the second edition

Despite assurances from many quarters in the summer of 2007 that the sub-prime debt problems in the U.S. were relatively small, local and manageable, turmoil in the global capital markets and economies nevertheless ensued throughout 2008 and into 2009. Bear Stearns was the first high-profile casualty to report significant losses, in two of its hedge funds. Credit rating agencies were among those most heavily criticized for failing to give sufficient warning to the investment community as to how serious, widespread and complex the problem was. In the U.K. the crisis escalated with a bank run on Northern Rock. An unprecedented government guarantee that depositors' money was safe succeeded in stemming the tide. However, this action led to criticism against the government on the "moral hazard" grounds that bailing out the private sector would only encourage greater risk-taking in the future. The same criticism was made against the U.S. Federal Reserve for lowering interest rates to relieve the crisis at a time when inflation was supposedly the major financial risk. It also seemed a little ironic that the government was trying to make credit easier when it was easy credit that was the root of the problem to start with.

By the end of March 2008, the global financial system was in serious trouble. At least one global investment bank, namely Bear Stearns, was on its way into the history books when it was taken over by J.P. Morgan for a fraction of its earlier worth. The CEOs and other senior executives at Bear Stearns, UBS, Citigroup, Merrill Lynch and Nomura had lost their jobs, following billions of dollars of subprime-related losses and writedowns by those firms. Thousands of securities professionals had also lost their jobs.

The FBI had opened criminal investigations into 14 organizations, and the SEC had separately opened a raft of civil investigations, with securities firms and investment banks being well represented in both sets of investigations. Organizations as diverse as Barclays in the U.S. to Wingecarribee Shire Council in Australia had filed lawsuits against the securities firms that had advised them on their subprime-related investments. One of these was Lehman Brothers, whose problems were only just starting.

Also by this time, Fitch had downgraded the AAA rating of major monoline bond insurers Ambac and Financial Guaranty Insurance Co. (FGIC), with formal warnings being issued by Moody's and Standard & Poor's of possible downgrades for these and other major bond insurers. The implications for the ratings and therefore the investability of the bonds that these insurers insured were dire indeed.

To prove that bad news comes together, this period also saw the world's largest-ever trading scandal, when the extent of the loss-making positions built up by a so-called "rogue trader" at France's Société Générale were revealed, demonstrating yet again the shortcomings of risk management procedures at large banks.

By early October 2008, many of the global investment banks had reached settlements with U.S. regulators regarding allegations that they had misled investors into believing that the auction-rate securities that they were buying were as safe and as liquid as cash. Indeed, by this time, there weren't even any pure global investment banks left. Lehman Brothers had filed for bankruptcy protection, with the carcass subsequently being carved up between Barclays and Nomura, and Merrill Lynch had been bought by Bank of America. The last two independent investment banks, namely Morgan Stanley and Goldman Sachs, had capitulated and had become deposit-taking banks that henceforth would be regulated by the Federal Reserve rather than by the SEC. It was the end of the Wall Street era as we knew it.

Any notion that resolving the credit crisis would be left to free market forces was dispelled when the U.S. government rescued and took effective control of American International Group (AIG), one of the world's largest insurers, as well as Fannie Mae and Freddie Mac, the two large U.S. mortgage finance companies (or Fonie and Fraudie, as some wags cited by *Forbes* called them).[1] In the largest bank failure in U.S. history, the government took control of Washington Mutual before arranging a fire sale of the company to J.P. Morgan. Shortly afterward, the controversial Troubled Asset Relief Program (TARP) was finally approved. Under the plan, US$700 billion of taxpayers' money would be allocated to buy up distressed assets from struggling financial institutions (although the focus of the plan soon shifted to consumers such as students, car buyers and credit-card users). The federal insurance ceiling for bank deposits was raised, from US$100,000 to US$250,000, and various tax breaks and executive pay restrictions were also included.

The crisis had by now become one of confidence and trust on a global scale, where liquidity had frozen. Banks were not lending to each other due to counterparty risk, where each bank was afraid that the other bank would not be able to honor its commitments. The threat of bankruptcy was hanging over at least one sovereign state, namely Iceland, given the disproportionate size of its banking sector to its overall economy. In the U.K., Bradford & Bingley followed Northern Rock in being nationalized. The government then took control of Royal Bank of Scotland. Fortis and Hypo Real Estate had to be rescued by the European governments concerned. You knew things had gotten really bad when this joke was making the rounds: "Uncertainty has now hit Japan—Origami Bank has folded, Sumo Bank has gone belly up and Bonsai Bank plans to cut some of its branches."[2]

The Irish government caused a stir by guaranteeing the deposits of the six largest Irish banks. Greece instituted similar measures. Partly fearing a migration of deposits from their own banking systems to the Irish and Greek banks, but more out of a need for collective action anyway, the European Union governments agreed to a set of principles for rescuing troubled banks. This included a deposit insurance scheme to guarantee bank deposits of €50,000 for one year. Central banks and governments around the world joined forces in cutting interest rates, and in guaranteeing bank deposits and inter-bank lending in a concerted effort to get money flowing again. Further full and partial nationalizations were undertaken.

World leaders attending the first G20 Summit on Financial Markets and the World Economy in mid-November 2008 in Washington showed their determination to resolve the financial crisis and to make changes to the world's financial system. By the end of November, Bloomberg had calculated that the U.S. government alone had pledged over US$7.7 trillion, or half the value of everything produced in the nation the previous year, to prop up the financial system. This included the TARP funds referred to above as well as over US$300 billion[3] to bail out Citigroup, once the largest bank in the world by assets. Controversially, General Motors and Chrysler managed to secure US$17.4 billion in emergency funding, albeit with strings attached. This staved off the prospect of blue-collar redundancies on a massive scale, at least for the time being.[4] The wider issue was where to draw the line with the bailouts. Two porn moguls—*Hustler* magazine founder, Larry Flynt, and the creator of the *Girls Gone Wild* video series, Joe Francis—probed these limits by asking Congress for US$5 billion "to rejuvenate the sexual appetite of America" during these hard-up times. Congress wasn't going to be taken for a ride, however.

By the beginning of 2009, we thought we were getting immune to hearing about multi-billion-dollar losses. But who would have expected a former non-executive chairman of NASDAQ to be charged with perhaps the biggest securities fraud of all time? Bernard Madoff[5] had by his own admission been operating a huge Ponzi scheme[6] for years by paying above-average returns to existing investors from the principal received from new investors. He himself estimated that client losses amounted to over US$50 billion. This was followed two months later by allegations of a US$8 billion fraud involving Sir Allen Stanford, a flamboyant billionaire, which bore striking similarities to the Madoff scandal. Who could one trust, and which hedge fund or bank would be next to collapse under the weight of losses or be exposed as a sham, worried investors asked themselves. (Some would argue that the developed world's national pension plans constitute huge Ponzi schemes, whereby each generation pays the next generation's retirement benefits until one day they can't. Even the printing of money by central banks to pay for the financial bailouts could qualify since the burden becomes the next generation's problem. This was emotively depicted by the U.K. Conservative Party's advertising campaign showing a baby with the caption that it had Dad's nose, Mum's eyes and Gordon Brown's debt.)

Illustrious names were struggling to survive. Lehman and Bear Stearns had already packed their bags and left Wall Street. Citigroup survived but had to be split in two. In retailing, Circuit City had to go into liquidation, while in the U.K. both Woolworths and the venerable Waterford Wedgwood went into administration. High-profile individuals including the German billionaire Adolf Merckle and the French aristocrat René-Thierry Magon de la Villehuchet had committed suicide, soon to be followed by the CFO of Freddie Mac, David Kellermann, who was found hanged at his home.

Meanwhile, there was civil unrest in Thailand and Greece, and heightened tension between India and Pakistan following high-profile terrorist attacks in Mumbai. Israel conducted its bloodiest campaign in Gaza since 1967, in retaliation against rocket attacks launched against Israeli towns by Hamas militants who in turn claimed to be retaliating against Israeli occupation of what they regard as Palestinian land. Piracy off the east coast of Africa was escalating at an alarming rate. Country after country was following the U.S. into recession. Zimbabwe was suffering hyperinflation, not to mention a severe cholera outbreak. The Seychelles and Ecuador had defaulted on their foreign debt. Iceland, Hungary, Latvia, Ukraine, Belarus and Pakistan had to go cap in hand to the International Monetary Fund (IMF). Many stock markets around the world had halved in value, with some experiencing even greater falls. Bond, currency and commodity markets had also been extremely volatile.

The inauguration in January 2009 of Barack Obama as U.S. president provided some glimmer of hope for a new world. His first measure was to introduce a stimulus package for the U.S. amounting to nearly US$800 billion. World leaders at the annual World Economic Forum in Davos, Switzerland, didn't really leave with any firm commitments or proposals other than hopefully a common understanding of the risks that protectionism poses to world growth. However, each country would have to balance these risks against the potential for social unrest locally. As the head of the world's most populous country, Premier Wen Jiabao promised to boost China's economy with "extraordinary measures". In a speech a few days later at Cambridge University, in the U.K., he also appealed to the business community everywhere to raise ethical standards: "We should call on all enterprises to take up their social responsibilities. Within the body of every businessman should flow the blood of morality."

It wasn't really until the second G20 Leaders' Summit was held in London, on April 2, 2009, that markets began to realize that the worst was probably behind them and that a new world order lay ahead of them. Global leaders achieved a remarkable sense of united purpose, both in terms of offering financial support to stimulate the global economy and in terms of agreeing in principle to reforming and improving the global financial system. It was a defining moment in history, which Professor Gordon Redding of INSEAD likened to the moment in 1517 when Martin Luther pinned his 95 theses to the door of the Castle Church in Wittenberg, Germany, thereby challenging the authority of the Catholic Church and sparking the Reformation. Like that event, the G20 Summit was the venue where the world's peoples, as represented by their political leaders, stood up to the greedy bankers and executives who had abused their position of dominance in the financial and business world. Enough was enough. Things were going to be different from now on.

At least things were going to be different just as soon as world leaders had dealt with other global crises that were escalating, such as the H1N1 (swine flu) pandemic, nuclear proliferation and climate change. Healthcare reform was also high on Barack Obama's domestic agenda. However difficult it would be for world leaders to agree between themselves on measures to be taken, they would still have political opposition at home to overcome.

Background to the first edition

The global financial crisis of 2007–2009 sets the scene for the second edition of *Writing Securities Research*. The background to the first edition, published in 2007, seemed dramatic at the time. However, in hindsight it merely represented a foretaste of a much bigger crisis to come. The global dotcom bubble that burst in 2000 was just another example of excessive valuations that have been the hallmark of market bubbles going back centuries.

The scandals surrounding Enron and WorldCom in the U.S., and then Ahold and Parmalat in Europe, prompted recriminations against auditors, investment bankers and securities-research analysts for their failure to identify the problems. Arthur Andersen paid a heavy price. Eliot Spitzer took the major U.S. and global investment banks and securities brokers to task, and exacted from them, if not a heavy price in the overall scheme of their balance sheets, then at least a commitment to change the way they run their businesses. Neither did the stock exchanges avoid embarrassment. It was only a few years earlier that U.K. companies such as Mirror Group, BCCI and Barings were the focus of attention, and before these it was Drexel Burnham Lambert in the U.S. that hit the headlines as the prime mover and ultimate casualty of the junk bond craze.

The changing regulatory environment

Each era brings new crises, bubbles, scandals and scapegoats, but the underlying themes and the human motives that drive them and intertwine them are invariably the same. The associations between market bubbles and both fear and greed are well established.

The U.S. reacted to the Enron and WorldCom scandals by introducing the Sarbanes-Oxley Act in 2002, and tightening up existing securities regulations. Repercussions were felt around the world, with regulations being introduced and revised from the U.K. and Europe to Hong Kong and Japan. New or enhanced measures addressed auditor and director independence, whistle-blowing policies and the lines between investment banking and research.

Then it was the credit rating agencies' turn. Following the passing of the Credit Agency Reform Act in the U.S. in 2006, the SEC introduced in June 2007 an oversight system for credit rating agencies. These now need to be formally registered as "nationally recognized statistical rating organizations" (NRSROs), rather than being passively recognized as such through so-called "No-Action Letters" issued by the SEC as had been the case since 1975. In December, the SEC, for the first time, granted this status to an agency, namely Egan-Jones, that gets paid not by the issuers whose bonds it rates but by its institutional investor clients. In June 2008, the New York Attorney General, Andrew Cuomo, reached a settlement with Moody's, Standard & Poor's and Fitch with respect to the way they get paid and the disclosures they need to make. Then the SEC announced measures in December that would "ensure that firms provide more meaningful ratings and greater disclosure to investors". However, one criticism that was not addressed was the fact that the need to use credit ratings is hard-wired into, that is mandated by, securities regulations. The SEC went some way to addressing this concern by announcing in September 2009 that it would eliminate references in "certain SEC rules and forms".

Meanwhile, Charlie McCreevy, E.U. internal markets commissioner, outlined measures that would be taken in Europe. The *Financial Times* quoted Mr. McCreevy in evocative terms referring to international regulators: ". . . no supervisor appears to have got as much as a sniff of the rot at the heart of the structured finance rating process before it all blew up." German Chancellor Angela Merkel highlighted the need for a European credit rating agency to challenge the dominance of the U.S. agencies. Similarly, Ronald Arculli, chairman of the Hong Kong Exchange, urged that Asia should have its own credit rating agencies.

During the financial crisis, the hedge funds attracted their fare share of attention too, with some commentators attributing the demise of Bear Stearns and Lehman Brothers to their rumor-driven short-selling tactics. Emergency measures were introduced on both sides of the Atlantic to curb naked short-selling (while, interestingly, the Chinese authorities pressed ahead with plans to allow short-selling). Market participants meanwhile argued for the reinstatement of the up-tick rule whereby traders could only sell a stock short when the stock price was rising. To an extent, this particular issue demonstrates how regulators can chase their own tails by constantly tinkering with new regulations; and that no particular style or set of regulations will be all things to all markets at all times. The debate about fair-value accounting is another such example.

Incidentally, it doesn't really matter if the readers of this book operate in a principles-based regulatory regime, as has been favored in the U.K. and Europe, or a rules-based system, as has been practiced in the U.S. Over recent years, there has been debate as to whether the U.S. should adopt a more principles-based stance with respect to its securities regulations (and indeed to its accounting standards). Personally, I appreciate the view espoused by Sir Howard Davies, the founding chairman of the U.K.'s Financial Services Authority, as descriptively portrayed in the *Wall Street Journal* of November 29, 2006, that once you have said that there should be no killing, there is no need to specifically prohibit sticking a hunting knife through another man's sternum. As Sir David Tweedie, chairman of the International Accounting Standards Board, said in an interview with the *FT* in April 2008 when warning that any new post-credit-crisis standards would need to be worked out carefully, "We have to be careful that if we slam the door shut on one form . . . that they (clever accountants) are not disappearing out of another door. . . . This is why we usually prefer principles to rules." Set against these comments, however, was the comment by Hector Sants, who became the chief executive of the U.K.'s FSA in the depths of the financial crisis, that a principles-based approach does not work with participants who have no principles. The financial crisis will inevitably have swung the pendulum away from the acceptance of a light regulatory touch to calls for a more stringent regime, and one that may be more globally interconnected than ever before.

The financial crisis has also heated up the debate as to whether financial services and products should be regulated: i) by a single authority, as with the FSA in the U.K.; ii) by multiple authorities, as in the U.S. and Hong Kong; or iii) in a so-called twin peaks model as practiced in Australia, where regulation is split functionally between prudential oversight and market conduct supervision. The regulatory structure in the U.S. has certainly taken a battering. The change of status for Morgan Stanley and Goldman Sachs from investment banks to deposit-taking banks reduced the SEC's scope of influence in favor of the Fed. The SEC's reputation was also tarnished by the Madoff and Stanford scandals, although the regulator has since earned brownie points with its high-profile cases against Galleon *et al* and Goldman Sachs. The debate as to whether swaps should be regulated as securities or as insurance products would be muted if there were only one financial regulator in the U.S.

Critics have claimed that in the lead up to the financial crisis, regulators and state authorities were out of the loop in terms of knowing what banks and other companies were really doing and how much risk they were taking. Ultimately governments had to step in to rescue the markets, for the sake of the common good. As mentioned, the measures included nationalization and direct investment in companies.

The then U.K. prime minister, Gordon Brown, summarized in a letter published in the *Washington Post* on October 17, 2008, what he thought was needed to root out the irresponsible lending that was at the heart of the crisis: cross-border supervision of financial institutions; shared global standards for accounting and regulation; a more responsible approach to executive remuneration that rewards hard work, effort and enterprise but not irresponsible risk-taking; and the renewal of the international institutions to make them effective early-warning systems for the world economy. He also urged world leaders to seek a global trade agreement and reject protectionism.

The leaders of the G20 nations, representing 85 percent of the world's economy, picked up the baton when they gathered at the Summit on Financial Markets and the World Economy in Washington in November 2008. They agreed in principle on the need to reform financial regulation. However, it was not until the second G20 summit, in April 2009, that a unified course of action started to unfold. New measures would address issues such as credit rating agencies, banks' capital adequacy, executive compensation, accounting rules, hedge fund registration and credit derivatives. Getting the details agreed upon by so many constituents would of course be more difficult, as proved to be the case at the G20 summit in Pittsburgh in September 2009.

Furthermore, as the global economy started to improve, other issues such as health care reform and climate change started to gain prominence, at least as far as the U.S. president was concerned. These would delay the implementation of the financial reforms, and the lost impetus would inevitably mean that the substance of the reforms would be diluted. For example, some argued that former Federal Reserve chairman Paul Volcker's plan announced in January 2010 to separate U.S. banking activities that are useful to society (e.g., commercial banking such as deposit-taking and lending) from those risk-taking activities that raise a bank's profitability potential (for example, the hedge fund, private equity and proprietary trading businesses) wouldn't go far enough to ensure that banks couldn't become too big to fail. Demarcation lines between the Fed and the SEC might in future be drawn less along functional lines, that is the type of business the financial institution is involved in, and more on the size of the organization and the level of systemic risk it might pose. As for the FSA in the U.K., its future apparently would not be guaranteed under a Conservative government.

What may be a truism is that no one structure or set of regulations can be all things to all participants at all times. However financial regulations and regulatory structures evolve, hopefully the advice contained in this book will be useful to readers operating in any securities market.

Introduction

More education rather than more regulation

However rules and regulations evolve, there will inevitably still be a need for good securities research, investment ideas and M&A advice. In this book, we are interested in both securities regulations and ethical behavior within the world of securities research. The former try to formalize what can and can't be done within definitions, whereas the latter is much more nebulous and encompasses more universal principles of moral behavior among research analysts and within the research departments of banks, brokerages, fund management houses and credit rating agencies. The book attempts to combine aspects of both spheres to reach a set of best-practice principles and guidelines for securities-research analysts, research managers and financial editors to follow, wherever they are based and whichever markets or sectors they cover. It should also help brokers and sales representatives understand what it would take for them to be regarded as research analysts by regulators.

Notwithstanding a few high-profile cases over recent years, especially in the U.S., it has been my observation as a supervisory analyst (SA) for the research departments of global investment banks that securities-research analysts are generally honest and hard-working, and do not try to pull the wool over clients' eyes. However, on a regular basis, I would see analysts inadvertently breaching regulations in their draft research reports or non-research e-mails. These analysts have been happy to operate within regulatory and best-practice parameters, once they understood the underlying rationale for them. I have also noticed that even seasoned financial editors, supervisory analysts and compliance officers charged with ensuring that research reports adhere to these principles, have sometimes done so without necessarily fully understanding the reasoning behind them and without therefore being able to justify fully to the analysts their editorial and compliance changes.

Not knowing the rules seems to be a widespread problem in the invest-ment banking world and in other research fields too. The *Fortune* maga-zine issue of June 9, 2008, ran a story about an energy derivatives trader at Citigroup who was jailed in the U.S. for conspiracy to falsify bank records and commit wire fraud. According to the article, he said that he didn't know exactly what the rules were. An article in the *Wall Street Journal* of August 16, 2006, on plagiarism in academic research quotes Elizabeth Heitman, a professor of ethics at Vanderbilt University Medical Center in the U.S., as saying: "We end up very often assuming people know the rules and don't tell them what the rules are until they get into trouble."

Rather than advocate for even more regulation for securities analysts, let's give education a chance. This book attempts to help all those involved in writing, publishing and marketing securities research to understand the regulatory and best-practice issues involved, so that they can steer through the chicanes safely. The book highlights the major risks and challenges that analysts and other securities professionals face, and, with the help of real case studies and examples, explains how they can avoid or manage these. It does not attempt to teach analysts the analytical skills they need to do their job, such as understanding business finance, interpreting financial accounts and valuing securities, for which plenty of resource material already exists. As such, the book does not focus on hard numbers, but rather highlights the soft issues that analysts need to be aware of—whether in terms of the regulatory risks that they themselves face as analysts or the investment risks to their views and recommendations that they need to draw to their clients' attention.

In any case, I'm not sure any book can really teach analysts the flair, cre-ativity and insight needed to anticipate the market consistently and make good investment recommendations that repeatedly produce the expected returns within the expected timeframes. As my mentor, Brian Williams, said, "You can try and teach someone to play football like Maradona, but only Maradona can play like Maradona."[7] (Younger readers might like to think more in terms of Lionel Messi!)

The book also does not attempt to foresee how the world of securities research will evolve from a business perspective, especially with regard to issues such as the paying for "sell-side" research (brokerage or independent research provided to multiple "buy-side" clients such as mutual funds and hedge funds), although we do consider recent developments.

The need to identify investment risk

From a research content perspective, one conclusion is that whereas many investors may be less concerned with dividend yield, corporate governance issues and investment risks during bull markets when "all boats are rising", these aspects become more acute as markets turn. During a prolonged bear market or period of volatility, analysts would need to be ever more diligent in eking out differentiating factors for their investment calls. They need to be even more proactive in identifying potential new "Black Swan" risks to their recommendations rather than merely assessing risks that are already known to the market. If one year it's subprime debt levels or perhaps the price of oil, the U.S. dollar or even rice that's surprising markets and making stock prices volatile, what might it be the following year?

When it became apparent toward the end of 2009 that the debt of state-owned Dubai World would not be guaranteed by the Dubai government, analysts scoured the globe to identify other countries exposed to "sovereign debt" risk. Greece was an immediate victim, when its government bonds were downgraded by the three major rating agencies. Other European countries with large budget deficits, low growth and high unemployment levels also came under pressure, with the markets being unsure whether or not the European Central Bank would be willing or able to bail them out. The very stability of the euro was under threat.

Fears of deflation, inflation or stagflation may recur, but what else could compound the problem? Globalization and free trade bring their own "seismic-shift" challenges, but Mark Mobius, who wrote the foreword to this book, has long been warning that protectionism and nationalism are major threats to world markets—and these could emanate from the developed world as easily as from emerging markets.

Judging by their reactions to the financial crisis, it seems that world leaders have learned some lessons from the Great Depression of the 1930s—especially an appreciation of the disadvantages of protectionism. However, the government bailouts could be regarded as protectionist measures, and the calling by the prime minister of the U.K. at the time, Gordon Brown, for "British jobs for British workers" seemed like a throwback to the '70s. The measure in the U.S. stimulus package to "buy American" caused much controversy and concern. Meanwhile, India announced that it had banned the import of Chinese-made toys for six months from January 2009. Just when that timeframe was coming to a close, the Chinese announced a "buy Chinese" policy. Trade relations between the U.S. and China deteriorated in September 2009 when China threatened to retaliate against the U.S. for raising the duty on Chinese tire imports. Their targets would be the imports of poultry and vehicles from the U.S. Meanwhile, China's policy of keeping its currency stable against the U.S. dollar was also a bone of contention.

Terrorism, including cyber terrorism, is a major threat to world markets, but perhaps the biggest risk of all—to life on Earth, let alone the markets—is climate change. The scientists seem to be blowing hot and cold on the subject, leaving long-term investors who are trying to make informed decisions quite confused. But such diversity of views is what markets thrive on, and is a major reason research analysts will always have a role to play.

Target readership

The target readers for this book include securities analysts, brokers, investment advisers, wealth managers, research associates and assistants, research managers, supervisory analysts, compliance officers, financial journalists, editors, translators, risk managers, accountants, auditors, management consultants, securities lawyers, regulators and students of investment and finance. The book should be of particular interest to sell-side equity-research analysts. However, it should also be useful to credit research analysts, credit rating analysts, as well as buy-side analysts who provide research for their own in-house fund managers.

The book, being full of words rather than charts, will inevitably appeal more to fundamental analysts than to technical analysts. However, research regulations are designed to protect the investing public, and as such, technical analysts who make investment recommendations on specific securities would invariably still be subject to these regulations. The principle of justifying an investment recommendation holds true for both types of analyst—it's just that they use different methods to make the justification.

Note that sales representatives, brokers and marketers of research and investment ideas should also benefit from reading the book, so as to understand fully what they can and can't say in their own communications with clients to avoid being regarded as research analysts by regulators. The book should also be of more than passing interest to the investing community at large, whether institutional or retail investors, as well as to corporate issuers of securities, especially investor-relations officers. These groups need to rely on analysts to represent the investment case fairly and fully; they need to know how analysts think, and to appreciate the constraints under which they operate.

Commercial benefits to compliance

I trust readers will agree that my explanations and suggestions as to how to deal with best-practice issues do not come at the expense of commerciality and competitiveness. Analysts who may think this book is all about learning how to obey the rules just to avoid fines from securities regulators (a laudable and commercial enough aim in itself) should appreciate that competitive advantage will inevitably accrue when, individually and collectively, analysts play the game properly. Indeed, the need for collective responsibility within the global financial sector was one of the key messages from the Corrigan report published in August 2008 by Counterparty Risk Management Policy Group III,[8] which was formed to examine the 2007/08 credit crisis. This was a concerted effort by the major securities firms to identify and address their own risk management problems internally, without the need for overly burdensome regulatory supervision. It recognized that individual institutions might need to make certain sacrifices for the sake of the common good and the stability of the markets. By the time the dust had settled, sacrifices had certainly been made at Lehman Brothers, Bear Stearns, Merrill Lynch, Citigroup, Morgan Stanley and Goldman Sachs.

As in any industry, investors will only deal repeatedly with analysts and brokers who have earned their trust. It is not sufficient for an analyst to be a good stock-picker; investors need to see that they are being treated fairly. Without this trust, an analyst's efforts to build relationships with clients will be wasted—no amount of taking clients out for dinners and shows, or even dwarf-tossing competitions (seriously), can make up for the loss of trust. As Kenichi Watanabe, chief executive of Nomura Holdings, said in April 2008 after the firm fired an employee who was under investigation for insider trading, ". . . we believe we will be affected . . . since we have lost the trust of our customers". As confirmation of his fears, Japan's Pension Fund Association said it would stop placing stock-broking and bond-trading orders through Nomura until the regulator had completed its probe. Ultimately, a level playing field where clients trust analysts can only benefit the securities industry as a whole.

I'd also add that if an analyst does breach regulations, but can demonstrate that he (or she) followed the firm's procedures and approval processes to the letter, then he may well have his firm's support in any investigation or litigation. If, however, the analyst skirts the firm's approval processes, then he risks losing the trust of his employer too. A managing director in Morgan Stanley's fixed-income division in Hong Kong lost his job over a case involving alleged insider dealing in the shares of CITIC Resources.[9] The press reported in July 2008 that Morgan Stanley had reported the incident to the local regulator and had said that the alleged wrongdoing was "an egregious violation of Morgan Stanley's values and policies". This and other firms would similarly distance themselves from any research analyst who acts inappropriately.

Local differences and specific circumstances

The comments and conclusions presented in this book merely represent my own interpretations of what is best practice in writing securities research for investors. A combination of experience as a global supervisory analyst registered with U.S. securities regulators, common sense and moral fairness has been my yardstick. However, my views may not necessarily reflect the views of all regulators. Research analysts must also be mindful that regulatory and cultural differences exist between markets, and that they may need to seek specific legal advice for their specific circumstances.

Summary

The book comprises five chapters. The first and main chapter examines general best-practice principles involved in writing securities research and giving investment advice. These would encompass such concepts as fairness, truthfulness, integrity, independence, transparency, accountability and consistency. Analysts should instinctively know what's right and what's wrong, just by putting themselves in the shoes of their readers and asking themselves: "Would I be misled, prejudiced or otherwise disadvantaged by this research, whether in respect to its content, timing of publication or distribution?" Specifically we look at the definitions of research around the world, and see that whereas equities have traditionally represented the core asset class that regulators have been interested in, they are increasingly turning their attention to credit research as well. We'll see that even instruments like swaps, which are over-the-counter contracts that only give economic exposure to securities, not the right to buy or vote, are encroaching into the realm of securities from a regulatory perspective. We then examine the major threats that analysts face, such as front-running, insider trading, rumor-mongering, defamation and copyright.

We devote a separate chapter, Chapter 2, to justifying recommendations, drawing risks to readers' attention and corporate governance issues. Conflicts of interest and the independence of research are also important enough subjects to warrant their own chapter, and these issues are explored in Chapter 3.

The fourth chapter examines the issues involving non-research communications such as e-mails (including commentary by research analysts on non-rated companies and communications from sales and traders), and the final chapter presents general writing and editorial thoughts that research analysts and financial editors may find useful in preparing securities research.

Case studies and examples

Case studies taken from the major markets around the world are presented throughout the book. These hopefully serve as practical examples to demonstrate general principles, and highlight the issues that regulators, investors and the press find especially important. Incidentally, they also demonstrate how fines and penalties have dramatically increased in scale over the past decade or so, from tens of thousands of U.S. dollars to hundreds of millions of dollars, and that "industry practice" provides no defense. Each case, of course, rests on the particular facts involved. Again, I reiterate that research analysts need to be mindful of their own local laws, regulations, customs and company policies, and will inevitably need independent legal advice for their specific circumstances.

All source material for the case studies is publicly available and comprises either primary evidence provided by regulators or secondary evidence provided by reputable newspapers and newswires. Primary sources include: the U.S. Securities and Exchange Commission (SEC);

the Financial Industry Regulatory Authority (FINRA) of the U.S., including its forerunners the National Association of Securities Dealers (NASD) and the member regulation, enforcement and arbitration divisions of the New York Stock Exchange (NYSE); the Financial Services Authority of the U.K. (FSA); and the Securities and Futures Commission of Hong Kong (SFC). Secondary sources include: *Financial Times (FT)*; *Wall Street Journal (WSJ)*; *South China Morning Post (SCMP)*; *New York Times (NYT)*; *Barron's*; Bloomberg; Thomson Reuters; and Dow Jones. I acknowledge these and the other sources, but cannot guarantee the accuracy or completeness of the information.[10] I have used my best efforts to cross-check specific information, but would stress that the aim of this book is more to demonstrate principles than to serve as a record of individual cases.

In presenting the cases, I make no judgment as to the guilt or innocence of the parties involved; I am merely using the cases to demonstrate general principles. The conclusions given for each case and example are my own conclusions, or at least ones that are shared by me; they are general conclusions that relate to the principles rather than to the specific cases and individuals involved.

Jake van der Kamp argued in his article in the *SCMP* of May 17, 2004, that regulators can sometimes be accused of wearing defendants down so much in a "trial by ordeal" that the defendants pay fines without necessarily admitting liability or actually being found guilty. A settlement is, of course, a settlement, but there have been enough cases around the world where regulators' decisions have subsequently been overturned or challenged to suggest that regulators are not infallible.

When Bank of America agreed with the SEC in August 2009 to pay a fine for misleading shareholders over bonuses before its acquisition of Merrill Lynch, the district judge rejected the settlement querying why the company (in effect Bank of America's shareholders) should pay a fine for acts that the executives and lawyers had committed. After all it was the shareholders who were the victims to start with.[11] The Madoff case also provides a classic example to demonstrate the shortcomings of regulators. The fact that would-be investors had previously drawn their suspicions to the SEC's attention prompted the chairman, Christopher Cox, to say: "I am gravely concerned by the apparent multiple failures over at least a decade to thoroughly investigate these allegations." The country's president-elect, Barack Obama, famously remarked that regulators and Congress had been "asleep at the switch".

Even in the judicial arena, there have been high-profile test cases where some might suspect that the outcomes have been driven as much by political considerations as by legal ones. Stoneridge versus Scientific Atlanta in the U.S.[12] and the anti-fraud enquiry into BAE Systems[13] in the U.K. have been cited as possible examples.

Most of the cases and examples relate to investment banks, securities brokerages and credit rating agencies, and to research analysts working in these firms. A few, however, involve sales/brokers, financial advisers, traders, investors, economists, bloggers, and even PR agents, compliance officers and lawyers. I have included these to demonstrate general principles that would also apply to research analysts, or that would concern them in some way. There are also many corporate governance cases relating to listed companies. I have included these to show the issues that analysts need to be aware of when assigning a discount (or premium) to a company's valuations or when highlighting the company's potential corporate governance risks.

The cases themselves are a matter of public record, but given that the purpose of including them in this book is to demonstrate principles rather than dragging the individuals through the mud again, I have used their initials rather than their full names. However, I have left Henry Blodget's and Jack Grubman's names intact; not only did they consent to censure, but their cases have been so well documented that it would seem a little disingenuous to refer to them by their initials. Similarly, Madoff and Stanford are now household names who have lost any chance of anonymity. I have left company names intact. Some cases may be pending appeal or may have developed further by the time you read this book.

Many of the case studies and examples include "asides", and there are also separate sidebars. These are hopefully interesting stories that may be incidental to the main issues being discussed, but which may still include lessons for analysts. Like many of the case studies and examples, some of these demonstrate what can go wrong with companies and managements, and hopefully highlight situations where analysts need to be vigilant.

Themes

Research coverage

Definition of research: Analysts need to understand the difference between "research" and "non-research", since this has a bearing on how communications are approved and distributed, and whether or not research disclosures are required. Different regulatory regimes around the world may have different definitions of securities research. For example, as we'll see in Chapter 1, the U.S. regulators define research as "a written (including electronic) communication which includes an analysis of equity securities of individual companies or industries . . . and that provides information reasonably sufficient upon which to base an investment decision". The regulations are defined in the context of communications with the public, and are evidently designed to help protect customers. As such, they effectively only apply to analysts or advisers who have more than one client. This book caters not just to sell-side research analysts but also to buy-side analysts as well, and covers not just equities but other securities too. For example, the U.S. definition covers options. Elsewhere regulations would also cover credit research. Even swaps have now entered securities regulators' purview.

For the purposes of this book, therefore, we'll broadly define research as any substantive analysis on any publicly traded security that provides sufficient information to make an investment decision. Of course, buy-side analysts still have plenty of market-related issues to worry about anyway, including the use of inside information, the initiating or spreading of rumors and some potential conflicts of interest. Sales, traders, marketers, commentators and bloggers also need to be aware that if their own communications constitute research, then they may need to adopt the same objectivity, disclosure and distribution standards as research analysts.

Supervision of research: Best practice would require all sell-side research on securities to be approved by a qualified supervisor before being published to clients fairly, and indeed this is a requirement under some regulatory regimes. An internal-review panel for all research, especially initiations and changes of recommendations or views, is also helpful in ensuring appropriate levels of due diligence and quality control. Non-research e-mails for selective distribution should also be subject to an approval process, albeit one that is less rigorous than that for research.

Competence: Fundamental analysts should not present themselves to the market as being experts in specific listed securities unless and until they can demonstrate a thorough knowledge of the respective companies. Analysts should always make clear when they formally cover or rate a company. For securities that they don't cover or rate, they should restrict their communications to objective commentary (non-research).

Accountability: Research should be attributed to an appropriately registered analyst. Analysts have a duty to their clients when they get them into a trade to be able to respond to their questions while they are invested and to advise them when to get out again, or at least inform them that they will no longer be in a position to advise them.

Fair distribution: All sell-side research, having been subjected to an approval process, should be made available to clients fairly[14] by being published through the research firm's formal publishing system with appropriate disclosures. This means that it should be published before being presented at any sales or traders meeting, to avoid potential risk of front-running.

Sourcing Information

Verifiability of information: Analysts should acknowledge the sources of their information. Without the protection of a publicly available source for their information, analysts risk being accused of spreading rumors to manipulate prices, trading on inside information or other offenses such as defamation (libel and slander), misrepresentation, plagiarism or breach of copyright or contract.

Rumors and speculation: Regulators are more concerned with the purposeful spreading of rumors to move a stock's price rather than the accidental garbling of information. During the financial crisis of 2007–2009, the spotlight fell on the short-selling practices of hedge funds, and the extent to which abusive rumor-mongering played a part. Some argued that Bear Stearns was murdered at the hands of short-sellers acting on rumor.

Analysts can report on published rumors, provided they quote the widely available source and give the respective parties a chance to represent themselves. I argue that analysts can put a company in play, for example, by identifying it as a potential takeover target, provided they do not have inside knowledge of any impending M&A activity and are not spreading rumors. As regulators themselves appreciate, coming to logical conclusions based on verifiable, publicly available facts and reasonable assumptions merely constitutes good research.

Reasonable basis for recommendations and risk assessment

Consistency of recommendations: The meaning of recommendations or ratings must be clear. To avoid confusion, individual recommendations and target prices should be consistent with each other, with the time horizon made clear. Analysts may find from time to time that their recommendation and target price for a security are not consistent with each other, perhaps during short periods of extreme price volatility and when an analyst is waiting for further details from the company. Analysts, however, must take care not to be seen to be tipping off sales of forthcoming recommendation changes, or perhaps giving potentially conflicting signals to clients.

Reason for valuations: Where equity analysts support recommendations with target valuations, they should say how and why their views differ from the consensus and why they think their own valuations are realistic and achievable, with reference, for example, to a discounted cash flow (DCF), dividend discount model (DDM) or sum of the parts (SOP) valuation, with perhaps earnings-based valuation multiples compared to peers in the market or sector as a relative cross-check. When analysts give valuations, they must make clear what their assumptions are. They need to make clear what valuation years are being used and, if they are prospective, whose estimates they are based on.

Changes in valuations: Analysts should always make clear what changes they are making since their last report, giving reasons why they are making the change. If they are changing their fair-value or target price, they should say what element of the valuation has changed; for example, discount-rate assumption, earnings forecasts, valuation multiple, year of valuation and so on.

Investment risks: Analysts should always highlight investment risks to their readers. The more the expected upside/downside to the target price, the more readers will expect the analyst to draw attention to the risks in achieving the target. Some analysts and investors prefer to think in terms of catalysts that are needed for a target price to be reached, and may ask themselves what would happen if these catalysts did not occur. Analysts should ask themselves what the risk is that their own non-consensus view is wrong, and that the market has indeed already valued the stock in question fairly. Either way, research analysts surely owe their clients a duty of care when giving investment recommendations and advice.[15] Analysts (and advisers) should make sure that their clients appreciate the investment risks involved, especially so in the case of retail clients.

Where possible analysts can assign a premium or discount to their valuations to reflect perceived risks, or at least draw their clients' attention to any perceived risks, with good reasons given of course. Corporate governance is one wide-ranging risk that more and more investors are expecting analysts to assess. This covers issues like social responsibility, executive compensation, equal treatment of shareholders, related-party transactions, independent non-executive directors and risk management.

Conflicts of interest

Potential conflicting interests: Banking/corporate finance colleagues, clients, sales/brokers, proprietary traders and the subjects of research reports all might be tempted to apply pressure on analysts to write research that suits their own agenda. Credit rating agencies have also been criticized for the way they have traditionally been paid for their services.

Separation of research and banking: Sell-side securities-research analysts are on the "public" side of the so-called Chinese wall, and cater to their buy-side clients. These include pension funds, other mutual fund/unit trust funds, hedge funds and sovereign wealth funds, at least insofar as they invest in listed securities. Investment bankers are on the "private" side, and may be privy to non-public information about their corporate clients. While on the public side of this wall, analysts must base their views and conclusions on publicly available information; they should not let their independence be compromised by receiving private or deal-related information or acceding to requests from their colleagues in the banking department. In some markets, analysts have to certify that their views are independent.

Managing contacts with bankers: Inevitably, bankers and analysts within the same firm may need to meet up, for acceptable reasons, while still wishing to maintain their independence from each other. It's important that such meetings are managed appropriately and transparently, with records of approvals and meetings being kept. On occasion and where allowed, analysts may need to be formally "brought over the wall". For all intents and purposes they would then be regarded as "insiders"—that is, on the private side of the wall—and their ability to write independent research would be compromised.

Disclosure of interests and relationships: The principle is that if someone is trying to sell you something, then you need to know whether or not they have their own axe to grind. Analysts therefore need to disclose what relationships or interests they or their employer may have in the companies they are recommending or focusing on.

Writing in general

Getting noticed: Analysts need to stand out from the crowd by grabbing their readers' attention. Summarizing messages in titles, key points, bullets and summaries helps readers, and these may be the only comments some readers will have time to read. There's never any harm in a bit of repetition to make the point: tell them what you're going to tell them, tell them, then tell them what you told them. Humor can work to the author's advantage, although care must be taken to avoid giving offense.

Transparency: Abraham Lincoln famously preempted Bob Marley by saying: "You may fool all the people some of the time; you can even fool some of the people all the time; but you can't fool all of the people all of the time". Clients appreciate analysts who are open and transparent in their communications and who own up to bad calls and errors more so than those who are shifty in their dealings and who try to cover up their mistakes.

Freedom of speech: However noble an ideal it may be, analysts would be wise not to assume that they have freedom of speech as a cast-iron protection for what they write. Not only are analysts subject to securities, defamation and intellectual-property restrictions, but they are also faced with social, political and religious sensitivities among their clients as well as in the countries in which they operate.

Now that you've read this far, here's a little riddle for you: what do a golden bull, a golden goose and a golden peacock have in common? The answer is that they all feature in this book. To find out why they're relevant, carry on reading.[16]

Endnotes

1. Fannie Mae in May 2006 and Freddie Mac in September 2007 agreed, without admitting or denying the allegations, to pay US$400 million and US$50 million, respectively, to settle accounting fraud charges brought by the SEC.
2. There are plenty more where that came from—see "Your credit crunch jokes" at bbc.co.uk.
3. The US$306 billion to guarantee debt was evidently in addition to US$45 billion received by Citigroup as part of the TARP program.
4. Chrysler sought Chapter 11 bankruptcy protection at the end of April 2009, and General Motors did likewise about a month later. Both came out of bankruptcy protection within a matter of weeks, albeit both a lot leaner.
5. His name is pronounced "Made-off", as in "he made off with our money".

6. According to the SEC's Web site, Ponzi schemes are pyramid schemes named after Charles Ponzi, who duped thousands of U.S. investors in the early 1920s in a foreign exchange arbitrage scheme involving international mail coupons. Get this—he called his company the Securities Exchange Company, or SEC for short.

7. In 1987, I suggested to my colleagues at Enterprise Zone Developments (EZD) that we should publish a guide to the tax and other issues involved in investing in industrial and commercial property in the U.K.'s enterprise zones. Some directors objected on the grounds that we'd be giving our secrets away, whereas Brian Williams, the chairman and managing director, supported the idea and persuaded the board to let me pursue the project. He used the Maradona allegory to allay the other directors' fears. The result was *A Guide to Investment in Enterprise Zones* (Longman, 1st ed. 1988, 2nd ed. 1990). The foreword was written by the Rt. Hon. Michael Heseltine MP, the secretary of state for the environment who implemented the enterprise zone concept in the early 1980s. In the year that the book was published the company's turnover quadrupled, and I'd like to think that publishing the book played no small part in getting the market to acknowledge EZD as one of the leading developers in the field.

8. See www.crmpolicygroup.org.

9. The investment banker was found guilty of insider dealing in September 2009 and jailed for seven years.

10. Consider the story about the undergraduate student at University College Dublin who attributed a fictitious quote to Maurice Jarre on Wikipedia as an experiment. The material was then used by the composer's obituary writers in various newspapers in March 2009. Separately, Dow Chemical's share price dropped over 4 percent in minutes on December 3, 2004, when someone purportedly representing the company said live on BBC that the firm had agreed to compensate victims of the 1984 Bhopal disaster. (The disaster had occurred at a Union Carbide plant in Bhopal, India, and Dow Chemical had taken over Union Carbide in 2001.) The hoaxster later identified himself as a member of the activist group, Yes Men. These stories serve to remind us all that we shouldn't necessarily believe everything we see or hear in the media.

11. The judge reluctantly agreed in February 2010 to Bank of America's US$150 million settlement with the SEC, saying it was "half-baked justice at best", according to the newswires. The amount of the settlement had been raised from US$33 million on new evidence. Meanwhile, New York's attorney general filed a separate lawsuit against the company and two of its top executives.

12. The landmark Stoneridge v. Scientific Atlanta case in the U.S. was decided on in January 2008 in a 5-3 vote by the Supreme Court in Wall Street's favor. At issue in that case was whether investors in companies that have been found guilty of fraud, such as Enron, could bring action against third-party business partners who had aided and abetted in the fraud. These would have included suppliers and advisers to those firms, including the investment banks offering underwriting, advisory and M&A services. If successful, the case could have deterred international firms from doing business in the U.S.

13. See the national interest sidebar on BAE Systems in the corporate governance section in Chapter 2.

14. Fair distribution to clients would at least mean simultaneous distribution to all clients of the particular category or class of client that the research was prepared for, with the distribution policy being disclosed to all clients.

15. In some markets distinctions might be drawn between analysts, brokers and advisers. Traditionally, investment advisers (who provide investment advice tailored to individual clients' needs) have been held to a higher fiduciary standard than analysts and brokers in terms of needing to act in the clients' best interests. However, I would note that in some markets any distinctions between these investment professionals might be blurred. I would also note the argument presented by Elisse B. Walter of the SEC, as reported in *InvestmentNews* on May 6, 2009, that retail investors should not have to make distinctions between the different types of professionals and that all financial professionals should be held to a fiduciary standard. Mary Schapiro, SEC chairman, followed this up the following month by saying that rules governing brokerages and investment advisers should be "virtually identical", as reported by Bloomberg.

16. Those who just can't wait can look up the references in the index.

Acknowledgments

Many thanks once again to all those whom I acknowledged in the first edition of this book.

For this second edition, I'd specifically like to thank: Mark Mobius, for his updated foreword; Emma Pegler, Lee Kha Loon, Alan Linning, Eugene Goyne, Liz Clay and Steve Vickers for their help and support generally; Charles Peattie, Russell Taylor and Suzette Field for the use of the Alex cartoons; and the team at John Wiley & Sons, especially Nick Wallwork, Janis Soo, Joel Balbin, Jules Yap, Cynthia Mak, Glenn Smith, Wong Pak Yau, Suhana Suhaimi and Feifan Li for publishing and marketing the book as well as Nicole Frank for editing it.

Other friends, colleagues, former colleagues, and contacts whom I'd like to single out for their ongoing help and support include Brian Williams, David Jeffery, Dick Ryeland, Dorothy Chan, Gail Humphryes, Jake van der Kamp, Tony Espina, Andrew Leeming, David Burnett, Colin Monks, Anthony Wood, Anthony Bolton, Matthew Sutherland, David Allen, Paul Addison, Mike Corless, Abe de Ramos, Tom Hester, Warren Blight, Lye-Keong Tho, Rossetti Leung, Paulina Chan, Al Troncoso, Paul Sheehan, David May, Siva Kumar, Utkarsh Majmudar, Tony Shale, Peter Churchouse, Joe Petch, Bruno Noble, Brent Robinson, Adrian Faure, Steve Proctor, Louise Crowther, Diego Marconato, Paul Bayliss, Paul Hedley, Patrick Boucher, Herald van der Linde, Daniel Kang, Jon Marsh, Tanya Osborne, Carlos Jalandoni, Myles MacMahon, Bruce Ruffy, Eliot Camplisson, Patrick George, Nigel Grinyer, Michael Duff, Nuala Connolly, Keith Stoddart, Keith Glasser, Andy Stormont, Chris Lucas, Simon Laugharne, Steve Petersohn, Xen Gladstone, Jean Kelman, Nick Robinson, Glenn Darwin, Semirah Darwin, Hanna Raftell, John Batten, Adrian Underwood, Viji Jayewardene, Nigel Denby, Effie Vasilopoulos, Arun Subramaniam, James Rose, Diane Stormont, Sanjukta Sharma, Debashis Basu, Geoff de Freitas, Joe Spitzer, Teresa Ko, Laura Metoudi, Jilly Mangles, Evan Miracle, Chris Murtagh, Florence Yee, Marsanne Gee, Remus Negoita, Andrés Gentry, Annie Carver, Louise Barrington, Robin Fox, David Webb, Tim Kay, Colin Sanders, Fiona Davis-Coleman, Norman Janelle, Prashant Gokhale, Wally Best, Peter Smith, May Mak, David Lague, Erik Floyd, Gael McDonald, Mike Spivey, Arun Nigam, Glenn Henricksen, Jenny Drew, Chris Young, James Pomfret, Kate Pound Dawson, Robyn Meredith, Richard Morrow, Stefan Gannon, Dilys Lui, Laksono Widodo and the late Graham Ormerod.

I'd also like to use this opportunity to thank members of the CFA Institute, local CFA Societies, local securities associations and regulators around the world for helping me to promote my best-practice message. In addition to those already mentioned, these include Kurt Schacht, Ellen Riccardi, Joey

Chan, Bobby Lamy, Tom Robinson, Bob Johnson, Ashvin Vibhakar, Christine Koppel, Katrina Tai, Samuel Lum, Jeffery Stith, Dorothy Kelly, Gabriela Franco, Frank Dohn, Shirley Ng, Celine Mang, Zoe Lau, Andrea Ng, Richard Mak, Karl Lung, Tom Wu, Donnie Xu, Chanitr Charnchainarong, Paiboon Nalinthrangkurn, Pisit Jeungpraditphan, Prasit Boondoungprasert, Nittaya Tiranaprakij, Patra Potiveshgool, Th'ng Beng Hooi, Jasmine Lee, Mazie Lim, Aaron Low, Daniel Schaefer, Ho Pui Kam, Triono Soedirdjo, Alysia Shinta, Demetrius Ari Pitoyo, Eric Burhan, Dana Pamilih, Rinaldi Firmansyah, Yoopi Abimanyu, Justitia Tripurwasani, Sita Mazumder, François Aubert, Giuseppe Ballocchi, Maurizio Parenti, Rahul Keshap, Manoj Dani, SF Wong, Tim Wong, Daisy Lo and Clara Tang.

Lastly, I'd like to thank my wife Connie and our son James, my brother Mark, my sister-in-law Jane and of course my mother Joyce and my late father John for their support and patience. My gratitude extends to the wider network of family and friends in the U.K., Hong Kong and elsewhere— you know who you are.

Abbreviations Used in This Book

AAOIFI	Accounting and Auditing Organization for Islamic Financial Institutions
ARS	auction-rate security
CDO/CMO	collateralized debt/mortgage obligation
CDS	credit default swap
CFA	Chartered Financial Analyst
CFD	contract for difference
CFTC	Commodity Futures Trading Commission
CSA	commission-sharing arrangement
DCF	discounted cash flow
DDM	dividend discount model
EPS	earnings per share
EVA	Economic Value Added
EV/EBITDA	enterprise value-to-earnings before interest, tax, depreciation and amortization
FBI	Federal Bureau of Investigation
FINRA	Financial Industry Regulatory Authority
FRN	floating rate note
FSA	Financial Services Agency (Japan)
FSA	Financial Services Authority (U.K.)
FT	*Financial Times*
GAAP	generally accepted accounting principles
IFRS	international financial reporting standards
IMF	International Monetary Fund
IOSCO	International Organization of Securities Commissions
IPO	initial public offering
IFSB	Islamic Financial Services Board
LIBOR	London Interbank Offered Rate
M&A	mergers and/or acquisitions
MiFID	Markets in Financial Instruments Directive

NASD	National Association of Securities Dealers
NAV	net asset value
NRSRO	nationally recognized statistical rating organization
NYSE	New York Stock Exchange
P/B	price-to-book value
P/E	price-to-earnings
ROE	return on equity
SA	supervisory analyst
SCMP	*South China Morning Post*
SEBI	Securities and Exchange Board of India
SEC	Securities and Exchange Commission (U.S.)
SFC	Securities and Futures Commission (Hong Kong)
SFO	Securities and Futures Ordinance (Hong Kong)
SIFMA	Securities Industry and Financial Markets Association
SIV, SPV	structured investment vehicle, special purpose vehicle
SOP	sum of parts
SWF	sovereign wealth funds
SWOT	strengths, weaknesses, opportunities and threats
TARP	Troubled Asset Relief Program
WACC	weighted average cost of capital
WSJ	*Wall Street Journal*

Note that some of the above abbreviations are registered trademarks in their own right. For example, CFA is a registered trademark of the CFA Institute and EVA is a registered trademark of Stern Stewart & Co.

Chapter 1

Principles
of
Research

Key points ▐▐▐➡

- Trust is hard to win, easy to lose and nearly impossible to salvage. If clients think that they are being confused, misled, prejudiced or disadvantaged by the analyst's research, whether in respect to its content, timing of publication or distribution, they will get their research elsewhere.
- Analysts should give investors what they really want; that is, original investment ideas supported by sound analysis, rather than just a regurgitation of news that is already reflected in the security's price.
- Analysts may need to satisfy specific criteria for sets of clients who have special investment needs, such as socially responsible investors or *Shari'ah*-compliant investors.
- Analysts should be consistent with their views or explain any apparent inconsistencies. Any recommendations and target prices should be supported with good reasons, valuations and risk assessment. Any material changes arising since the previous report should be highlighted.
- Fundamental (as opposed to technical) analysts should not present themselves to the market as being experts in securities unless they can demonstrate a thorough knowledge of the respective companies. For securities that they do not actively cover or rate, they should restrict their communications to objective commentary.
- Best practice would require all securities research to be approved by at least a qualified supervisor, if not by a full internal-review panel before being published to sales and clients simultaneously.
- Without the protection of a verifiable and publicly available source for their information, analysts risk being accused of spreading rumors to manipulate prices, trading on inside information or other offenses such as misrepresentation, defamation, plagiarism or breach of copyright or contract.
- For accountability purposes, all published research should be attributed to an appropriately registered analyst, with all appropriate disclosures made.

Definition and supervision of research

Supervision and control of research

We'll be examining specific definitions of "research" more closely in the next section. Broadly speaking, for the purposes of this book, we're talking about substantive analysis of securities, particularly stocks and bonds, which enables investors to make their investment decisions. Securities regulators around the world invariably require those preparing research and giving investment advice to be appropriately registered and licensed.

Some regulators also require research to be approved by a qualified supervisor before being published. For example, the Financial Industry Regulatory Authority (FINRA) of the U.S.[1] requires research on equity securities published by their members to be approved by a qualified research principal or supervisory analyst. Indeed, one of the many common violations for which the global investment banks were fined in April 2003 was "failing to establish and maintain adequate policies, systems and procedures for supervision and control of their research and investment banking divisions". Given the risks that securities firms and analysts face, instituting a robust approval process for their research product (including any product that could be regarded by a regulator as research) seems pretty sensible in any jurisdiction, whether it's mandated or not.

Incidentally, as we can see from the following case study, securities firms around the world that distribute research into the U.S. or publish research on the Web (thereby making it available in the U.S.) need to understand to what extent their research needs to satisfy U.S. regulations.

CASE STUDY

Marketing research to the U.S. by foreign broker-dealers

Background: Foreign broker-dealers who are not associated with a U.S. broker-dealer can distribute research to U.S. institutional investors, subject to restrictions (including restrictions on active marketing of their services).[2] Those who are associated, like the international operations of most of the big global banks, can have their research distributed by the U.S. entity. However, the U.S. entity must take responsibility for the research, and the research must state this clearly as well as the fact that the foreign analyst is not registered or qualified under FINRA regulations.

Details: We see from FINRA's round-up of disciplinary actions for September 2008 that Citigroup had permitted its foreign-based analysts to publish research without obtaining either the required U.S. qualifications or the exemption (as afforded by Rule 15a-6). FINRA reported in May 2008 that SG Americas Securities had also fallen foul of these provisions. Without admitting or denying the findings, both companies consented to censure and a fine—US$650,000 in the case of Citi and US$175,000 for SG Americas.

One caveat is that a foreign-based analyst who is already registered with FINRA as an "associated person" cannot take advantage of

Marketing research to the U.S.
by foreign broker-dealers—*cont'd*

the exemption. My former colleague Louise Crowther draws to my attention the case where FINRA fined and censured RBC Capital in September 2009 for relying incorrectly on Rule 15a-6. RBC Capital, owned by Royal Bank of Canada, agreed to pay US$150,000 without admitting or denying any wrongdoing. Even though the analysts were based in Canada, they were still registered with FINRA in the U.S. as "associated persons" and, as such, should have passed the Series 86 and 87 exams in order to function as research analysts. FINRA says its Rule 1050 applies to foreign analysts if they are associated persons, regardless of whether their research is distributed under a Rule 15a-6 safe harbor. FINRA acknowledged that had the Canadian analysts never registered to take the Series 7 exam and instead issued research solely in reliance on SEC Rule 15a-6, like the foreign analysts at some other firms, then it would not have had a basis to bring charges against RBC.

Conclusions: These may seem like cases of form over substance, but it does look like the SEC is intending to relieve broker-dealers of excessive red tape in this global market. In June 2008, the SEC issued a request for comment on proposed amendments to revamp Rule 15a-6.[3] Furthermore, the regulator announced on August 25, 2008, that it had agreed with the Australian Securities and Investments Commission (ASIC) a mutual recognition arrangement whereby broker-dealers could operate in both jurisdictions without the need to be separately regulated in both countries. This move may open the door for other cooperative arrangements with other regulators around the world.

However, pending further developments, the above cases demonstrate that analysts who distribute their research to the U.S. will still need to ensure they are armed with the appropriate qualification or exemption.

A preview by an internal investment committee or panel for all new fundamental research helps not just in satisfying regulators' requirements for an approval process, but it should also help in raising the standard of the research. An analyst can treat the exercise as an internal dress rehearsal before presenting the research to sales and clients. The approval process also provides a degree of protection for analysts. If, for whatever reason, they end up in the dock after publishing their report, at least they shouldn't be there on their own; they should have the support of research management, provided the procedures have been followed properly. As we will see from the case study in Chapter 3 on conflicts of interest (global settlements), it's not only the analysts themselves who are liable but the managers of analysts too.

Such a panel might consist of the research product manager, a strategist, a supervisory analyst and a compliance officer to ensure that the reasons for writing the research are appropriate and that issues such as due diligence, the business argument, valuation rationale, risk assessment, wider investment implications, sources of information and disclosure requirements are addressed. The panel would need to be satisfied that all the analysts have the appropriate registrations and licenses for the markets in which they operate. Furthermore, the panel should ensure that records of the approval process are maintained.

Reasons for research: The panel should ask what special event or reason has prompted the analyst to write the research at that particular time. The panel would need to be satisfied (in the case of sell-side analysts) that it is for the genuine benefit of the buy-side clients such as mutual funds/ unit trusts and hedge funds, rather than, say, at the request of banking colleagues, the subject company or individual clients (except for individually requested bespoke research). The compliance officer would need to check separately whether the firm's banking/corporate finance division is seeking to be engaged by the company, for example, in a capital raising exercise or for M&A advice.

From a commercial viewpoint, the analyst would wish to make clear what original idea or approach he has come up with that will differentiate his research from that of the competition.

Due diligence: It is important to determine that the analyst has conducted a sufficiently in-depth due-diligence exercise on the security issuer that is the subject of the research report. This is to ascertain, as far as is feasible, that the subject company and its directors have no skeletons lurking in the cupboard that may come back to haunt investors later, with potentially embarrassing consequences to the analyst's and the research firm's reputations. Examples might include substantial off-balance-sheet items, including structured investment vehicles (SIVs) and special purpose vehicles (SPVs), or highly geared exposure to derivatives. They might also include criminal records or pending lawsuits, especially in cases of so-called "pre-deal" IPO research (where such research is allowed to be published), on companies not yet policed by a stock exchange. (Please see Chapter 3 for more on "pre-deal" research. See also the case study on ICEA Capital and Deloitte Touche Tohmatsu in Chapter 2 for a discussion on the "due diligence" that investment banks need to undertake when sponsoring new listings or advising on M&A deals.)

Analysts do not represent themselves as auditors of the issuers (and they do not have the access to a company's internal records and information that its auditors have), and the issuers may not technically be "customers" under anti-money-laundering rules. Furthermore, analysts have traditionally not been held to the high fiduciary standards of investment advisers in terms of having to act in their clients' best interests. Nevertheless, analysts surely still owe their investor clients a duty of care when making recommendations on the securities of these issuers. I would note the call by Elisse B. Walter of the SEC, as reported in *InvestmentNews* on May 6, 2009, that all professionals who give investment advice should be subject to a fiduciary standard, whatever they are called and however they are paid. Analysts should therefore know the history and status of the companies and their managements pretty thoroughly.

The business argument: Before even discussing the valuation of the shares, the panel would need to hear the analyst's opinion of how sound the company's financial health and business model are. The panel would need to see that the analyst has prepared full financial forecasts, including balance sheet, profit & loss and cashflow forecasts (where appropriate). Questions the panel might ask an equity analyst, for instance, are:

- How does the industry in which the company operates stack up in the context, for example, of Michael Porter's "five forces"? Do the buyers or suppliers have more power? What is the competitive environment like in terms of substitute products or the threat of new competitors, and what are the barriers to entry?
- What is the demand/supply situation for the company's own goods or services? Is the company potentially a long-term winner or loser in its business? What are the company's strengths, weaknesses, opportunities and threats (the so-called SWOT analysis)?
- Is the industry in which the company operates undergoing consolidation, and how susceptible is the company's business to M&A activity?
- How much debt does the company have, and is it generating sufficient cash flow to service it? What are the long-term contractual liabilities of the company?
- Does the company have a good track record of earnings? How easily can it sustain or increase those earnings? Is it taking market share (with reference to earnings drivers and growth/ratio analyses)?
- Is the company increasing earnings faster than sales? That is, how efficient is it in controlling costs (with margin analyses)? What is the company's operational gearing like? In other words, given the company's fixed costs, what effect on the bottom line would every additional dollar in sales have?
- How does management tend or intend to reinvest or distribute earnings?
- What is the company's reputation like in the market? What is the analyst's impression of management, and how seriously does management take corporate governance issues?
- What items in the company's financial statements are most subject to interpretation, or which are most likely to cause a difference in opinion between management and the auditor?

- What might explain any difference between the analyst's earnings forecasts for the company and those provided by consensus? That is, what does the analyst see that the market might not, and vice versa?

Valuation, risk and wider investment implications: The question about consensus forecasts leads into a determination of the extent to which the analyst's own expectations for the company's operations and earnings have already been discounted by the market as reflected in the current price, and what risks there may be to the analyst's own valuations (see Chapter 2 for a full discussion of valuation, risk and corporate governance issues). The panel would need to determine that the analyst has used appropriate methodologies and comparisons for valuing the stock, given the industry the company is in and the current stages of the business and economic cycles. Questions might include:

- What might explain the difference between the current stock price and the analyst's own discounted cash flow (DCF), dividend discount model (DDM), economic value added (EVA), net asset value (NAV), sum of parts (SOP) or other calculations? What discount rate is assumed to reach the net present values under the discounting of future returns methodologies, and why?
- To what extent is the current price-to-book ratio (P/B) justified, given the analyst's own growth expectations for return on equity (ROE)?
- To what extent is the current price-to-earnings ratio (P/E) justified, given the analyst's forecast for earnings growth and considering the P/E multiples of peers in the industry?
- What dividend yield does the analyst expect, and how does this compare to yields of other comparable investments in the sector, or to bond yields or bank deposit rates?
- What changes is the analyst making to his or her target price/valuation, and why? Is the change due to a change of earnings estimates, a change of multiple arising from a change of perceived risk, a roll-over of the year of valuation or a combination of these?
- What technical factors or leading indicators (for example, the expected supply of and demand for the shares, any share lock-ups or the level of legitimate trading by insiders such as directors and other senior executives) might affect their price? Indeed, who are the major shareholders, and do their stated strategies or investment histories support a potential M&A argument?
- What is the appropriate investment recommendation for clients, and is the recommendation consistent with the brokerage's recommendation methodology as defined in the disclosures?
- What are the catalysts that are needed for the target price to be achieved, and what are the risks to the investment case?
- Are there any specific corporate governance issues to consider, for example, in terms of the treatment of minority interests?

- Lastly, and increasingly importantly, what potential alternative investment opportunities might be of interest to clients, whether from an outright long-term or short-term buying or selling perspective or whether as part of some hedge, basket or other combination strategy? Examples might include different securities of the company (different issues of bonds or different classes of equities), derivatives of those securities including convertible bonds and options, recommendations based on different time horizons for the same securities (for example short-term trades) or the securities of the company's competitors, suppliers or customers, whether locally, regionally or globally.[4]

EXAMPLE

Stock-picking tips

Details: Many of the above factors are ones that Anthony Bolton, the outperforming U.K.-based fund-manager who ran Fidelity International's Special Situations Fund for 25 years, would consider when picking his stocks. He gives a list of lessons that he has learned over the years in his book *Investing with Anthony Bolton* jointly authored by Jonathan Davis. In the September 6/7, 2008, weekend edition of the *FT*, Bolton says he always asks himself how good the company is that he's investing in, especially in terms of its size, competitiveness and the sustainability of its business. He favors cash-generative, service-type businesses over those that consume cash such as manufacturing companies. In terms of valuations his ultimate measure is cash-on-cash returns, that is annual cash flow as a percentage of total cash invested.

Bond investors would have some different criteria to consider. As with any investment, they would consider whether the expected return is worth the expected risk. In terms of valuing bonds therefore, analysts consider the yield differential with benchmarks such as U.S. treasuries. Crucially, bond investors want to know whether they'll be paid their income and capital on time.

The CFA Institute lists the four Cs of credit that need to be addressed by bond analysts and credit rating analysts. Whether the analyst is rating the issuer itself or a particular credit issue, he or she would consider:

- Character. This relates to the identity of the issuer, including its reputation and corporate governance history.

- Capacity. This deals with the issuer's ability to pay, with due consideration given to its operational and financial capacity, as well as its competitive positions.
- Collateral. What assets and guarantees are in place to secure the issuer or issue?
- Covenants. What contractual facilities or restrictions are placed on the issuer or issue?

These four Cs are not to be confused with the four Cs you'd be interested in if you were a diamond dealer in Antwerp: carat, cut, clarity and color. Incidentally, both diamond-trading and bond-trading have a fifth C that could or should be considered: conflict and conditions, respectively. Conditions refer to the future economic conditions that borrowers may be subject to, that is the worst-case scenarios that investors should consider.

Source of information: A major theme running through this chapter is the need to ensure that analysts base their views on publicly available information. Without the protection of a publicly available source for their information, analysts risk charges of insider trading or manipulating prices by spreading rumors. The panel would need to be satisfied that the analysts' views, arguments and conclusions are based on verifiable facts and reasonable assumptions.

Disclosures: As discussed in more detail in Chapter 3, analysts need to draw to investors' attention if they, their employers or family members have any interests in or relationships with the companies they are recommending, including any apparent conflicts of interest arising from banking relationships. The panel would need to determine that recommendations and timeframes for target prices are defined. The panel would also need to be confident that the analyst is expressing personal, independent views, and that there have been no undue influences from banking colleagues, the issuer or even from individual clients. The panel would need to ensure that appropriate disclosures have been made in all these respects.

Continuing education

Many securities firms, on both the buy-side and sell-side, prefer to hire analysts who have gained a professional qualification such as the Chartered Financial Analyst (CFA) designation or who have achieved an appropriate academic standard such as a Master of Business Administration (MBA) degree. Individual companies might have their own tailor-made requirements. The *FT* reported on January 4, 2010, that, as one of many steps being taken to restore confidence in credit rating agencies following the financial crisis, Standard & Poor's was working with New York University's Stern School of Business to develop an in-house credit analyst certification program. The program would focus on financial statement analysis, advanced statistical analysis, valuation, derivative basics and credit scoring models.

All S&P analysts would need to pass the course in order to act as primary credit analysts.

Supervisors need to make sure that analysts keep up any ongoing training required by their local regulator. For example, FINRA in the U.S. requires registered securities professionals to follow a two-part Continuing Education Program. The "Regulatory Element" involves computer-based training on industry rules and regulations, whereas the "Firm Element" requires firms to provide training to those who have direct contact with customers, and to their supervisors, on topics such as new products, sales practices, risk disclosure and new regulations.

The cartoon below highlights the need for securities professionals, including analysts, to undertake this training. However, it also serves as a reminder that employers will distance themselves from individuals who stray from the ethical path. We saw in the Introduction how Morgan Stanley reported one of its employees to the local regulator over an alleged insider trading incident. I would reiterate that analysts who conduct themselves appropriately and follow the company's approval processes would stand a better chance of having their employer's support if ever they found themselves in trouble with the regulator or courts.

CASE STUDY

Cheating in tests

Details: FINRA fined and suspended 16 representatives of State Farm VP Management in March 2008 for test-taking irregularities in its Continuing Education Program. The fines ranged from US$5,000 to US$10,000 and the suspensions ranged from 30 days to six months. One representative was barred as a principal. Nine of the individuals were supervisors who directed or allowed subordinates to take one particular test for them.

Cheating in tests—*cont'd*

One was a supervisor who directed a subordinate to take the test for other reps. Six were reps who took the tests for their supervisors. FINRA acknowledged that the reps had acted without any authorization from State Farm. The individuals neither admitted nor denied the findings.

Conclusion: As we see later in the intellectual property example on plagiarism, studies suggests that business students may be more inclined to cheat than students in other disciplines, possibly because their main purpose for continuing further education is to get a better job at the end of it rather than the pursuit of academic gratification. Perhaps the same conclusion might apply to some brokers and analysts. Anyway, this case demonstrates that regulators and employers won't tolerate cheating, even though old-timers like Alex below may have gotten away with it in the past.

The realm of research

When "research" criteria are triggered, various requirements come into play, including the need for appropriate registration and licensing, supervisory approval, addition of disclosures as well as fair distribution. Thus, research analysts need to know whether their communications constitute "research" or "non-research". A clear understanding of the distinction has repercussions for sell-side analysts in the way they communicate—whether with their external fund management clients or with their internal clients (including cash sales, proprietary traders, the structured products team or asset management arm) and by whatever method (whether through formal publications, e-mail correspondence, morning sales meetings, phone calls, one-on-one meetings, road shows, conferences, mass-media appearances and so on).

Sales representatives, traders and marketers should also understand what it would take for their own communications to cross over the line into "research" and for themselves to be regarded as "research analysts" by the regulators, whatever their official titles may be and whatever departments they may be in.[5]

It seems clear that equity research comes within the ambit of research regulations in developed markets. There has been some debate, however, as to what extent credit/bond research is, or should be, subject to research regulations, as discussed below. In any case, I trust that the principles laid out in this book will be as useful to credit and bond analysts as I hope they are to equity analysts.

The principles should also be of great interest to buy-side analysts, even though their internal analysis for their in-house client may not technically fall within "research" definitions under regulations designed to protect external clients and members of the public. Their efforts would still of course be subject to market legislation, for example with respect to market abuse such as insider trading and manipulating prices by spreading rumors. Whereas they may not be exposed to all the same potential conflicts of interest that sell-side analysts in the global banks are exposed to, they nevertheless do share some common conflict risks. Furthermore, buy-side analysts would still need to compete with sell-side analysts by providing their in-house client with sufficient information and risk assessment for them to make their investment decisions.

Bonds are generally included in any definition of securities, and the bond markets are evidently within securities regulators' purview. Here are a couple of cases involving the bond markets, although not necessarily involving research analysts. Both happen to be insider trading cases. We consider insider trading as a separate subject later on in this chapter.

CASE STUDY

Ambit of securities regulations (bonds)

Details: In the U.S., Barclays Bank paid the SEC US$10.9 million in May 2007 to settle insider trading charges. This included a civil money penalty of US$6 million. Barclays' former head trader of U.S. distressed debt also paid a penalty of US$750,000. Neither admitted nor denied the SEC's findings that they had illegally traded millions of dollars of bond securities over 18 months using inside information gleaned from bankruptcy creditors meetings.

In the U.K., the FSA reached its first market abuse settlement involving the credit market in September 2008. In this particular case, a former hedge fund manager with Moore Europe Capital Management was fined

Ambit of securities regulations (bonds)—*cont'd*

£52,500 for trading in the bonds of Rhodia, a speciality chemicals manufacturer headquartered in France, just before the company announced a refinancing program. The fund manager had received the inside information from Credit Suisse, which had contacted him for advice on the correct pricing of the deal. The individual settled early. If he hadn't, his fine would have been £75,000. Neither Moore Europe Capital Management nor Credit Suisse was criticized.

Separately, the FSA censured two portfolio managers for market abuse in October 2009. They were portfolio managers of a structured investment vehicle, called K2, for Dresdner Kleinwort (which then became part of Commerzbank). They were given inside information about a potential new issue of Barclays floating rate notes (FRNs), which were going to be on more favorable terms than the previous issue. They sold the fund's holdings of the previous issue to two counterparties. When the new issue was announced these two counterparties had to make mark-to-market losses on their trades. The FSA acknowledged that the two Dresdner traders did not make a personal profit from the trade. However, Margaret Cole, the FSA's director of enforcement, refuted the argument that practices in the debt market meant it was always acceptable to trade after being "sounded out" on a new issue. "Future offenders will be likely to face significantly more severe sanctions," she said.

Conclusions: Although not specifically relating to research analysts, these cases set useful precedents to demonstrate that regulators on both sides of the Atlantic will bring cases involving the bond markets. There's no doubt that the bond markets are well within the purview of securities regulations. As such, bond and credit analysts should not presume that their actions and recommendations would not be of interest to securities regulators.

Let's now consider bond and credit research specifically.

EXAMPLE

Ambit of securities research regulations (equity and credit research analysts)

The debate: Under U.S. securities regulations,[6] and in the context of communications with the public, a research report is generally defined as

Ambit of securities research regulations
(equity and credit research analysts)—*cont'd*

"a written (including electronic) communication which includes an analysis of equity securities of individual companies or industries . . . and that provides information reasonably sufficient upon which to base an investment decision". The definitions say that a "research report includes, but is not limited to, a report which recommends equity securities, derivatives of such securities, including options, debt and other types of fixed-income securities, single stock futures products, and other investment vehicles subject to market risk". The emphasis is evidently on equity securities, although the references to "is not limited to" and "other investment vehicles" are general catch-alls.

Furthermore, the U.S. requirement for analyst certification generally refers to a written or electronic communication that includes "an analysis of a security or an issuer . . ." a definition that would not necessarily be restricted to equities alone. Then, following the global financial crisis, FINRA's consolidated rule on spreading rumors was revised to cover all securities, not just equities.

In practical terms, the NYSE and NASD stated in a joint report in December 2005 that they would monitor the extent to which firms have adopted and adhered to the Bond Market Association's voluntary principles relating to fixed-income research[7] before determining whether more definitive rulemaking would be required.

European regulations[8] require fair representation of investment recommendations and the disclosure of conflicts of interest. It defines "recommendation" as meaning "research or other information recommending or suggesting an investment strategy, explicitly or implicitly, concerning one or several financial instruments or the issuers of financial instruments, including any opinion as to the present or future value or price of such instruments, intended for distribution channels or for the public". The ambit seems pretty broad, and would seem to catch the recommendations of individual bond issues as well as the issuers themselves.

Interestingly, the chairman of the Committee of European Securities Regulators, Eddy Wymeersch, was quoted by David Ricketts in the *FT* on November 10, 2008, as saying: "Although Mifid (the European Union's Markets in Financial Instruments Directive) has been a catalyst for changes in the market structure, the biggest issue we are still struggling with is if it should be exclusively applicable to equities, or whether it should be extended to other securities, such as bonds and derivatives."

In Hong Kong, the Securities and Futures Commission's Code of Conduct states that disclosures are required for securities that are

Ambit of securities research regulations
(equity and credit research analysts)—*cont'd*

reviewed in investment research reports.[9] According to the interpretations provided in Paragraph 16 of the code, "investment research" includes documentation containing any one of the following: i) result of investment analysis of securities; ii) investment analysis of factors likely to influence the future performance of securities, not including any analysis on macroeconomic or strategic issue or iii) advice or recommendation based on any of the foregoing result or investment analysis. Furthermore, the interpretations then clearly define "securities" as meaning "shares issued by a listed corporation and any warrants or options on these shares". There is, however, no reference to bonds. That said, Alan Linning, partner at international law firm Sidley Austin and former director of enforcement at the SFC, notes that, while the code currently defines securities rather narrowly for research purposes, the Securities and Futures Ordinance (SFO) defines "securities" more broadly for the purposes of market misconduct such as insider trading and covers bonds as well as other instruments.[10]

The CFA Institute, in their research objectivity standards, defines research as, "a written or electronic communication that firms sell or distribute to clients or the general public, which presents information about a corporate issuer and may express an opinion or make a recommendation about the investment potential of the corporate issuer's equity securities, fixed income securities, or derivatives of such securities". The definition may have no regulatory standing in specific jurisdictions. However, importantly, it does set an industry standard for professional securities analysts to follow that is both global in scope and specifically covers fixed income securities in addition to equity securities.

The final communiqué of the 31st annual conference of the International Organization of Securities Commissions (IOSCO),[11] held in Hong Kong June 5–8, 2006, refers to the debate about disclosures in the bond market as being "one of the liveliest discussions at the Conference". It also refers to "the exceptional challenges that are to be found in the bond markets sector, particularly in the pursuit of greater transparency and the issues to be faced by regulators within that process".

Conclusions: Securities regulations around the world invariably are broad enough to capture research on securities and instruments other than equities, even though up until now regulators may have concentrated on equity research. The global financial crisis of 2007–2009 will inevitably herald a wider application of securities regulations than may have been adopted in the past.

Suffice it to say I think the best-practice principles presented in this book would be useful for all sell-side analysts, both equity and credit, to follow. Where specialist legal and compliance advice may be necessary is in determining the extent to which research disclosures are required for specific types of product in specific jurisdictions. As mentioned above, these best-practice principles should also be of great interest to buy-side analysts as well, even though technically they may not be catering to multiple clients or the public.

Research would, by my interpretation, include all initiations of coverage and changes of recommendations for securities, including implied recommendations and views as to what extent current prices, valuations, discounts or premiums are justified. I would also suggest that the definition would include new forecasts, estimates, target prices and target valuations, at least insofar as they materially affect investors' investment decisions.

Moreover, research analysts are defined in U.S. regulations as being responsible in connection with the preparation of research reports, or making recommendations or offering opinions in public appearances or establishing a rating or price target of a subject company's equity securities. This could be relevant, for example, if sales and traders widely communicate substantive analyses with recommendations on a security, including short-term trading calls, that cannot be attributed to the respective research analyst. In other words, research is defined by its content, not by the job description of the person preparing or disseminating it.

It might not always be immediately clear whether a certain asset class or investment instrument is included under the regulations. Although not specifically relating to research, the following case study probes the boundaries of U.S. and U.K. securities regulations by exploring whether swaps might be included in their purview.

CASE STUDY

Ambit of securities regulations (swaps and other derivatives)

Introduction: Traditionally, swaps have not been regarded as securities since they only give an economic benefit, and do not confer any ownership or voting rights. However, recent cases have brought to the fore the debate as to whether or not swaps should come under the purview of regulators.

IOSCO published its recommendations for unregulated financial markets and products in September 2009.[12] The recommendations cover

Ambit of securities regulations (swaps and other derivatives)—*cont'd*

asset-backed securities, collateralized debt obligations and credit default swaps. However, it conceded that its recommendations "go beyond the traditional remits of regulators".

Mary Schapiro, the chairman of the SEC, said in an interview with Bloomberg's Judy Woodruff in August 2009: "The SEC should have a role in policing these instruments, particularly where these instruments are economic substitutes for securities."

Details: The SEC brought its first enforcement action involving security-based swaps in April 2008. This was a bribery and corruption "pay-to-play" case where payments were allegedly made by a broker-dealer firm called Blount Parrish & Co. to the mayor of Birmingham, Alabama (while he was serving as president of the County Commission of Jefferson County), in exchange for participation in local municipal deals. Criminal charges were also brought, and in October 2009 the mayor was found guilty. He was later sentenced to 15 years in prison. A case of "mayor culpa", you might say.

In its first insider trading case involving credit default swaps, the SEC charged a Deutsche Bank bond salesman and a Millennium Partners fund manager with insider trading in May 2009. The alleged trading involved the reaping of a US$1.2 million profit from trading in credit default swaps of VNU, an international holding company with media interests. The judge rejected the bond salesman's claim that the SEC had no jurisdiction over these CDSs.

In July 2008, the U.K. regulator fined an IT professional who had used contracts for difference (CFDs) in effect to short-sell shares in The Body Shop (see the U.K. case study on "Use/dissemination of price-sensitive information" later in this chapter).

Disclosures: Various cases have prompted regulators to require investors to disclose material derivatives positions in companies. The Children's Investment Fund (TCI) lost a court battle against U.S. rail network CSX over the disclosure of covert stakes in companies. The judge ruled that swaps should be viewed as constituting beneficial ownership, and that they should be included in overall holding calculations for disclosure purposes.

Following the creeping M&A actions by Schaeffler Group in respect to Continental and by Porsche in respect to Volkswagen, European regulators have also begun requiring investors to disclose material positions.

Ambit of securities regulations (swaps and other derivatives)—*cont'd*

Aside: The Capital Market Authority of Saudi Arabia (CMA), where the stock market had hitherto been closed to foreign investors except through funds, announced on August 20, 2008, a resolution that allows "Authorized Persons to enter into Swap Agreements with non-resident foreign investors whether institutions or individuals, to transfer the economic benefits of the Saudi Companies' Shares listed on the Saudi Stock Exchange (Tadawul) while Authorized Persons retain the legal ownership of the shares". The board resolution comes with conditions and requirements that need to be met. Furthermore, the CMA's glossary of defined terms used in the Capital Market Law includes contracts for difference (CFDs) under the definition of "securities". Instruments such as swaps and CFDs are evidently well within the purview of at least the Saudi Arabian securities regulator.

Conclusions: From our research perspective, securities regulators have traditionally focused on equity research. We've seen that they are likely to look at credit research more from now on. Research on quasi-securities such as swaps might also now be on their radar screen.

Since IOSCO's recommendations for unregulated financial markets and products in their own words "go beyond the traditional remits of regulators", it will be interesting to see what actual regulatory measures are introduced around the world.

As mentioned, research is invariably defined by its content. Regulators do not necessarily draw a distinction between sales and research—if the comment satisfies the definitions of "research", then it might be considered as research, whatever the official role of the person making the comment.

Take an example where a salesperson writes a detailed analysis of a company, gives a personal view as to whether or not it would be a good investment, and then distributes this to a wide audience. This could count as research, especially if the analysis is deemed to be sufficient for an investor to make a decision on. Note, the personal view might be explicit, as with outright advice to buy, sell, switch, punt and so on, or it might be implied, as with a subjective view as to whether or not a valuation or premium/discount to peers is demanding, justified, warranted, reasonable, fair, achievable and so on.

If it is deemed to be "research", then the material should be approved for fair distribution to clients simultaneously with appropriate disclosures, including risk disclosures.

EXAMPLE

Ambit of securities research regulations (marketers of research, including hedge fund research)

Introduction: There has been much debate as to the extent to which hedge funds should be regulated. Trading losses of US$6 billion at Amaranth Advisers in September 2006 and the fall from grace of Long-Term Capital Management (LTCM) in 1998 brought this debate into focus. These flashpoints were followed by the collapse of Bear Stearns in early 2008, after two of its hedge funds lost money on derivative trades related to subprime loans. Hedge funds were accused of forcing the collapse of both Bear Stearns and Lehman Brothers. More on this later. Anyway, in terms of prospective hedge fund regulation, regulators around the world may come to different conclusions or apply different thresholds for the amounts and conditions required to qualify for exemption from any regulations and registration. They may rely to some extent on self-monitoring by the industry itself. In the U.K., for example, the Hedge Fund Working Group published in January 2008 a 140-page document on best practices on matters such as disclosures, conflicts of interest, valuation of assets and management of risk. IOSCO published its recommendations in their Hedge Funds Oversight report in June 2009.

In any case, remember that it's invariably the content that defines "research" rather than the author's job description. Marketers of hedge-fund communications need to know whether their own commentaries constitute research.

Details: Keith Black of the Stuart Graduate School of Business and John Mauldin of Millennium Wave Investments, both in the U.S., recount how even the covering letter accompanying a hedge-fund research report submitted to the NASD for checking was considered by the NASD to be a research report itself.[13] The letter included four reasons the sender liked the fund and the appropriateness or non-appropriateness of the fund for investors. The NASD considered the covering letter to be a research report, and therefore subject to research regulations. This was notwithstanding arguments that sales literature was never intended to be captured by research regulations or that analysis of hedge funds should not be subject to the same rules as equity analysis because they involve less risk of abuse, such as front-running. One supporting factor for this second argument is that the price of a private fund is its NAV (a function of the value of the underlying portfolio securities), not a market price based on the supply and demand for the fund itself.

Ambit of securities research regulations (marketers of research, including hedge fund research)—*cont'd*

Conclusion: The U.S. definition of research—"analysis . . . and information reasonably sufficient upon which to base an investment decision"—is, in theory, broad enough to catch any investment adviser's or salesperson's communications to clients urging them to invest in an investment product. This could include marketers of hedge funds. If a regulator thinks a marketer or broker is acting as a research analyst by producing research material, then the person might need to be registered and provide research disclosures.

There can be a fine line between what constitutes "research" and what doesn't, and some firms are evidently exploring the boundaries by employing analysts and other experts on the sales and trading desks, as the following example demonstrates.

EXAMPLE

Ambit of securities research regulations (analysts as experts on sales desks)

Summary: From a *Financial Times* article of May 8, 2006, we see that Lehman Brothers had "liberated" analysts from restrictions on what they can say and when they can say it by adding them to the equity sales and trading desks. As experts or specialists on the sales and trading desks, they would not write research as such, but would consider themselves free to respond quickly to market events and to call selected clients about perceived trading opportunities.

The article quotes one regulatory executive (although it's not clear which regulatory authority is represented) as saying that as long as the desk analysts do not share any client information with their bank's proprietary traders, there should not be a problem.

Conclusion: By my understanding of the issue, and notwithstanding Lehman's current status as an ex-global investment bank, provided such experts do not communicate "research" to their selected clients, they should be free to act as sales/traders and call clients selectively.

Ambit of securities research regulations (analysts as experts on sales desks)—*cont'd*

It remains to be seen whether regulators globally are comfortable that the specific communications between such expert sales/traders and selected clients do not constitute "research", and also whether the broader client base is comfortable with any perceived selective treatment. Also, as my former colleague Paul Sheehan reminds me, traders' phone calls are invariably taped, making it that much easier for a regulator to catch instances where the experts' comments might drift over into the realm of "research".

(See also the case study on "huddles" between Goldman Sachs analysts and traders in the front-running and selective distribution section below.)

Invariably regulators require analysts, brokers and investment advisers to be registered as such. However, it's not just the so-called Anglo-Saxon markets where regulators control the activities of securities and investment professionals. The Securities and Exchange Board of India announced in May 2008 their SEBI (Intermediaries) Regulations, requiring financial intermediaries to get licensed. In Thailand, a headline in the July 30, 2009, issue of the *Bangkok Post* read: "Unlicensed brokers emerge as new threat". In the first half of the year Thai regulators took legal action against five companies for operating illegal brokerages and selling futures contracts without a license. The following case study shows how Chinese regulators are clamping down on unregistered purveyors of investment advice.

CASE STUDY

Ambit of securities research regulations (stock-tipping bloggers)

Summary: Chinese law prohibits the provision of securities consultancy services without approval from the China Securities Regulatory Commission (CSRC). Xinhua News Agency reported on May 23, 2008, that "Big Brother Leader 777", a self-styled prophet of China's stock market, had been jailed for three years, fined RMB600,000 and had his illegal earnings confiscated, for illegally selling share tips over the Internet.

Ambit of securities research regulations (stock-tipping bloggers)—*cont'd*

Details: The *FT* reported on July 13, 2007, that the Chinese police in the northeastern city of Changchun had arrested an Internet blogger, WXJ, after an investigation into his unauthorized investment consulting business. Also known as "Big Brother Leader 777" and the "patron saint" of stock traders, his stock tips apparently made his site one of China's most popular, and he is reported to have made RMB10 million for his investment advice. Specifically, the court heard that he'd made RMB205,000 by selling tips to 16 people from May 2006 to May 2007.

At the time of his arrest, lawyers interviewed by the *FT* said it was unclear if his detention was part of a broader move against informal investment companies. However, Xinhua News Agency reported on July 27, 2007, that the CSRC had confirmed 11 cases of unlicensed securities consulting businesses operating on the Internet. Then the *SCMP* reported on October 11 that Shanghai police had arrested two unlicensed stock traders for allegedly offering trading tips to retail investors. These actions culminated in the introduction of new rules in April 2009 requiring all securities brokers in China to pass standard professional exams and to be registered with the Securities Association of China, as reported by *China Daily*.

Aside: In a similar case in South Korea, a blogger codenamed Minerva was arrested in January 2009. Rather than being charged over licensing requirements, he was accused of undermining financial markets with his doom-mongering. Christian Oliver, writing for the *FT*, says the case illustrates the government's unease with the growing influence of online gossip in the world's most wired economy. Like Big Brother Leader 777, Minerva had gathered a dedicated following. He had made accurate predictions ahead of the Lehman collapse. At least this case had a happy ending for the accused. He was acquitted.

Conclusions: However mercurial China's laws may seem at times to some, the authorities are evidently taking the provision of securities advice seriously.

Unlicensed pundits (bloggers or otherwise) who give investment advice on securities are potential targets for regulators, whether in China or elsewhere in the world. As stressed previously, securities research is invariably defined by its content, so it doesn't matter what someone's role is—if they're publishing material that constitutes research or investment advice, then they need to ensure that proper procedures are followed.

These blogging cases from China and Korea highlight the growing problem for all regulators posed by so-called citizen journalism, which we discuss further in the next example.

Some people might wonder how even formal journalists or commentators in the press get away with discussing securities and giving advice.

EXAMPLE

Ambit of securities research regulations (media commentators)

Background: Generally speaking, in the democratic world at least, recognized media participants have won the right to ply their trade by reporting news and giving views. It's difficult for the authorities in a democratically-elected society to argue against "public interest", with perhaps "national interest" being an overriding factor (see the corporate governance case studies in Chapter 2). Nevertheless, media participants from time to time have run-ins with authorities regarding issues such as freedom of speech, defamation and the protection of sources.[14]

News reporters and media commentators would generally not fall within the ambit of securities regulators. For example, the "news media" is granted specific exemption from Regulation AC (Analyst Certification) in the U.S., and European regulations provide similar exemptions. See the case study in Chapter 3 on Overstock.com, where the SEC in the U.S. conceded that the issuing of subpoenas to journalists had been extraordinary.

However, the democratization of the media, that is the gathering and dissemination of news and views by citizen journalists, bloggers and twitterers, poses serious problems for authorities.[15]

Also, as I discuss throughout this book, the in-depth analysis and the recommendation of specific securities throws up various issues—or hoops of fire that those making the recommendations need to jump through. Invariably, for the purposes of investor protection, regulators require anyone who provides securities "research" and makes specific securities recommendations supported by in-depth analysis to be subject to higher standards of oversight.

Details: One high-profile and often controversial figure in the U.S. is Jim Cramer, who airs his views and stock recommendations on CNBC. However, he is also a director of TheStreet.com, which is registered with the SEC as an investment adviser. Cramer is identified in the TheStreet.com's investment adviser registration documents as being one of the individuals who determine investment advice. His investment activities and experience are detailed in the registration documents.

Ambit of securities research regulations (media commentators)—*cont'd*

In Hong Kong, Paul Pong regularly writes his Market Mood commentary in the *SCMP*. He clearly states at the top of his column that he is an investment analyst and head of Pegasus Fund. He is registered with the Securities and Futures Commission, under his Chinese name Pong Po Lam, as a licensed responsible officer for Pegasus Fund Managers, which itself lists "Advising on Securities" as one of its regulated activities. Until October 5, 2008, Pong also presented his Portfolio Picks. However, according to an editor's note, he discontinued his portfolio given potential conflicts of interest with his obligations as a professional fund manager.

In the case study later in this chapter entitled "Regulations tightening up around the world (China)", we will see that a representative of Beijing Shoufang Investment Consulting was fined for stock manipulation. For the purposes of this example, he was also a regular guest on the China Securities program aired by China Central Television (CCTV). As reported by the *SCMP*, not only was he banned for life from the securities industry, but he also had his license as a stock commentator canceled.

Aside: Whether or not an individual is registered to give investment advice, any commentator would still need to ensure that they don't fall foul of securities-related laws (for example, with respect to market manipulation such as insider trading, spreading rumors and so on). The *International Herald Tribune* of October 15, 2008, ran an article written by Noam Cohen entitled "Web lets rumor mill grind faster". One of the stories was that the SEC and CNN were investigating the posting of a rumor onto a CNN-sponsored citizen-journalism site called ireport.com that Steve Jobs, the CEO of Apple, had been rushed to the hospital. The *IHT* referred to this story as a "false item", which had caused Apple's share price to fall 5 percent. That's the power of rumor. (Having said that, in January 2009 Jobs did not give the keynote speech at Macworld in San Francisco and later admitted that his condition was worse than originally thought. Within a few months he'd had a liver transplant. The old saying "where there's smoke there's fire" may sometimes hold water.)

Conclusions: There may be some commentators in some markets who make specific securities recommendations supported by in-depth analysis while not being regulated, but in the developed markets you'll invariably find that such pundits are subject to regulation and need to be able to demonstrate suitable experience.

Ambit of securities research regulations (media commentators)—*cont'd*

I'd also note that research definitions do not specify that the provider of research necessarily needs to receive any payment from the recipient of his services for regulations to be breached. However, when determining the amount of any fine to be levied, a regulator would no doubt take into consideration any commissions or fees that the adviser had earned. Regulators might also pay regard to whether the commentator had already bought shares beforehand in the companies they recommend without disclosing the fact. If he has an interest in the shares' performance, he could be seen to be conflicted by recommending them.

Notwithstanding the press community's desire to have freedom of speech as its bedrock defense, both formally-recognized journalists and anonymous bloggers still need to be responsible and to take care not to breach legal and ethical boundaries. Of course, there's a gulf between these two categories of journalists in terms of self-regulation and conduct. Whatever category they're in, people can't just say what they want.

However, saying what you want in a public forum seems to be how the world is evolving. StockTwits.com, a so-called twittering or micro–blogging site, describes itself as "an open, community-powered idea and information service for investments" and as "Bloomberg for the little guy and gal". The site says that users "can eavesdrop on traders and investors, or contribute to the conversation and build their reputation as savvy market wizards". It remains to be seen how effectively regulators will be able to police the spreading of rumors by twitterers and bloggers.

Subject to appropriate in-house approval processes, analysts can usually come to their own conclusion as to whether their words constitute "research" by asking themselves: "Is what I am writing commercial or value-added, and do I expect sales to be able to use the information to encourage clients to trade in the name? And is this the kind of information that would be useful to all clients who may be interested in this company, not just my focus clients?" If the answer to either question is "Yes", then the analyst should probably publish the note to all clients as a research report with a formal investment conclusion.

For accountability purposes, all published material, whether it is deemed to be research or non-research, should be attributed to appropriately registered and licensed authors, with their roles identified and contact details given. See Chapter 4 for a discussion on "non-research" commentary and e-mails.

I thought it would be useful to end the sections on "Supervision and control of research" and "The realm of research" with some thoughts to help practitioners reduce their approval and publishing risks, especially during critical times. The decision-tree format represents a kind of research supervisor's cheat-sheet, I suppose.

EXAMPLE

Minimizing approval and publishing risks

The questions: As a supervisory analyst confronted with an out-of-the-ordinary publishing request during a critical time I would ask myself two fundamental questions:

1. Is this new "research" (that is analysis and sufficient information on which to base an investment decision), or is it "non-research"?
2. Is the information that the analyst is using "public", or is it "private" (that is material and price-sensitive information that's not yet publicly available)?

The decision-making: If it's objective "non-research" commentary on publicly available information, then it can be distributed to anyone.

However, if it constitutes new "research" (especially with commercial ambitions), then it needs to be published fairly to clients. The process would include ensuring that:

- the author has the necessary licenses and registrations;
- any actual, perceived or potential conflicts of interest are managed appropriately, with business relationship lists checked and research disclosures added as appropriate;
- any information used is publicly available, and not material and price-sensitive unpublished information;
- comments or views are based on fact or reasonable assumptions, and are not defamatory;
- any recommendations, target valuations or earnings forecasts are justified and consistent, with risks to the investment case highlighted;
- the research is published to all clients before the analyst presents it to internal sales or prop traders, or selected clients; and
- the approval process is documented and the research is retained for easy retrieval, if ever required by a regulator or court.

Minimizing approval and publishing risks—*cont'd*

In effect, the 80-20 rule might apply, that is that 80 percent of an approver's time might need to be spent on 20 percent of the volume of the material. He shouldn't get so bogged down in the details that he can't see the wood for the trees. The sections to be focused on would include:

- the first/cover page;
- the investment summary;
- any M&A discussion;
- any forecasts, including financial models;
- the valuations and risks section; and
- the disclosure pages.

Less time would need to be spent on the details in between, at least if they are historic or factual in nature. As my old friend, Tony Shale of *Euromoney*, says: "The rest is just words." For example, however useful some analysts might think reams of pages giving details of quarterly results broken down by division may be to readers (and I'm not suggesting how useful they may be), these details would probably represent relatively low-risk material from a regulatory perspective. Other low-risk details might include details about the history of the company, its product ranges, customer profiles and so on.

If, however, the information that the analyst is using is deemed to be "private", that is material and price-sensitive, then:

- the supervisory analyst or research principal would need to make sure the analyst does not discuss the matter with his colleagues for fear of bringing them over the Chinese wall as well (and hence possibly preventing them from writing on the company too);
- the analyst or a compliance officer would need to ask the company to make the information public; and
- if the company doesn't comply, then the compliance department might have no alternative but to alert the regulator.

When the information is made public or is no longer material and price-sensitive, then the analyst can proceed with publishing his research.

Ultimately, the approver of the material needs to ensure that the publishing of the material does not expose the brokerage firm or the authors to any potential accusations, especially relating to conflicts of interest, front-running, insider trading, disclosure of investment risks and defamation. These aspects are discussed more fully in the rest of this and the following chapters. As to what to do when publishing mistakes do occur, please see the section in Chapter 5 entitled "Correcting errors".

Honesty and fair treatment of clients

Some analysts have expressed the view that securities regulations, especially those in the U.S., are a minefield and an impediment to doing their job properly. I appreciate that there may be a risk of over-regulation in some markets. However, I think the regulations are sometimes so general and non-specific that they provide huge scope for analysts to operate within, provided their motivations are honest and they treat clients fairly. The rationale for securities regulations is to maintain the integrity of markets and the public's confidence in them, and to protect the interests of investors. If capital cannot be raised and allocated efficiently and effectively, then the foundations of the capitalist system would be undermined.

The financial crisis of 2007–2009 prompted calls for widespread revisions to financial regulation. However, these will invariably focus more on such issues as banks' capital adequacy, bankers' remuneration, hedge funds and derivatives. Regulations relating to research analysts are already pretty well established in developed markets, with the exception perhaps of those relating to credit rating agencies—which evidently need to be tightened further following the financial crisis.

EXAMPLE

Common securities-related violations cited by the SEC and FINRA of the U.S.

- Offer and/or sale of securities by unlicensed broker-dealers, or permitting associated persons to function as research analysts without being properly registered.
- Violating broker-dealers' responsibility to treat customers fairly.
- Insider trading: buying or selling a security in breach of a relationship of trust and confidence while in possession of material, non-public information about the security.
- Manipulating the market prices of securities.
- Inappropriate influence by investment banking over research analysts.
- Inadequate supervision of research and banking departments.
- Misrepresenting to customers how safe or liquid the securities being sold to them really are.
- Issuing research reports that are misleading, exaggerated or unwarranted, and/or contain opinions for which there is no reasonable basis, and/or omit material facts, and/or omit warnings about investment risks and/or include insufficient disclosure of interests.
- Receiving payments for research without disclosing them.
- Failing to produce e-mail communications promptly when requested.

In the Global Research Analyst Settlements between the U.S. authorities and the big global houses between 2003 and 2006, it was not just the securities firms that were fined; it was also individual analysts and their research managers.

Apart from technical aspects such as securities licenses, registrations, legal disclaimers and research disclosures (with which the research firm will presumably be available to help analysts), an honest analyst who treats clients fairly and acts with integrity really has little to fear from this so-called minefield.

Analysts should always treat clients fairly, putting themselves in their clients' shoes. They should ask themselves whether what they have written could mislead, prejudice or otherwise disadvantage investors.

Analysts should make sure their new research, including initiations and changes of recommendations, estimates and target prices/valuations, is published through the firm's formal publishing system so that it is made available to all clients at the same time. In other words, they should refrain from selectively telling sales and favorite clients in advance.

Regulators around the developing world have followed the U.S.'s lead by clamping down on analysts and brokers who violate securities regulations, especially with regard to fair distribution of research, insider dealing and conflicts of interest. Many local representative or branch offices of global securities houses would likely be subject effectively to U.S. rules and regulations anyway, given membership say by a group member of the self-regulatory organization, FINRA, or given their own marketing in the States. However, they would also likely be subject to other local regimes around the world.

EXAMPLE

Regulations tightening up around the world (Hong Kong)

Market misconduct: Hong Kong's Securities and Futures Ordinance (SFO) came into effect on April 1, 2003. The SFO consolidated various existing regulations and also raised the bar to international standards. Key points for analysts are:

Insider-dealing cases can now be dealt with as either civil or criminal offenses. The standards of proof are higher for criminal offenses, but the penalties for conviction can be that much more severe. The first criminal conviction was handed down in July 2008. That case involved a finance manager of Sino Golf, a golf club manufacturing company, who sold shares in the group's holding company ahead of an announcement about the bankruptcy of one of the group's major debtors, thereby

Regulations tightening up around the world (Hong Kong)—*cont'd*

avoiding a loss in share value of over HK$60,000. More relevant to the readers of this book was that in the same month Mr. DJ, a former managing director in Morgan Stanley's fixed-income division, was arrested at Hong Kong International Airport after touching down from Beijing. He was charged with buying HK$87 million worth of shares of CITIC Resources, at a time when he was advising the company on financing for its acquisition of some oilfield assets in Kazakhstan. Mr. DJ denied the charges, but in September 2009 was found guilty of insider dealing. He was jailed for seven years, and fined HK$23.3 million.[16]

One major criminal market manipulation case involved the shares of Asia Standard Hotel Group. Four investors were found guilty in November 2009 of manipulating ASH shares by repeatedly trading among themselves to give the impression of wider investor interest and causing the shares to rise nearly 80 percent in price.

Other instances of market misconduct, such as disclosing, circulating or disseminating false or misleading information to induce securities transactions, can also be dealt with as either civil or criminal offenses.

Criminal sanctions allow for imprisonment of up to 10 years and/ or fines of up to HK$10 million.

Also note that under the regulations it is not just a breach if a person knows that the information is false or misleading (either through the inclusion or the omission of a material fact), but also if he is merely reckless or negligent in this respect.

Conflicts of interest: The SFC introduced new research-disclosure requirements to its Code of Conduct in April 2005 to address analysts' conflicts of interest. The new measures took into consideration the general principles published by IOSCO in September 2003. These include the disclosure of analysts' and their employers' interests in and relationships with the subject companies. However, they also took into account the practical needs of the Hong Kong market. Examples of specific new measures include:

- a trading blackout for analysts of 30 business days prior to, and three days following, the publication of research (except on the occurrence of major events that would affect the price of the securities and where the events are known to the public);
- the banning of trading in securities by analysts against their own recommendations; and
- the disclosure by analysts of their names and license status in media appearances.

Regulations tightening up around the world (Hong Kong)—*cont'd*

Note that the measures cover just listed shares, stock warrants and options; they do not apply to fixed-income securities.

(For further details of the general principles behind conflicts of interest and the normal disclosure requirements in global securities markets, please see Chapter 3.)

Other measures: These include the SFC's "Fit and Proper Guidelines", which were issued in April 2006 with an appendix added in January 2007 to cover sponsors and compliance advisers (see the case studies in Chapter 2 on Deloitte Touche Tohmatsu and ICEA Capital), as well as the HKEx's Code on Corporate Governance Practices, which became effective in 2005.

EXAMPLE

Regulations tightening up around the world (China)

Details: We saw in the earlier case about the stock-tipping blogger called "Big Brother Leader 777" that anyone giving securities advice in China now needs to be registered with the CSRC, and that securities brokers need to pass professional exams.

The Chinese authorities are evidently getting serious in other aspects of market regulation as well. In January 2007, the CSRC implemented new regulations regarding the disclosure of information. On September 6, 2007, Dow Jones Newswires quoted the vice chairman of the CSRC, Fan Fuchun, that the regulator will improve its cooperation with stock exchanges and the Public Security Bureau in the crackdown on illegal activities in the stock market. He continued: "With stock trading becoming increasingly active recently, insider trading has become more rampant and price manipulation has become more sophisticated, seriously disturbing market order and hurting investors' interests." Spoken like a true capitalist! Lo and behold, on February 4, 2008, a court in Zhejiang Province handed down jail sentences of 18 to 30 months to three people for insider trading of shares in Hangxiao Steel. As reported by the *SCMP* on May 13, 2008, the Supreme People's Procuratorate and the Ministry of Public Security jointly announced that those who make

Regulations tightening up around the world (China)—*cont'd*

profits of more than RMB150,000 from taking advantage of insider information could be sued in court.

Xinhua News Agency reported on November 22, 2008, that the CSRC had fined a representative of Beijing Shoufang Investment Consulting RMB125 million for stock price manipulation or, more specifically using the terminology of this book, front-running. According to Xinhua, the individual had purchased shares before trying to push their prices higher by recommending them to investors. The fine was the same amount as the illegal gains, and these were also confiscated. The CSRC also fined Wuhan Xinlande Investment Consultancy RMB7.35 million for a similar offense.

Another insider trading-related sentence was handed down in January 2009 when the former president of a leading Chinese securities firm, Guangfa Securities, was jailed for four years. According to the *FT*, the individual was accused of tipping-off his brother that Guangfa would seek a listing by taking over a company that already had one.

The penalty bar was raised in December 2009 when a senior trader at Great Wall Trust and Investment Corp. (later renamed China Galaxy Securities) was executed for embezzlement and misappropriation. It's a serious business, folks.

Conclusion: Following the global financial crisis of 2007–2009, China has a great opportunity to develop an efficient and effective regulatory system that draws on the most robust aspects of the world's securities regulations and avoids any aspects that have proven to be flawed.

EXAMPLE

Regulations tightening up around the world (Japan)

Summary: Japan's Financial Instruments and Exchange Law, nicknamed J-SOX (the Japanese version of the Sarbanes–Oxley Act in the U.S.), consolidates and builds on previous legislation and became effective on September 30, 2007. As part of the consolidation of the previous acts, securities firms and investment advisory firms have been grouped together with other investment organizations as "financial investment firms",

Regulations tightening up around the world (Japan)—*cont'd*

and such firms are required to categorize clients either as "professional investors" or "general investors".

Details: As with Hong Kong (see above), the maximum prison sentences and fines for market manipulation were increased. However, curiously, the Japanese legislators evidently regard insider trading as a lesser crime than other forms of manipulation. For example, they have increased the maximum prison sentence for general unfair trading, spreading of rumors, resorting to deceptive devices and market manipulation to 10 years (from five years). However, the maximum sentence for insider trading has only been increased to five years (from three years).

The fines were increased as follows: for the first category from a maximum of ¥5 million and ¥500 million for individuals and corporations, respectively, to ¥10 million and ¥700 million; and for insider trading from ¥3 million and ¥300 million to ¥5 million and ¥500 million, respectively.

Other measures relevant to securities analysts and investment advisers include the need to give appropriate explanation regarding the structure of transactions and the risks of losses. The level of explanation would depend on the level of customers' knowledge, experience and financial status as well as the purpose of the transaction. In its own explanations of the law, the Financial Services Agency (FSA) states: "If a financial instruments firm fails to provide necessary explanation upon sales of a financial instrument, the firm will bear liability for damages, whether at fault or not, with any losses incurred on the principal being presumed as losses to be compensated."

Following the financial crisis, the FSA also announced that it would introduce measures to address issues such as derivatives trading and hedge funds.

Conclusions: Even though these fines were increased they don't seem as onerous as those applicable elsewhere, for example the HK$10 million maximum payable in Hong Kong as detailed above. Nevertheless, a few years behind bars and the shame of being caught should provide sufficient deterrent for most market participants.

Aside: The *Economist* issue of January 19–25, 2008, gives an interesting insight into regulatory practices in Japan, and why they are different in certain respects to regulatory practices in other developed markets. Japanese regulators are much more inclined to punish the firm than the individual, perhaps because of the national ethos of collective responsibility and the traditional willingness of executives to accept

---

Regulations tightening up around the world (Japan)—*cont'd*

punishment even if they are not responsible. Furthermore, financial penalties are considered relatively ineffective, since companies might pass the cost of the fine onto customers in the form of higher prices. Temporary closure of the business is often a preferred punishment, given the damage to revenue and reputation. One recent high-profile example was in June 2009 when the FSA banned Citigroup from selling financial products to retail clients for a month. The charge was that the firm had failed to improve its control systems so as to enable it to detect suspicious transactions, including money-laundering. Only five years earlier Citigroup had to close its private bank after the FSA deemed that large profits had been amassed illegally as a result of a failure of internal controls and a lack of oversight from the bank's U.S. headquarters.

One of the overriding principles of securities regimes around the developed world is that of a fair market; that is, a level playing field where all clients are treated fairly. Analysts should constantly be mindful of their responsibilities and duties, and take note of specific themes such as front-running, insider dealing and the spreading of rumors.

Some of these themes may overlap, with the concept of price-sensitive information being a recurring element. Price-sensitive information includes the internal information that a company has which it needs to disclose to the market fairly. Research analysts should treat their own investment conclusions equally sensitively, and distribute their research to their clients fairly. An analyst must of course draw his conclusions from publicly available information. However, if the analyst expects readers to accept his arguments why a stock should be priced differently to the market price, then in effect the research itself becomes price-sensitive information.

Anyway, I've split these themes up into separate sections below for ease of understanding the different situations where they might manifest themselves in practice. These situations effectively represent the major risks that securities professionals such as research analysts, research managers, supervisors, compliance officers and financial editors face in their day-to-day jobs. Hopefully the case studies and my explanations will help these professionals identify these risks and avoid them or deal with them accordingly.

Front-running and selective distribution of research

Fair distribution: All new sell-side "research", having been approved as appropriate, should be distributed fairly to clients at the same time, and not selectively to the firm's own sales, traders and favored clients.[17] Once research is available to all clients of the same class or category, then analysts, sales and traders can invest on their own or the firm's account (subject to any delayed timing or other restrictions that may apply under local regulations[18] or the firm's internal policies, including restrictions on analysts trading against their recommendations) and target distribution of the material to selective clients as required, not before. In effect, the firm's proprietary traders are internal clients, but they cannot be treated any more favorably than external clients—that is, if the firm has external clients.

Some firms may have an informal medium, such as e-mail or communal bulletin boards, through which useful or interesting items of news, bits of information, rumors (see separate section below), earnings results, price alerts and so on, can be made available to sales in a timely fashion. However, if any new recommendations or opinions are expressed that can be seen to be sufficient for new investment decisions to be made, then individual sales and traders might act on that information ahead of the information being made available to the firm's general client base. This could expose the firm to potential charges of front-running or selective distribution.

Front-running of research involves personal trading by the analyst or proprietary (prop) trading by the brokerage firm using research before it is published to the wider client base. Selective distribution is where analysts or sales unfairly brief favored clients of new research before it is distributed to the general client base. Both are similar in nature. Regulators would treat seriously any instances where actual trading occurs. However, regulators might punish individuals for misconduct or firms for supervisory deficiencies, even if no trades are made or perhaps where it may be difficult to prove that the trader or investor relied on the research.

CASE STUDY

Front-running and selective distribution of research (huddles)

Summary: U.S. regulators subpoenaed Goldman Sachs in August 2009 demanding information about the firm's weekly "huddles" between its research analysts and traders, as reported by the *WSJ*. The regulators suspected that Goldman was taking advantage of as yet unpublished research for its own benefit and for the benefit of favored clients.

Front-running and selective distribution of research (huddles)—*cont'd*

Details: One example that Susanne Craig of the *WSJ* cited was that of a Goldman Sachs analyst who had published a "lackluster neutral" rating on the shares of mutual-fund manager Janus Capital in April 2008. Company documents revealed that at an internal meeting that month the analyst had told dozens of Goldman's traders that the stock was likely to head higher. The next day research-department employees called about 50 favored clients. Only six days later with the publication of a formal research note did the rest of the firm's clients find out about the analyst's new bullish views. However, by this time the price had already risen 5.8 percent.

Conclusion: However the SEC's investigation turns out, the case at least demonstrates that regulators expect firms not to treat their prop traders and special clients any more favorably than their other clients. It also demonstrates that a short-term trading tip that may be different to a long-term fundamental call should be treated as a separate piece of research in its own right. As such, separate research disclosures might be needed to show the rating definitions and histories of the short-term trading calls.

CASE STUDY

Front-running of research

Details: Banc of America Securities was fined US$26 million by the SEC in March 2007 for "failing to safeguard nonpublic research information and publishing fraudulent research". This followed an earlier fine of US$10 million in 2004 for failing to produce documents and e-mails promptly in respect to these investigations. The SEC cited a breakdown in internal controls. Sales and traders learned of upgrades and downgrades on multiple occasions between 1999 and 2001, with proprietary trading being executed on at least two occasions before the research was published. In addition, research reports were published on Intel Corporation, among others, that were "materially false and misleading". The firm consented without admitting or denying the commission's findings.

Front-running of research—*cont'd*

It's not just the brokerage firms who are liable to be penalized. A former analyst at Dao Heng Securities in Hong Kong lost his appeal in July 2004 against the SFC's decision to suspend his license for front-running his research reports. The companies he had been buying shares in ahead of publishing his buy recommendations to his clients were Chongqing Iron & Steel, Lerado Group and Global Green Tech Group.

Conclusion: The combined fine of US$36 million that Banc of America Securities had to pay is not insignificant. The main Global Research Analyst Settlements in 2003–04 (which neither Banc of America nor its parent Bank of America were parties to) marked a watershed for securities research, and significantly raised the bar in terms of fines. See Chapter 3 for further details of the settlements.

Whereas front-running of research involves trading by the analyst or the brokerage firm ahead of clients, selective distribution of research means that favored clients get access to the research ahead of the general client base. The NYSE issued a press release in July 2004 listing 16 individuals against whom they had recently taken disciplinary action. Summaries of three of these cases, as well as a separate case from the U.K., are given in the case study below.

CASE STUDY

Selective distribution of research

Summary: JC, director of equity sales at Merrill Lynch, and PC, previously a senior analyst at Merrill, were censured, suspended and fined US$150,000 and US$25,000 respectively for tipping-off a small number of clients of an impending recommendation downgrade before the downgrade was published. They neither admitted nor denied guilt. Merrill Lynch itself had previously been fined US$625,000 for supervisory deficiencies and for failing to prevent the misconduct.

TK, former director of institutional sales for HD Brous & Co., again without admitting or denying guilt, was censured and barred for, among other things, preparing and distributing research reports without supervisory-analyst approval.

Selective distribution of research—*cont'd*

Separately, the FSA in the U.K. fined RC, a Citigroup analyst, £52,500 in March 2007 for improper conduct that might have led to market abuse. He had alerted four clients of a forthcoming initiation-of-coverage report with a buy recommendation on Banca Italease. The *Times* of March 21, 2007, reported that he had described the company as "hot stuff" in an e-mail to one of the clients. None of the clients acted on the tip. If they had then this would no doubt have constituted "market abuse", which would have increased the severity of the case. (Consider, for example, the £750,000 meted out by the FSA on August 1, 2006, to both PJ, a former managing director at hedge fund manager GLG Partners, and GLG itself, for trading on confidential information relating to a new issue of convertible preference shares in Sumitomo Mitsui Financial Group. This was notwithstanding contentions by PJ that the trading occurred on the Tokyo Stock Exchange, which is not under the FSA's jurisdiction, and that the issue of convertible shares was already being widely rumored.) As it was, the fine for RC would apparently have been £75,000, but for his willingness to settle at an early stage of the investigation.

Conclusions: The U.K. case demonstrates that if an analyst inadvertently tips off sales, traders or clients about new research ahead of publication, then all steps should be taken to ensure that no actual trading is done in the name, and that the local regulator is alerted as soon as possible. Penalties are invariably more severe when illicit trading actually occurs.

Apart from the message that analysts must make sure research is approved and distributed fairly, the U.S. cases also illustrate the point that the regulator does not draw a distinction between sales and research; the same rules apply. Thus, under some regulatory regimes, any salesperson giving a client sufficient information on which an investment decision could be made could be regarded as a research analyst and be subject to research regulations. This applies to sales passing on an analyst's research, or sales being seen to be making their own "research" by making comments such as, "Our research analyst thinks this stock is a buy, but I reckon you should sell it for the following reasons. . . ."

The NYSE censured the following well-qualified professional in August 2005. He claimed he merely wanted to get feedback to improve the quality of his research before publishing it.

CASE STUDY

Selective distribution of research (fact-checking)

Summary: HR, former supervisory analyst and head of research with HD Brous & Co., consented to a censure and three-month bar for selectively pre-releasing reports to various parties, including the companies that were the subjects of the reports, their competitors and clients and employees of his member organization. The research reports disclosed the ratings, target prices and estimates he planned to assign the stocks and/or the projected date of publication of the report.

HR did not admit or deny guilt. As part of his defense, he contended that he pre-released some of the reports for fact-verification purposes, and to gain useful feedback before publishing the reports to clients.

Conclusion: If analysts do wish to have facts checked before publication, they need to strip out their recommendations, target prices, estimates and other views from reports before forwarding the remaining facts for verification. Analysts would have even more protection if they conducted such exercises through the compliance department. Fact-checking cannot be used as an excuse for the selective distribution of research.

Here's an example of an analyst leaving a brokerage firm after a routine review of e-mails apparently uncovered evidence of selective distribution.

EXAMPLE

Selective distribution of research (greater conviction of view)

Details: A semiconductor equipment analyst in the San Francisco office of Morgan Stanley voluntarily resigned after the firm found evidence of "inappropriate dissemination" of his views in e-mails, according to a *Wall Street Journal* article dated December 16, 2003. In the e-mails, distributed to four or five clients, the analyst had stated that he had picked up information on a stock and thus had "greater conviction" of his overweight opinion.

Selective distribution of research
(greater conviction of view)—*cont'd*

The *WSJ*, citing a person familiar with events, stated that the analyst had disagreed with the firm's interpretation of its policies and procedures. Morgan Stanley stated that it does not comment on employee matters.

Conclusion: Even additional information that strengthens an analyst's conviction of his existing view could be deemed to be material enough to warrant fair distribution of the comment to clients, on the basis that the incremental information might encourage investors at the margin to buy or sell who otherwise would not have done so.

Hints of forthcoming material changes should also be avoided. In one situation, I was asked to approve a limited-distribution e-mail on a rated Chinese media company as non-research market commentary. I questioned why the analyst was using consensus estimates instead of his own to let his clients know the current valuation for the company. On the face of it, that might seem fine, given that the consensus numbers were publicly available. However, the analyst mentioned that the consensus estimates had recently been downgraded by 66 percent to reflect the bad news that he was discussing. By using those estimates instead of his own, he could have been seen to have been implying that his own estimates were no longer valid, thereby alerting his clients of his own impending earnings-forecast downgrade, and by what extent he was intending to lower his forecasts.

In such situations the more appropriate and more commercial course of action is for analysts to make their forecast changes and publish them formally in a "research" report, as eventually happened in this case. The very fact that many other analysts in the market had already made their forecast changes also suggested that the analyst in question was a little behind the market—which was even more reason for him to get on and make his forecast changes instead of procrastinating with e-mail commentary.

Like a good chess player who is always prepared to counteract any move made by his opponent, a good analyst should rarely be totally surprised by any company results, news or events. An analyst should already have thought through the possible risks and permutations to his financial forecasts, and be ready to incorporate new factors into his spreadsheet as and when they happen. As in chess, of course, the number of potential moves ahead that analysts can anticipate is what separates the leaders from the also-rans, if you'll excuse the mixed metaphor.

Conflicting signals: It's one thing being prepared for all eventualities, but analysts should still avoid specifying the changes they will be making to their recommendation, valuation, target price or earnings estimates. This is especially the case for internal meetings and limited-distribution e-mails (that is, non-research), but I think it also makes sense for reports that are to be published formally. Although in published research this might seem to satisfy the principle of providing the same information to all readers at the same time, it might give conflicting signals to readers. Some readers may act immediately in anticipation of the potential change, while others more prudently may wait for the change, which, for whatever reason, may never come. So if an analyst thinks he is going to make a change, he should make it and publish it. This is the more commercial option, in any case, and helps the sales team in their job.

Scenario-building: It should, however, be okay for analysts in their published reports to present scenarios by saying how sensitive their estimates and valuations might be to changing assumptions. Indeed, this helps satisfy the requirement to draw risks to readers' attention, since readers can see how earnings estimates would change under more aggressive or more conservative assumptions. For the sake of consistency, the formal recommendation and target price should reflect the analyst's base case over the stated period of time. Target prices and trading opportunities can always be given for different classes of investors/risk-takers over different timeframes, provided appropriate disclosures and definitions are given.

Insider dealing and selective disclosure

This section deals with the passing on or use of material, price-sensitive information. We are interested in illegal insider dealing/trading, as opposed to the legal trading of shares by formal insiders of a company such as its directors. Certain academics and economists, including Henry Manne and Milton Friedman, have argued that such insider trading can actually make markets more efficient by speeding up the flow of information. One argument is that people who are in a position to know about a company's problems should be given an incentive to make the public aware of them. Mere whistle-blowing to regulators may not provide sufficient incentive.

Anyway, the practice is illegal in most regulated markets, at least the developed ones. It can be a complicated subject, and each case will depend on the circumstances and the jurisdictions in which the supposed insider trading took place. As a common principle, though, comments and views should be based on publicly available information and be seen to be so. Technically speaking, insider dealing usually only involves the dissemination and/or use of material and price-sensitive information.

Materiality and price-sensitivity of the information: Whereas the regulator has the benefit of hindsight in observing apparently inexplicable market movements before investigating what may have caused them, the analyst has to determine at the time he publishes his report whether any information given to him is material and price-sensitive.

There are no hard-and-fast rules about materiality and price-sensitivity. It's difficult to define thresholds for what might constitute a material impact on a company's stock price. Various factors, including the company's size, the liquidity of its shares and the volatility of the market, would be relevant. Ultimately, the test is whether the incremental information is sufficient to persuade investors who might otherwise not have done so to trade in the security. As a very general rule of thumb, any information that has the potential to affect stock prices (or analysts' earnings forecasts as a proxy) by under 5 percent is unlikely to constitute material information, whereas any potential effect of over 10 percent probably would. However, even a small change in an analyst's estimates that triggers a recommendation change might qualify—at least a regulator would argue that the analyst himself must have thought the information material enough to warrant a change in rec- ommendation. And the more a company presents the confidential informa- tion to an analyst as being factual, as opposed to potential, the more likely it is to be material.

The SFC of Hong Kong lists many possible examples of price-sensitive information, including: regularly occurring matters such as financial results and dividends; exceptional matters such as making acquisitions; signing contracts, entering into joint ventures or cancelling already announced agreements; fundraising exercises; comments on the prospects of future earnings or dividends; and changes of accounting policies, as well as changes of auditor. But it's not just information flow from a company's man- agement to the market that counts. For example, could an activist share- holder, who holds a closed-door meeting with a company's management to exert pressure on them to adopt a certain strategy, be generating his own inside information that he uses as a base for further investment?

If the analyst really believes a piece of hitherto undisclosed information is not that significant, then he should at least present it as such; for example, through using words such as "only" and "just" when describing the potential magnitude of the effect on earnings. Furthermore, the information should be more incidental to the message contained in the publication rather than representing the focus. If the information is only potential and immaterial, it presumably would not warrant a formal change of the analyst's estimates or views.

Notwithstanding the above, it may be a slippery slope in any case for indi- vidual analysts to determine to what extent unpublished information given to them would be material and price-sensitive. Not only might regulators be judging these criteria by a different yardstick, but if they see an analyst regu- larly using confidential information, albeit information that is deemed to be relatively immaterial and non-price-sensitive, they may be more inclined to monitor that analyst more closely than might otherwise be the case.

Sourcing and fair disclosure of information: Readers need to risk-weigh analysts' comments to make their investment decisions, so they need to know to what degree comments are factual. Analysts should distinguish between what the company has said officially (whether in stock exchange filings, press releases, analyst meetings or interactive data like XBRL), what the press, bloggers or twitterers have reported (either as fact or rumor) and what they themselves think (supported by analysis or evidence). Apart from providing extra information to the investor, sourcing information protects analysts in cases where comments turn out not to be true.

It's one thing, for example, when an analyst changes earnings estimates following a formal results announcement or some reported event. However, as a supervisory analyst, I would look closely at earnings estimate changes by an analyst following a one-on-one meeting with a company before results are formally announced. What extra information has the analyst received that he or she didn't have before, and that the market wasn't privy to? How material and price-sensitive might this information be?

The onus is invariably on companies to determine what information to disclose to analysts. Most developed markets now have rules requiring companies to disclose material, price-sensitive information to the market fairly. For example, the U.S. has Regulation FD (Fair Disclosure). The listing rules of the Hong Kong Exchange (HKEx) require issuers to make timely public disclosure of price-sensitive information. Even in a relatively restricted market like Saudi Arabia, a glance at the Web site of the Capital Market Authority shows fines being dished out to companies for failures in this regard, for example, Saudi Chemical Company being fined SR100,000 in August 2008.

Generally speaking, I would suggest that unless analysts suspect the information is inside information, they should be able to regard information given to them by company management as being publicly available. Nevertheless, analysts should be wary that some companies might be tempted to leak information out slowly through them, to avoid any sudden dramatic share price movement. For example, ahead of a formal results announcement a company might want to leak the prospect of disappointment out to the market, so that when the results are announced the market won't be taken completely by surprise. Analysts should not risk their own independence and integrity by doing the company's dirty work for them. It takes two to tango, so, as a safety measure, analysts should make clear to companies that they do not wish to receive material, price-sensitive information, unless the information is also being made available to the market. Analysts' suspicions should be aroused if the company representative says the information is "off-the-record" or if he is not prepared to be quoted.

Duty of confidentiality: In the U.S., the concepts of "misappropriation" (of confidential information in breach of a fiduciary duty) and "awareness" are important elements in deciding insider trading cases[19] (also see the ASCO and Cuban cases in the Sourcing information section below). In other markets such as the U.K., Australia, Hong Kong and Singapore, a fiduciary duty would not necessarily need to be proven. Even in the U.S. fraudulent misrepresentation might negate the need to prove a fiduciary duty. For example, if a hacker hacks into a company's system and trades on price-sensitive information that he has unearthed, then he may well be deemed to have committed insider trading even if he could argue that he didn't owe anyone any duty of confidentiality. For example, the SEC won a summary judgment against a Ukrainian hacker in March 2010. The SEC claimed that he had bought put options in the shares of IMS Health after hacking into Thomson Financial's computer network and finding out that earnings that were about to be released would be below analysts' expectations. (Also see the aside about an IT technician at The Body Shop in the U.K. case study on "Use/dissemination of price-sensitive information" later in this chapter.)

Analysts must treat confidential, price-sensitive information very carefully. They have a duty of care toward their clients, and should not expose them to risk by passing on inside information to them.

An analyst who has been given inside information is, in effect, compromised, and would be restricted from writing independent research until the information becomes public or is no longer price-sensitive. If an analyst believes he has been given inside information, he should not discuss the matter among his fellow analysts. If he does, he could risk making them insiders as well, and therefore possibly preventing them also from writing research on the company or sector. Instead, he should draw the matter to the attention of research management and compliance, who should either request the company to make the information public or else alert the local regulator.

EXAMPLE

Use/dissemination of price-sensitive information (general)

Summary: Insider trading is rife in the U.S. stock market. Christopher K. Thomas, the founder of Measuredmarkets, concluded that the aberrant activities revealed by analysis of price movements ahead of M&A announcements "most likely involved insider trading".[20] According to the deputy director of enforcement at the SEC, the number of insider-trading cases filed by the SEC since 2000, as a percentage of all their cases, has ranged from 7 to 12 percent. The practice is rife in London too.[21] Insider trading is evidently quite common in all developed markets, and regulators continue to take the matter very seriously.

Regulators' tools: If the monitoring of trading activity by analytical research firms such as Measuredmarkets is not sufficient to deter them,

Use/dissemination of price-sensitive information (general)—*cont'd*

would-be market abusers should note the comment by Rick Ketchum, then chief of regulation for the NYSE, as reported in the *FT* on August 6, 2007: "We are continually working to improve and strengthen our system of monitoring trades in NYSE-listed securities, options, bonds, ETFs and other products. Our surveillance systems allow us to review and investigate anomalous patterns that may constitute insider trading and market manipulation."

Also note that the records that regulators can get access to don't just include e-mail and phone records. In the U.S. they also include so-called "blue sheets", which include account names and trading information and which are generated by member firms at the request of regulators in connection with investigations of questionable trading. The NYSE announced on January 31, 2006, that it had fined 20 firms (including two former members) a total of US$5.85 million for inaccurate blue sheet submissions. The FSA in the U.K. fined Credit Suisse, Instinet (an agency-broker owned by Nomura) and Getco (a privately-owned market maker) a total of £4.2 million in April 2010 for not providing transaction reports accurately and promptly. Presumably, following these fines, trading records will be more accurate going forward.

The FSA recently introduced plea-bargaining and immunity to prosecution, measures which have proved useful in the U.S. in proving insider trading cases. Back in June 2008, the *Guardian* quoted Margaret Cole, head of enforcement at the FSA, saying that the FSA was looking at introducing a "leniency factor" to persuade suspects to cooperate. By March 2010, the FSA had secured a criminal insider trading conviction with the help of the trader's accomplice. (See the aside in the "Gathering confidential information" case study later in this chapter involving the former Cazenove trader nicknamed "Streaky".)

The Galleon hedge fund case that came to light in October 2009[22] showed how U.S. regulators had used wiretapping to catch their man. The man in question was Raj Rajaratnam, a larger-than-life character who headed a firm where internal analysts and fund managers who failed to provide inside information were allegedly berated or pushed out of the firm.

One interesting point that came out of the case in Hong Kong involving alleged insider trading in the shares of CITIC Resources, was that the prosecutor could determine not just when the defendant, DJ, opened and replied to his BlackBerry and e-mail messages but also how far down each page he had scrolled. (That should make the "Big Brother" conspiracy theorists smug.)

Use/dissemination of price-sensitive information (general)—*cont'd*

Another interesting point from that case was that the fine imposed on DJ represented the notional profit that he could have made—which was about 10 times the amount he actually made, as claimed by his defense counsel. (Apparently DJ sold half of the shares at a tidy profit shortly after the price-sensitive information became public, but sold the other half at a loss in the depths of the financial crisis. There were also heavy costs that the SFC ordered him to pay. DJ appealed the decision.)

In a new development, the SFC announced in late April 2010 that it was seeking a court order to bar a New York-based hedge fund, Tiger Asia Management, from trading in Hong Kong and to freeze assets allegedly gained from insider trading in the shares of Bank of China. One challenge for the SFC is that Tiger Asia has no employees or physical presence in Hong Kong.

Conclusions: The risk/reward ratio seems stacked against analysts and firms who wish to trade on inside information:

- regulators have the benefit of hindsight in being able to look back at suspicious price activity ahead of an M&A announcement;
- regulators can seek help from suspected insider trading accomplices through plea-bargaining arrangements or from third parties through whistleblower or bounty programs;
- regulators have the benefit of being able to access e-mail and phone records, as well as trading records, with increasing levels of cross-border cooperation (not just through the various M&A activity that has been going on recently between exchanges but also through IOSCO initiatives)[23];
- analysts stand to get fined much more than they stand to gain, not to mention any jail time that may need to be served; and
- if the burden of proof is too great for a criminal case,[24] a regulator can still bring a civil action.

However difficult it may have been in the past to catch insider traders, and notwithstanding the increased use of swaps and derivatives in insider trading cases, it must surely be getting easier for regulators to find the evidence needed, given the technology at their disposal and their ability to access records.

In any case, one thing that analysts and other securities professionals need to be aware of is that they are at the top of regulators' watch lists. In his special feature on insider trading, published by Bloomberg on June 20, 2007, Bob Drummond says that any whiff of Wall Street culpability prompts priority scrutiny. He quotes Stephen Luparello, who was NASD's

Use/dissemination of price-sensitive information (general)—*cont'd*

senior executive vice president for regulatory operations at the time, as saying: "Where you've got somebody in the industry that's involved, those always get raised to the top of the pile." A regulatory lawyer quoted by Bloomberg in March 2010 when an ex-investment banker and his wife were charged with insider dealing by the FSA, said: "This is the sort of case that the FSA should be bringing in order to achieve effective deterrence, rather than cases against a dentist and intern."[25] Going forward, I'm sure regulators around the world will step up their efforts to ensure that market professionals who deal in inside information are rooted out.

Let's look at some cases from around the world.

CASE STUDY

Use/dissemination of price-sensitive information (U.S.)

Summary: Fox-Pitt Kelton (now part of Macquarie Bank) settled with the SEC to the tune of US$50,000 in November 1996 over insider trading-related charges.

Details: According to the SEC, the Fox-Pitt Kelton analyst received material, nonpublic information from an issuer during a conference call, which the issuer held simultaneously with analysts from several broker-dealers. During the call several sales persons and another analyst walked in and out of the office where the conference call was being made, and heard the information being discussed. Sales traded on behalf of clients in the company's shares, and the second analyst traded in a firm proprietary account over which he had discretionary control.

Conclusions: The interesting thing to note about this case is that the SEC did not try to catch the firm on actual insider trading, but rather on supervisory deficiencies. The firm was in effect fined for not having procedures and practices to avoid insider trading, for example effective Chinese walls, policies relating to restricted and watch lists (which we'll discuss in Chapter 3) and appropriate training. An actual insider trading charge could have been more difficult to prove, for example given the fact that the issuer was giving the information to several analysts at the same time.

Use/dissemination of price-sensitive information (U.S.)—*cont'd*

This case serves as a lesson for analysts and brokerage firms that regulators have many weapons in their armory, and can choose their battlegrounds as they feel fit depending on the level of evidence available. Rather like Eliot Ness pinning Al Capone down on tax evasion charges rather than for murder or racketeering—it serves the purpose.

CASE STUDY

Use/dissemination of price-sensitive information (U.K.)

Summary: The U.K.'s Financial Services Authority issued a press release on December 16, 2004, stating that it had, for the first time, fined individuals for abusive dissemination of information. RH, an equity analyst with a firm of U.K. stockbrokers, traded in shares of I Feel Good (IFG), then publisher of a popular British comic magazine called *Viz*, using information on a bid for the company passed to him illegitimately by JS, the finance director of IFG at the time. RH and JS were fined £18,000 and £15,000 respectively.

Details: RH and JS knew each other as friends and former colleagues, and the press release referred to phone, text and e-mail correspondence between the two, including 11 text messages the day before the deal was announced. RH traded in the shares of IFG for himself and made a profit of just under £5,000. The press release made clear that RH had cooperated with the FSA by agreeing to settle the matter and that but for this, his fine would have been substantially higher.

Conclusions: This case again demonstrates the point made that offenders stand to lose more than they stand to gain. I'd also reiterate here that analysts who still choose to take the gamble of trading on inside information should cooperate with regulators if and when they get caught.

Note that this case involves the trading by an analyst of stocks using inside information on his own account. However, charges of insider trading or at least of misconduct could also apply to analysts who encourage clients to trade in securities using inside information. (See the selective distribution case study above involving the Citi analyst. Also see the Moore Europe

Use/dissemination of price-sensitive information (U.K.)—*cont'd*

Capital Management case earlier, which was the FSA's first bond-related market abuse settlement.)

Aside I: An interesting twist on the theme of insider trading was reported by the *Financial Times* on November 23, 2006, in an article entitled "FSA fines trader for passing on 'outsider' information". SP, an equity salesman with CSFB, which became Credit Suisse, was dismissed by the firm and fined £20,000 by the FSA for passing on to some hedge funds information about Boston Scientific, which apparently was not inside information but which the salesman evidently presented in a way that made it seem like it was. SP claimed he had not intended to give such an impression. This was misconduct rather than actual market abuse, as in the IFG case above. Although the case focuses on a salesman rather than a research analyst the same consequences would no doubt also apply to a research analyst who presented information in such a misleading way.

Aside II: One doesn't need to be an authorized individual to run afoul of insider dealing, and one doesn't even need to trade in actual securities either. In July 2008 the FSA fined an IT technician at The Body Shop, the ethical retailer, £85,000 for market abuse. Apparently he misused his technical skills to access confidential e-mails of senior executives, and saw e-mails giving details of the company's Christmas trading results and a draft announcement that the company had underperformed expectations. The technician, expecting the shares to fall when the announcement was made, borrowed money to enter into contracts for difference (CFDs) to reflect a short position of 80,000 shares in the company. On closing the position he made a profit of £38,472.

Aside III: The FSA successfully concluded its first criminal case in March 2009. A legal counsel at TTP Communications had told his father-in-law that Motorola was about to take over TTP. They both shared profits of nearly £49,000. Both were found guilty and were jailed for eight months.

We've already discussed the Hong Kong case involving insider trading by a former managing director at Morgan Stanley in the shares of CITIC Resources. Let's have a look at an earlier case involving information gleaned by a Goldman Sachs analyst at a small analyst briefing.

CASE STUDY

Use/dissemination of price-sensitive information (Hong Kong)

Summary: In June 2003, a Goldman Sachs analyst was reprimanded by the Securities and Futures Commission (SFC) in Hong Kong for selective disclosure of information passed to her by New World Development (NWD) at a small analyst meeting in 2001.

There were two underlying issues, as far as I can see and as far as the analyst was concerned. Firstly, that the analyst had apparently distributed new "research" internally (she'd slashed her forecasts) before publishing this to clients and, secondly, that she had passed on "information" provided to her by the company that was not available to the investing public.

Background: At the time of the case, and at the time of publishing this book, issuers in Hong Kong are subject to the rules of the Hong Kong Exchange (HKEx), whereas analysts are registered with the SFC.

The listing rules of the HKEx require issuers to make timely public disclosure of price-sensitive information. Furthermore, according to the HKEx Guide on disclosure of such information, issuers should "decline to answer analysts' questions where individually or cumulatively the answers would provide unpublished price-sensitive information". At the time of the reprimand of the analyst by the SFC, some industry participants expressed concern that no action had been taken by the exchange against NWD. Indeed it took seven years from the date of the analyst meeting for the HKEx to finally issue a press release that it had formally censured NWD. In the meantime, in a separate incident, the HKEx publicly censured CNOOC, a large Chinese oil company, for selective disclosures, as reported in the *SCMP* on October 7, 2005.

Details: We are less interested in the implications for issuing companies than in the implications for analysts who pass on price-sensitive information. In the SFC's press release of June 17, 2003, the then executive director of enforcement, Alan Linning, said: "The disclosure made in this case potentially gave those who were on the sales and trading floor of Goldman Sachs an intelligence advantage over those other members of the investing public who were not aware of the information. However, it does not appear that any member of Goldman Sachs staff acted on the information." In an *SCMP* article on June 19, Linning said: "We want to send a clear message to all analysts that they should not accept any price-sensitive information or selective disclosure."

Use/dissemination of price-sensitive information (Hong Kong)—*cont'd*

Conclusions: It may have been assumed by some local analysts that any information a company passed to them, in the normal course of their duty as analysts, and which the company would pass to any other analyst who asked for it, could be deemed to be publicly available information. This assumption cannot be taken for granted. It is all well and good in theory to say the onus is on the companies to decide what information to disclose to analysts. However, research analysts should still be satisfied that the information is publicly available.

Although the SFC accepted that the analyst had not acted dishonestly, this case demonstrates that analysts still need to take care when passing on information from companies. Analysts should make clear to companies that they do not wish to receive inside information.

Aside: On the flip side of the coin, a company could feel disgruntled if it has indeed followed correct disclosure procedures, but appears not to have done so because of some rumors that an analyst might have spread. My former colleague Marsanne Gee draws to my attention an official announcement made on August 19, 2008, by ZTE Corporation, a Chinese telecom equipment maker. In it the company denounces a rumor, allegedly spread by a telecoms analyst at a securities house in Shanghai, that China Telecom's tender for CDMA network equipment had been finalized, when apparently it had not been. The analyst's communication stated that ZTE's main local competitor, Huawei Technologies, had snatched a greater share of orders than had been awarded to ZTE, and that this helped explain why ZTE's share price had been declining for six days in a row. ZTE stated that it had not violated the principle of fair disclosure of information, and that it reserved the right to take legal action against the institution or individual involved for making misleading analyses. The *SCMP* reported on August 21 that ZTE had in fact won more than half of the orders, with the rest being split between Alcatel-Lucent, Huawei and other parties.

Both Linning, who moved on to become a partner at Sidley Austin, and Eugene Goyne, senior enforcement director of the SFC in Hong Kong, reminded me of the interesting Hong Kong insider trading case involving a Chinese food and beverage manufacturer called Tingyi Holdings, an analyst at Deutsche Bank and a fund manager at Royal Skandia.[26]

CASE STUDY

Use/dissemination of price-sensitive information (Hong Kong)

Background: At the request of a fund manager at Royal Skandia, a Deutsche Bank analyst and his supervisor visited Tingyi Holdings on July 11, 2000, ahead of interim results being published. The analyst then reported back to the fund manager with positive information about the company's business. The fund manager bought shares in the company on July 12. The following day the analyst distributed his findings to about 100 clients in an e-mail. (Only on July 17 did Deutsche Bank formally publish a more detailed research report with a formal buy recommendation and annual earnings forecast of US$32 million.)

On August 3, the company reported interim results for FY2000. Following two loss-making years the company had made a dramatic turnaround and reported a first-half profit of US$17.1 million. The share price rose by 36 percent in the two trading days following publication of the good results.

Details: The issue was whether the analyst was told anything material that was nonpublic and price-sensitive and not already known to the market. Adding to the intrigue was the fact that the analyst and the fund manager happened to be first cousins.

The defendants were cleared on the grounds that there was sufficient evidence that the market was already expecting that the company would be returning to profit. So it was not so much the turnaround that was the surprise that caused the dramatic share price rise, but just the magnitude of the turnaround. The judges noted that Tingyi's price didn't really move after the 100 clients had received the e-mail from the analyst, so he couldn't really have said anything that was material or price-sensitive. Expert witnesses also confirmed that the defendants had not received from the company any new information that was not already known.

Conclusions: This was a long-running case that might have gone either way. No doubt all concerned could have done without the limelight. The case rested on insider dealing, but questions might also have been raised about fair distribution of research. Analysts in all markets need to take both issues seriously.

The following insider trading case is interesting. Whereas the above cases involved one-off situations, this case study from the U.S. involves serial insider trading by multiple parties. Indeed there seems to have been a rise in the number of serial insider trading cases or insider trading rings in the U.S. in recent years—in addition to the one below, we look at a couple of other situations later in the "Sourcing information" section, as well as one instance involving suspicions of insider trading on a massive scale (see the ASCO references). Of course, we've already discussed the famous Galleon case.

CASE STUDY

Use/dissemination of price-sensitive information (serial insider trading)

Summary: In March 2007 the SEC charged 13 defendants in connection with two related insider trading schemes in which securities professionals traded on material, nonpublic information tipped, in exchange for cash kickbacks, by insiders at UBS and Morgan Stanley. The allegations were that between 2001 and 2006 the defendants made at least US$15 million in illegal insider trading profits on thousands of trades through these schemes.

Details: According to the SEC, the UBS scheme involved unlawful trading ahead of upgrades and downgrades by UBS research analysts and corporate acquisition announcements involving Morgan Stanley's investment banking clients. The web of intrigue seemed to implicate individuals not just at UBS and Morgan Stanley but also at Bear Stearns. The cases involved clandestine meetings and the use of coded text messages on disposable cell phones.

From our research perspective, one of those who eventually pleaded guilty was MG, an executive director in the equity research department at UBS, who provided traders with information regarding the upgrades and downgrades in exchange for sharing in the illicit profits. As a member of UBS's investment review committee he was able to see research before it was published. He was sentenced in November 2008 to 78 months in prison and ordered to forfeit US$15.8 million.

Another of the accusations included the stealing of inside information—about upcoming corporate acquisitions—by RC, an attorney (lawyer) in the compliance department of Morgan Stanley, and the passing on of the information by her to her husband, CC, an attorney in private practice who tipped others in exchange for sharing in the illicit trading profits. "*Quis custodiet ipsos custodes?*" (Who will guard the guards?) one might ask, or, as John C. Coffee Jr., a securities professor at Columbia University in New York, said in a Bloomberg article of March 1, 2007: "You've got a Morgan Stanley compliance attorney involved. This is a little like a cardinal getting caught with prostitutes in the church." Both husband and wife

Use/dissemination of price-sensitive information (serial insider trading)—*cont'd*

pleaded guilty. However, as reported by the *New York Times* on October 5, 2007, the sentences were relatively light given the husband's ill health and given that the defendants were "at the bottom of the food chain, had not conceived the scheme and profited only to a modest extent". Both were sentenced to six months of home confinement, with probation of four years for RC and three years for CC.

Conclusions: I don't know anything about prostitutes in churches (do they assume missionary positions perhaps?), but in terms of cardinal sins generally, these cases yet again demonstrate how greed can cloud people's judgment. With potential fines, prison time and ruined reputations for offenders if convicted, the risk/reward ratio seems heavily skewed against committing such crimes. Not only must the powers of regulators be increasing, as argued elsewhere, what with increased technology and access to records at their disposal, but serial insider traders have a heightened risk of being caught given the number of accomplices and trades involved. In the U.S. (and recently also in the U.K.), the use of plea-bargaining and immunity from prosecution have proven to be effective measures in the combat against crimes such as insider trading. Many regulators, including the SEC in the U.S., also have the authority to award a bounty for any information received that leads to an insider trading settlement.

CASE STUDY

Use/dissemination of price-sensitive information (pillow talk)

The *Sunday Times* ran a wonderful story on August 26, 2007, entitled "America's enforcer listens out for insider pillow talk". The story starts "America's watchdogs are moving their insider-dealing investigations out of the boardroom and into the bedroom". As at the date of the article the SEC had so far that year announced investigations into seven cases involving married couples, compared with only one in 2006. As well as the lawyer couple mentioned above, a separate unrelated case involved a New Jersey couple of Chinese origin—JW, previously

Use/dissemination of price-sensitive information (pillow talk)—*cont'd*

a financial analyst in the finance department at Morgan Stanley who had confidential information about pending deals, and her husband RC, previously an analyst at ING Investment Management.

The two pleaded guilty and in December 2007 were sentenced to jail for 18 months each for insider trading, despite a plea on the cultural grounds that there had hitherto been a more relaxed attitude to insider trading in their native China. The judge deemed that the two were simply driven by greed not by cultural differences. The judge also ordered the pair to forfeit their ill-gotten gains of just over US$600,000, although she did allow them to serve their sentences consecutively for the sake of their infant son.

A young lady in Hong Kong who obtained millions of Hong Kong dollars from "rich uncles" (wink, wink) when she was 17 years old appealed her conviction for insider dealing in the shares of Vanda, as featured in a January 2010 article on complinet.com. A slew of other interesting characters who were involved had also been convicted. The judge questioned her argument that she had been "used and exploited" by her gentlemen-boyfriends, considering the amount of money she had received.

In another serial insider trading case demonstrating the risks of "pillow talk" and the accessibility of information, a former Lehman Brothers salesman, MD, pleaded guilty in a Manhattan court in May 2009. An ex-colleague, a tax lawyer and a day trader also pleaded guilty for their involvement. MD was charged with having tipped-off friends and relatives about 13 impending corporate transactions from 2004–2008 using confidential information that he'd misappropriated from his wife who worked at Brunswick Group, an international PR agency. The transactions included major deals involving the likes of Anheuser-Busch, Eon Labs, Alcan, Take-Two Interactive Software and Rohm & Haas. Each company at the time was involved in a major M&A deal or other corporate restructuring. The SEC alleged that the illicit trading yielded more than US$4.8 million in profits.

The SEC complaint alleged that by providing the inside information, MD curried favor with his friends and business associates and, in return, was rewarded with cash and luxury items, including a Cartier watch, a Barneys New York gift card, a widescreen TV, a Ralph Lauren leather jacket and Porsche driving lessons. No wonder the tipper referred to his wife as the golden goose. Yup, his goose is cooked all right.

Use/dissemination of price-sensitive information (pillow talk)—*cont'd*

By the way, in his research on financial journalism, Damian Tambini of the London School of Economics shows how close to the source of inside information PR firms are nowadays with a comment made by Sarah Whitebloom, a financial reporter for the *Guardian*, which was published in *Corporate Watch* in 2003: "If you really want to know what is going on in business and the City, don't bother reading the financial press. Ninety percent of their stories have come hot off the fax machines of public relations firms or have been 'provided' by one of the innumerable PR men who stalk the Square Mile."

As we've seen from the above cases, anyone can fall foul of insider trading rules, not just securities professionals. Having been a supervisory analyst in the research departments of global investment banks for many years, I have often been asked what risks economists face. Apart from having to follow society-wide rules on such matters as defamation and copyright (more on which follows later), economists may also need to heed securities-specific and market-general rules and regulations, as the following case study demonstrates.

CASE STUDY

Use/dissemination of price-sensitive information (economists)

Summary: According to the *Wall Street Journal Asia* of April 12, 2004, JY, a vice president and economist at Goldman Sachs at the time of the event, was sentenced to 33 months in prison for relaying an insider tip about U.S. Treasury bonds that allowed the firm to make millions of dollars in profits. JY pleaded guilty to securities fraud, among other charges. He also settled civil charges with the SEC, agreeing to pay US$240,000 in penalties. The settlement barred him permanently from working with broker-dealers. Without admitting or denying wrongdoing, Goldman Sachs agreed to pay US$9.3 million to settle SEC charges.

The SEC's litigation release, dated November 12, 2003, explains that Goldman Sachs purchased U.S. Treasury 30-year bonds minutes before

Use/dissemination of price-sensitive information (economists)—*cont'd*

the Treasury Department's October 31, 2001, announcement that it would no longer issue such bonds. The Treasury Department's announcement had a dramatic market impact, causing the largest one-day price movement in the 30-year bond since October 1987.

Conclusion: The 33-month sentencing was apparently at the lower end of the scale, and the case may represent an extreme example given the relative rarity, one assumes, of such price-sensitive insider activity in the U.S. government-bond market. However, the case still demonstrates that economists are not immune from securities regulations, at least when discussing bonds and other securities. Furthermore, it cannot be taken for granted that such insider activity is as rare in some less-regulated markets of the world where economists operate as it may be in the U.S.

Aside: Economists don't even have to be involved with securities to find themselves out of a job. AX, a high-profile economist for Morgan Stanley covering Asia, resigned from his job in October 2006 after the leaking of an internal e-mail in which he gave personal, and evidently sensitive, views about Singapore. (AX is in good company. The *New York Times* agreed in March 2010 to pay S$160,000 damages to Singapore's leaders over an article published in its global edition, the *International Herald Tribune*. The publishing company conceded that the piece, entitled *All in the Family*, may have been understood by readers to infer that the son of the founding father of Singapore did not achieve his position through merit. Other publishers, including the *Wall Street Journal*, Bloomberg and the *Economist*, have also incurred the wrath of Singapore's leadership in recent years.)

JH, another high-profile economist, at Goldman Sachs, came in for some criticism at the hands of Ben Stein in his *New York Times* column on December 2, 2007. To be fair, Stein paid JH many compliments about his intellectual capacity. However, the accusation seemed to be that JH was "selling fear" with his ultra-pessimistic research on the subprime issue in the U.S., and that he was doing this to support Goldman's own trading strategy of shorting CMOs (collateralized mortgage obligations). This was denied by the Goldman spokesman, who maintained that the firm's economists were independent and that their research was held to the highest standards of objectivity.

The greater issue raised, however, was that, while Goldman was busy short selling such questionable paper on its own account, it didn't

Use/dissemination of price-sensitive information (economists)—*cont'd*

seem to mind encouraging its customers to buy it (see the case study on managing apparent conflicts in Chapter 3).

Separately, an unnamed investment bank in Hong Kong was featured in the SFC's April 2009 issue of *Enforcement Reporter* concerning the publication of an economics research report. The SFC stated that the research report did not contain any reference as to the source or basis for its statements about a large economic stimulus package. Readers were unable to identify whether the statements were facts, or were merely views of the author and/or the investment bank. The SFC recognized that the impact of economic research reports on the stock markets may not be as direct as stock analysis reports. However, they made the point that economic research reports containing sensitive issues may be reported by the media and may have considerable impact on the local stock market.

The SFC concluded that investment banks should adequately review their research reports, including economic research reports, to ensure that any statements are based on reliable sources or reasonable analysis. The regulator added that the presentation of the reports should not confuse estimates or personal views of authors and house views with facts and information from reliable sources, in order to avoid misleading the investing public.

Specific requests and proprietary information

Specific requests: The situation might arise when an individual client asks an analyst to undertake bespoke research on an unrated company, and to reach an investment opinion. Generally, research regulations on communications with the public would not cover communications to single recipients. (And this underlying principle generally holds good for buy-side analysts who service their in-house client, as well as for financial or investment advisers who tailor-make investment advice for individuals, as opposed to analysts who write for clients generally.) Note that, for rated companies at least, a sell-side analyst should not give advice to one client that is inconsistent with that given to other clients.

Some regulatory regimes might have wider definitions of this distribution threshold in determining what constitutes a research report (and what, therefore, is needed to satisfy research regulations, restrictions and disclosures). For example, the NYSE/NASD joint memo of March 2004, which focuses on research analysts and research reports, states: "A client communication that analyzes individual securities or companies will be considered a research report if it provides information reasonably sufficient upon which to base an investment decision and is distributed to at least 15 persons." These elements have since been incorporated into FINRA's body of rules, which combine NASD and certain NYSE rules. Furthermore, the SEC's final rule on Regulation Analyst Certification (AC), effective April 14, 2003, states that "an analysis prepared for a specific person or a limited group of fewer than 15 persons would generally not be a research report".

However, large research houses should be aware that an explanatory note to Regulation AC suggests that this number was chosen in part because an investment adviser who has had fewer than 15 clients in the preceding 12 months does not hold himself out generally to the public as an investment adviser. A global research house that regularly made use of this exemption might be seen to be breaking the spirit of the regulation if not the letter. Furthermore, by restricting the distribution of certain items of research from their general client base, a global firm may be seen to be breaking faith with the principles of investment legislation and regulations to treat clients fairly. Ultimately, I would consider the yardstick that the regulators use in practice, as the following case study illustrates.

CASE STUDY

Definition of publishing

Summary: In the NYSE's Exchange Hearing Panel decision 05-112, dated October 17, 2005, against Nomura Securities, we see that "The Exchange's Board of Directors has held that distribution to two or more persons satisfies the 'generally distributed' or 'made available . . . to customers or the public's standard.'"

Conclusion: This was stated in the context of the distribution of market letters or sales literature, but the same principle must surely apply to research reports.

The less-risky course of action would be to restrict the commentary to objective "non-research" reportage. If an analyst provides full-blown research (that is, analysis and sufficient information on which to base an investment decision) and then decides to cover these stocks formally for the benefit of the wider client base later on, the analyst could then be accused of selective distribution and unfair treatment of clients if he or she had already provided "research" to one or two select clients beforehand.

Restricted distribution reports: Some reports cannot be distributed within certain markets at certain times, for regulatory reasons. So-called pre-deal research is discussed in Chapter 3.

Proprietary information: A securities-research brokerage house might occasionally commission an outside market-research agency to glean more information about a specific industry or product. I would argue that in such cases, although the information gleaned and any conclusions reached may be proprietary, it would not be deemed to be non-publicly-available information on the basis that anyone could employ an agency to undertake similar market research.

Unfair portrayal of past recommendations

Caveat emptor ("buyer beware") is a long-standing business principle. However, one of the stated aims of securities regulations around the world is the protection of investors, especially with respect to protecting relatively unsophisticated retail clients from unscrupulous boiler-room-type brokers. It seems only reasonable that someone trying to sell you something does so on a warts-'n'-all basis; that is, that they tell you about the negatives as well as the positives.

When research analysts or brokers demonstrate to clients how good their recommendations have been, they must give a fair and balanced portrayal by showing how all their recommendations within their universe have performed over the given timeframe. The underlying rationale for this is to prevent unscrupulous brokers from showing how well their recommendations have performed by just providing the good trades as examples.

Some regulations might require specific definitions be given of universes, timeframes and returns, but in my view it ultimately boils down to the motives of the strategist, analyst or broker giving the information.

For example, it is now a requirement in the U.S. that in research reports that recommend securities, the performance of all the recommendations that have been assigned a rating over a period of at least the previous year should be depicted anyway. Whether or not this is a requirement in other markets, best practice would dictate that analysts do not boast about their successes without giving a balanced portrayal of all their recommendations, including the unsuccessful ones.

Regulations invariably require that a warning be given to investors that past performance is no guarantee of future performance.

CASE STUDY

Performance of past recommendations

Details: MT, formerly of Merrill Lynch, consented to censure, was suspended for two months and was fined US$10,000 by the NYSE in

Performance of past recommendations—*cont'd*

March 2002 for, *inter alia*, not making proper disclosures about the performance of past recommendations. The following paragraph, taken from the NYSE's findings, makes clear what the regulator requires in terms of disclosure:

> Exchange Rule 472.40 further states that 'a recommendation (even though not labeled as a recommendation) must have a basis which can be substantiated as reasonable' and that 'the market price at the time the recommendation is made must be indicated'. In addition, the rule requires that if the communication features records or statistics which portray the performance of past recommendations or of actual transactions, the portrayal must be 'balanced and consist of records or statistics that are confined to a specific "universe" that can be fully isolated and circumscribed and that covers at least the most recent 12-month period'. The rule further requires that communications 'state that the results presented should not and cannot be viewed as an indicator of future performance'.

More recently, in July 2007, the NASD fined two Fidelity broker-dealer companies a total of US$400,000 for distributing misleading sales literature to military personal regarding investment plans. They settled without admitting or denying the charges. The material was categorized as sales literature but the same principle applies to research analysts and their communications. The literature showed how one plan significantly outperformed the S&P 500 Index over a 30-year period. However, over 10- and 15-year periods—the timeframe most relevant to the investors—the plan substantially underperformed. The brochure also showed the plan's average annual total returns for one, five and 10 years as well as the life of the plan, but didn't show comparable returns for the S&P 500 over these periods. The comparable S&P 500 Index average annual returns would have shown that the index significantly outperformed the plan during the more current time periods.

Conclusions: These cases provide practical examples of the enforcement of the rules regarding the performance of past recommendations, and the potential consequences of not following them.

Model portfolios would normally be regarded as universes in their own right. At any one time they can be isolated, although as time progresses, these universes, like all universes, may change. Strategists on the sell-side should always flag the addition/dropping of individual stocks as and when they occur, and substantiate these transactions with supporting text.

Performance of past recommendations—*cont'd*

When giving performance figures, sell-side strategists and analysts should give balanced portrayals by showing the performance of all the stocks in the portfolio or universe on a regular basis (that is, not just when they happen to be performing well). In other words they can't cherry-pick when showing investment returns. In my mind, showing a balanced portrayal is the overriding factor behind the regulations concerning past performance.

In addition to showing the current price, strategists should also show what the performance for each individual stock has been since the last transaction date, as well as over the past 12 months (or since inclusion if there aren't 12 months of performance to show yet). By including both these columns together with the current price, strategists should satisfy the requirement to indicate what the original market prices were both for when the stock was introduced and when the weighting was last changed. Where strategists have not yet been running the portfolios for 12 months, they should probably add a line showing the performance of the fund to date and a second line showing "N/A" for the overall performance of the portfolio over 12 months.

A footnote to the effect that the results cannot be viewed as an indicator of future performance must be included, with a note to show what, if any, transaction costs have been assumed.

Conflicts of interest and disclosure of interests

The issues of conflict of interests and disclosure of interests are discussed in detail separately in Chapter 3. Before any research is communicated to the public, the compliance department should be satisfied that any actual or apparent conflict-of-interest issues have been managed appropriately, and that all interests in and relationships with the subject company are disclosed. This includes not just formal written research but also media appearances and recordings.

Catering to investors with specific investment criteria

Certain investors or investment funds will only entertain recommendations that satisfy certain moral or legal criteria. Examples might include ethical or socially responsible investments (SRI), such as in alternative energy, carbon-neutral and other environmentally friendly companies, or perhaps companies that have a high level of corporate governance.

There has been some debate as to whether SRI funds perform better than other funds. Sophia Grene compared the findings of two French research organizations in the *FT* of December 15, 2008: Altedia, an investment consultancy firm, demonstrated that SRI funds outperformed, whereas Edhec Business School found no evidence that they outperformed. Only when like-for-like studies are done over a long period might we get a better understanding.

A report published by Innovest in September 2008, commissioned by the WWF-Norway, showed that better company management of carbon issues translates into better investment performance globally. The analysis especially praised ABP of the Netherlands and CalPERS of the U.S. for investing with a social and environmental conscience.

The following month the *Edge*, a Malaysian business and investment publication, reported that Malaysian equities manager Corston-Smith Asset Management and U.K.-based pension fund manager Hermes Equity Ownership Services (the executive arm of BT Pension Scheme) had jointly launched the Asean Corporate Governance Fund. The fund would invest in companies with a minimum standard of corporate governance and would actively work with them to improve standards even further.

Normally fund managers would prefer to sell, or at least not to buy, the shares of companies with perceived poor corporate governance. In Korea, for example, Tiger Asia Management has been active short selling such shares. However, some activist shareholders and fund managers, like Lazard Korea Corporate Governance Fund, who believe they can use their stakes to prompt changes to a company's management or strategy, might prefer to invest in companies with low ethical or corporate governance levels, since this is where they see potential upside value.

With the growing importance of Islamic funds to the global investment community, research analysts and investment advisers might want to understand to what extent their covered securities or investment recommendations might be acceptable to investors or funds that need to comply with *Shari'ah* law. By the way, whereas *Shari'ah* funds appeal to Muslims, Dharma funds would appeal, for example, to Hindus, Buddhists, Daoists and presumably also Jedi knights, for whom nature and the natural way are the overriding influences.

Strictly speaking, *Shari'ah* law prohibits the lending or borrowing of money and other illicit or immoral behavior. Since both earning interest and raising debt are standard ways for companies to help increase shareholders' returns, one wonders how many companies there are whose securities would qualify for investment purposes.

However, as with any legal or theological system there are always different points of view where scholars and experts might disagree. Over the years, given practical considerations and the changing needs of society, the parameters of what may be deemed acceptable have gradually shifted. Under the more relaxed interpretations and concessions, companies may still qualify provided their exposure to non-compliant activities is not significant (see the example below).

EXAMPLE

Shari'ah law implications for securities research analysts (stocks)

Summary: At the end of November 2008, in the depths of the financial crisis, the Dow Jones Islamic Market (DJIM) Index (an index of major investable companies around the world that a panel of *Shari'ah* supervisors has deemed to be *Shari'ah*-compliant) included 2,300 companies with a total market cap of US$11.4 trillion. This is by no means an insignificant universe. To put these figures into perspective, the market cap of 1,500 companies that comprised the U.S. sub-index of the Dow Jones Global Index at the same datapoint amounted to nearly US$10 trillion.

A few reasons might explain the rapid rise in interest for *Shari'ah*-compliant investments over the past few years. Three that immediately spring to my mind are: i) the surge in the price of oil that fuelled the availability of Middle-Eastern petrodollars, much of which needed to be invested in *Shari'ah*-compliant vehicles; ii) the relatively low interest rate environment around the world, which enabled more companies to qualify as *Shari'ah*-compliant (given the restrictions on debt and cash levels) than would qualify in a high-interest-rate environment; and iii) a general trend toward more ethical and sustainable investments anyway. Crucially, *Shari'ah*-compliant institutions weren't as affected by the global financial crisis as others were, largely because they weren't so exposed to toxic assets such as CDOs and CMOs.

Details: The full guide to the methodology used to compile the DJIM Indexes can be found at http://indexes.dowjones.com. DJIM component stocks are selected by filtering the Dow Jones Global Index through both business activity and financial ratio screens to remove stocks that are not suitable for Islamic investment purposes.

Specific business activities that are precluded include companies that are involved with alcohol, tobacco, pork-related products, financial services (including banking, finance companies and insurance companies), weapons and defense companies, and entertainment businesses such as hotels, casinos, cinemas and so on.

The second layer of selection is to screen out companies with unacceptable financial ratios with respect to the levels of debt and cash. The following ratios need to be less than 33 percent: debt/market cap; cash and interest-bearing securities/market cap; and accounts receivable/market cap. Note that "market cap" is defined as being the trailing 12-month average market capitalization of each company.

Aside: One useful critical examination of the DJIM Index methodology is "Investment in Stocks: A Critical Review of Dow Jones *Shari'ah*

Shari'ah law implications for securities research analysts (stocks)—*cont'd*

Screening Norms" by M.H. Khatkhatay and Shariq Nisar. The paper was presented at the International Conference on Islamic Capital Markets held in Jakarta, Indonesia, during August 27–29, 2007, and is available on the Dow Jones Indexes Web site. The event was jointly organized by the Islamic Research and Training Institute (IRTI) of the Islamic Development Bank (IDB), Jeddah, Saudi Arabia, and Muamalat Institute, Jakarta, Indonesia.

Empirical data of the five hundred companies included in the BSE500 index of the Bombay Stock Exchange was used in the study. The paper concluded that from 2002 to 2006 an average of 86.3 percent of the BSE500 stocks passed the business eligibility criteria. Of these, 32.6 percent satisfied the financial ratio criteria. As such, 28.1 percent of the BSE500 stocks were *Shari'ah*-compliant, according to the Dow Jones criteria. The authors, however, stress that these are companies that are "*Shari'ah*-tolerant" as opposed to being strictly "*Shari'ah*-compliant".

Conclusions: Analysts could do worse than identify which stocks in their own coverage universes might qualify under *Shari'ah* law criteria, and thereby increase the marketability of their research. In order to appeal to *Shari'ah* investors, they would need to have any basket or recommended list of stocks approved by independent *Shari'ah* experts. They might also like to consult the Islamic Financial Services Board (IFSB) and the standards published by the Accounting and Auditing Organization for Islamic Financial Institutions (AAOIFI).

Analysts should be aware, however, that the demand for and supply of *Shari'ah*-compliant investments may fluctuate depending on a number of factors, including, for example, the level of interest rates.

There are complications in the Islamic fixed-income market, as the following case study demonstrates.

CASE STUDY

Shari'ah law implications for securities research analysts (bonds)

Background: Muhammad Taqi Usmani, a respected *Shari'ah* scholar, set the cat among the pigeons in 2007 by stating that 85 percent of existing *sukuk* (Islamic bond) issues did not adhere to *Shari'ah* principles.

Shari'ah law implications for securities research analysts (bonds)—*cont'd*

The problem is that the notion of a guaranteed repurchase runs counter to the Islamic principle that risks and profits should be shared by the parties concerned. Subsequently, the AAOIFI declared such issues to be unlawful. This ruling appeared not to be retroactive to existing issues (which could have been complicated, given their contractual nature), and would only apply going forward. The market in the existing issues has evidently suffered from reduced liquidity since then. However, what happens when an issuer goes bust or defaults?

Details: East Cameron Gas was the first U.S. company to issue *sukuk* securities. The company filed for bankruptcy in November 2008. The judge ruled that the *sukuk* holders could have a claim on the income stream from the underlying assets. Meanwhile, in Kuwait, Investment Dar Co., which owns 50 percent of carmaker Aston Martin Lagonda, became the first company in the Middle East to default on Islamic bonds when it missed a payment on a US$100 million *sukuk*. Investment Dar announced in September 2009 that it had entered into a so-called "standstill agreement" with its banks and investors.

The notion of a "standstill" gained wider notoriety in November 2009 when the Government of Dubai rattled global markets when it announced that Dubai World and its subsidiary, Nakheel Properties, would be seeking a standstill for six months on the repayment of US$26 billion of debt. At the time, Dubai World had total debt of US$59 billion, which according to Wikipedia represented nearly three quarters of the United Arab Emirates' total debt of US$80 billion. Luckily, Dubai's neighbor within the UAE, Abu Dhabi, rode to the rescue on December 14, 2009, with US$10 billion in aid. Dubai World said it would use US$4.1 billion of this to repay Nakheel's Islamic bond, which was maturing that day. A close one!

Conclusion: Interestingly, in Shamil Bank of Bahrain versus Beximco Pharmaceuticals, the U.K. Court of Appeal declared in 2004 that English law takes precedence over *Shari'ah* law. The court encouraged participants who wish to rely on *Shari'ah* principles to incorporate these clearly into their contracts. We'll need to see a few more *Shari'ah*-related cases around the world to see how courts and judges treat these issues.

Analysts and research departments can screen their universes by other criteria to create other baskets of stocks, such as companies that practice good corporate governance, that are environmentally friendly, that would benefit from anticipated climate change or perhaps that are geared toward food, water or energy, whether in terms of development, production, refining, storage or distribution.

Just as we saw above that some clients might wish to invest in companies with poor corporate governance, so too some clients might be willing to invest in companies geared to vices such as alcohol, tobacco and gaming.

EXAMPLE

The virtues of a vice portfolio

Details: Spencer Jakab, writing in the December 19/20, 2009, edition of the *FT*, cites a study by Frank Fabozzi and others of Yale University. The study shows that over 37 years a portfolio of sin stocks[27] drawn from 21 stock markets around the world would have earned an average annual total return of 19.02 percent versus a market return of only 7.87 percent. The portfolio would have outperformed in 35 out of those 37 years.

Ben Kwok in the Lai See column of the *SCMP* reported on November 21, 2008, how Merrill Lynch had published a research report showing that in six recessions in the U.S. since 1969 stocks such as Altria, Philip Morris and Molson Coors had produced average returns of more than 10 percent, while the S&P 500 had fallen an average of 1.5 percent.

Conclusion: Should analysts encourage investors to invest in vice stocks? If clients' morals or religious beliefs allow it, and the companies are legitimately trading, then it's surely just a matter of timing the investment to achieve the best returns. Judging by the above examples, investors can achieve above-market returns, bearing in mind of course that past performance provides no guarantee of future performance.

Analyst surveys

It is probably also appropriate here to say a few words about analyst surveys. One of a research analyst's most coveted achievements is to be ranked in one of the various independent analyst surveys around the world, such as the *Institutional Investor* polls. By being ranked, they can demonstrate the ultimate proof of their worth to a securities organization—the acknowledgment from the firm's clients. However, as in any competitive arena, there are marketing and canvassing practices that may seem aggressive but are still acceptable; and then there are practices that stretch the limits of fairness.

EXAMPLE

Playing the voting "game"

Summary: CLSA withdrew from the annual *Asiamoney* brokers' poll in August 2005, after having come in first in the overall ranking the previous year. According to the *South China Morning Post* of August 19, 2005, the company had admitted that "totally inappropriate instructions" had been given to sales and research staff to engage in "unacceptable practices", namely the submission of entry forms on behalf of clients.

Details: The *SCMP* reported on August 18 that a CLSA country head manager had sent an e-mail to staff in which he began with "It's a game" and continued with "vote-rigging should be as discreet as possible". The rigging had evidently come to light when three forms had been received, purportedly from separate clients but all written in the same handwriting. CLSA, after initially denying any misconduct, suspended the manager concerned and withdrew from the poll.

Conclusion: CLSA bowed out of the poll before the survey was concluded. As an extreme example, a survey result that is concluded and that is not reached independently but through vote-rigging, may constitute misrepresentation by the securities firm. Such a result may cause clients and readers of the survey to have a more favorable view of an analyst than may be deserved.

Aside: CLSA soon regained favor in the *Asiamoney* polls and won various awards from 2006 onward, including the *Most Independent Research Award* for 2007 and 2008.

Both Bloomberg and StarMine undertake objective studies on the world's best stock-pickers and earnings forecasters. They track the performance of recommendations against stock price movements and earnings forecasts against reported results. For example, Bloomberg's stock-picking rankings for the year ended March 31, 2008, were based on the stock recommendations for 300 companies with a market cap of US$5 billion or more that were made by over 3,000 analysts worldwide at 432 research firms and investment banks. These surveys aren't popularity contests, as other surveys might be considered, but objective studies of analysts' recommendations and forecasts. Provided the data is accurate and up-to-date, there is presumably less room for manipulation or favoritism in such surveys—the facts speak for themselves.

At least such surveys should help critics of analysts (like Sir Nigel Rudd, chairman of Alliance Boots, who famously described sell-side retail analysts who were covering the company as "stupid", as reported in the *FT* in April and May of 2007) to identify the ones who do provide valuable insights and accurate forecasts.

In the April 14, 2007, issue of his Long View column in the *FT*, John Authers looked at research issues such as timeliness and conflicts of interest. He agreed with Candace Browning, head of research for Merrill Lynch (who had recently announced in an e-mail to clients that the firm needed to regain control of distribution since its research was being "Napsterised", that is being made available instantly on the Web), that although life may now be harder for sell-side analysts their obituaries were premature. Authers quoted Browning as saying that sell-side research "plays a critical role" in ensuring that securities are "priced as fairly as possible . . . thereby delivering one of the most important functional elements of a market economy: efficient capital allocation". Supporting evidence came from a recent Greenwich poll of more than 2,000 institutional investors, in which U.S. respondents reported that they allocated 42 percent of their total commission spend on high-quality sell-side research. Authers also cited Henry Blodget, the former Merrill Lynch Internet analyst featured in Chapter 3, who believes that the most valuable service good analysts provide is to challenge conventional views.

The global head of equity research at HSBC sparked an interesting debate in the *FT* in June 2006 when he distributed a supposedly internal e-mail saying that their research was worthless and that most of the analysts did not deserve to be paid that year. Many *FT* readers agreed with him. One respondent, whose business tracks the performance of analysts, stated that half of the recommendations that they look at add no value if investors followed them. To me, that means that half of the recommendations do add value. The trick for investors (and for employers of analysts) is to identify those analysts who consistently add value, not just through their recommendations and forecasts but also through their reasoning and arguments.

As we can see from the following Alex cartoon, analysts' own colleagues sometimes don't value their contribution.

For specific support from the buy side for the use of sell-side research, I'd refer readers to Mark Mobius of Templeton, who wrote the foreword to this book. Similarly, Anthony Bolton, Fidelity's outperforming fund-manager, said in his book[28] that he has always been a proponent of using the best outside research to complement Fidelity's in-house research. As reported in the *FT* in January 2009, Fidelity had seen a dramatic increase in demand from its retail investors for independent research, and had become the first fund-manager to offer its clients a researcher performance ranking, based on the accuracy of stock picks. GLG Partners, the hedge fund we featured earlier in this chapter, concluded from its analysis published in September 2009 and covering the past four years of data, that a portfolio following European brokers' daily stock picks and holding them for three months would outperform 75 percent of mutual funds.

More support for sell-side research comes from a comparison with research produced by their buy-side counterparts. Eric Martin, writing for Bloomberg on July 31, 2009, reported the results of a survey by professors from Harvard Business School and the University of North Carolina. The study compared the recommendations of 12,000 sell-side analysts with those of 340 buy-side analysts from 1997 to 2004, and found that performance from the sell-side analysts was three times better than that of the buy side.

Sell-side analysts, whether at bulge-bracket banks or independent research firms, can't be complacent, and their product must move with the times. In a chain of letters to the editor in the *FT* in September 2007, Guy Ashton and Stuart Parkinson, respectively head of company research and head of equity strategy research at Deutsche Bank, argue against the "rebirth of classic analysts" as advocated by Luke Johnson in his *FT* article on September 5, as follows:

> Equity research has moved on from a world where some analysts simply peddled nods and winks from directors or circled the globe to drum up

institutional investor votes that could ultimately have helped to win investment banking. That model—we call it the Ranking-and-Banking model—is rightly dead. But the new model is better. Today's dialog with investors and company managers is more insightful, and is carefully targeted at those participants who value and reward us for the insights, and the alpha, we generate. Equity research in the early 21st century is about substance, not showbusiness.

As for the independent research firms, they'll need to look to their laurels with the expiry in July 2009 of the obligation by the global investment banks[29] to offer their clients independent research alongside their own.

When the *FT* published its annual awards in conjunction with StarMine in May 2008, the authors argued that with the credit squeeze putting investors' nerves and portfolios under severe strain, research has experienced a resurgence in importance that looked unlikely after the Enron-era research scandals.

According to Martin Dickson, deputy editor for the *FT*, top-quality research is "very valuable".

Even in December 2008, at the depths of the financial crisis when the Wall Street model had proved to be flawed, Alan Greenberg, the former CEO of Bear Stearns, was reported by Bloomberg as saying that companies that specialized in M&A advisory work would stay in business as demand for independent opinions grows.

Hopefully these pundits will all be proved right and sell-side research will evolve in useful ways, and will stay alive and well for a long time to come—and, if it's not too much of a conflict of interest for me to say so, that there'll continue to be a steady demand for books on best practices in writing research!

Sourcing information

Acknowledging the source

Without the protection of a publicly available source for their information, analysts risk being accused of spreading rumors to manipulate prices (especially if the information turns out to be false), trading on inside information (especially if the information turns out to be true) or other offenses such as defamation, negligence, misrepresentation, plagiarism or breach of copyright or contract.

This is not to say that analysts cannot come to their own conclusions by piecing together different bits of information from different sources and through different channels ("the mosaic theory"). Far from it—that is their job. However, analysts would need to be able to demonstrate that they are basing their analyses, views and conclusions on verifiable facts and reasonable assumptions.

I'm not suggesting that analysts need to identify industry contacts by name in published research whenever they quote "industry sources" (suppliers, customers, competitors, and so on) as the source for their information, but they may need to substantiate their claims if ever required to do so by a regulator or by the courts. In sensitive M&A situations where the prices of the respective securities have moved rapidly, ahead of official announcements, regulators might be keen to find evidence of market misconduct or abuse.

Local knowledge: It's not just company-specific information that's relevant; it's the whole business environment that needs to be understood and appreciated. With international investors seeking the best risk-adjusted returns globally, local knowledge and experience can be a great advantage. Andrew Leeming, the author of *The Super Analysts*, remarks that Joe Petch, formerly a number-one-rated analyst for Indonesia and a top-five All Asian analyst, "is acutely aware that understanding the unique political and cultural issues that influence Asia's stock markets is an important part of successful investing". Each country and region around the world has its own peculiarities, and an analyst who can understand the local issues, relationships, customs and influences would be well placed to provide clients with a competitive advantage.

Drawing the line: Analysts need to be able to draw the moral line in determining how far they are prepared to go to unearth information. Does the end always justify the means? There's a thin line, or at least sometimes a gray area, between making creative efforts to find the truth and behaving unethically (or even appearing to behave unethically), as the following case studies help to demonstrate.

CASE STUDY

Gathering confidential information

Summary: From a NASD news release of October 2002, we see that DR1, a research analyst, and his brother, DR2, a research associate, were suspended for eight and five months, and fined US$35,000 and US$5,000, respectively, for misusing confidential information. Both had been employed by Sterling Financial Investment Group, Florida. Both Sterling and the head of the research department were also fined and sanctioned for failing to supervise the brothers' activities. The respondents neither admitted nor denied the findings made by NASD.

Details: While DR1 was researching Neurocrine Biosciences Inc., he made an appointment at a clinic performing clinical trials of a medication

Gathering confidential information—*cont'd*

to treat insomnia being developed by Neurocrine. However, DR1 sent his brother, DR2, along to portray himself as DR1. DR2 represented himself as DR1, and acquired confidential medical information, including information from a questionable source. DR1 then used this information in a research report, without verifying its accuracy.

Separately, according to an article in the *Wall Street Journal Asia* of August 21, 2002, another stock analyst, JA, was let go by Friedman, Billings, Ramsey Group Inc., Virginia, after posing as a doctor to glean information about a different trial. The firm attributed the action to JA's "failure to follow firm policy related to the conduct of research analysts". JA acknowledged lying about being a doctor, but said it was for the greater good of unearthing the truth.

Conclusions: Analysts must be praised for trying to find a competitive edge in gathering their information, but they must take care not to be overzealous. It's all well and good talking about "the greater good", but losing one's job, being fined and suspended, and being charged with misrepresentation are potentially real consequences of such actions.

We mentioned earlier how analysts at Galleon were berated or pushed out if they couldn't provide inside information. Of course, a balance has to be struck—analysts need to satisfy their employers while at the same time not breaching regulations. In an article dated April 26, 1993, entitled "What Portfolio Managers Want from Security Analysts", Byron Wien of Morgan Stanley presciently argued that the industry was at risk of losing the good analysts to the buy-side, and that those remaining would have "little of the creative flair that made the field attractive in the old days". He continued by recalling how he himself had "hung out in bars in Silicon Valley talking to engineers and picking up gossip". In his own words, he regarded himself as an investigative reporter or an undercover agent. (Thanks Byron, I'll have to remember that one the next time I let my wife know I'm going for a drink after work!)

The following case study is also interesting. It is an insider-trading case, but rather than include it in the insider-dealing part of the "Honesty and fair treatment of clients" section (which already includes enough interesting cases taken from around the world anyway), I have presented it here given the interesting methods of systematic, premeditated information-gathering allegedly employed by the individuals.

CASE STUDY

Gathering confidential information

Summary: A litigation release from July 2006 gives details of the SEC's complaint against a number of defendants, including EP (a former associate in the Fixed Income Research Division at Goldman Sachs), DP (a former analyst at Goldman Sachs) and SS (a former M&A analyst at Merrill Lynch), as well as friends and family members of DP and EP living in the U.S. and Europe. The SEC claimed that the defendants (both alleged tippers and tippees) collectively garnered at least US$6.8 million in illicit profits. SS, EP and DP all pleaded guilty.

Details: According to the SEC's complaint, as part of an effort to obtain confidential, nonpublic information, DP and EP placed online job adverts and met with individuals employed at investment banks who they believed might be able to provide confidential, nonpublic M&A-related information; with exotic dancers who might garner information from Wall Street professionals; and with individuals who might be able to steal copies of a magazine before it was distributed to the public.

The SEC gives details of the specific schemes. In one, DP and EP recruited SS, who provided them with nonpublic information regarding at least six M&A deals that Merrill Lynch was working on, including Reebok (ahead of its acquisition by adidas-Salomon). In another, the two defendants recruited two individuals to obtain employment at one of the printers of *BusinessWeek* (a popular magazine that has the power of moving the price of securities featured in it). These people provided DP and EP with key copy ahead of publication. A third scheme involved the passing of nonpublic information by a friend of DP who was sitting on a federal grand jury convened to investigate, among other things, potential accounting fraud at Bristol-Myers Squibb.

SS pleaded guilty to one count of insider trading, and in January 2007 was sentenced to 37 months in prison. EP eventually pleaded guilty to conspiracy and eight counts of insider trading, and was sentenced to 57 months in prison to be followed by two years of supervised release. He was ordered to pay a US$10,000 fine and to forfeit the illicit gains. DP also pleaded guilty. Given the extent of his cooperation with the authorities, he was eventually sentenced to time served, being just over two years from his arrest, with a further three years of supervised release. He was also ordered to pay a US$10,000 fine and to forfeit the gains—but he then fled while on probation. Other syndicate members, including the grand juror and the print workers, also pleaded guilty to criminal charges.

Gathering confidential information—*cont'd*

Aside: In case the U.S. thinks it has a monopoly on insider trading rings, the Financial Services Authority (FSA) and the Serious Organised Crime Agency (SOCA) raided 16 addresses in the U.K. in March 2010. They arrested seven people including employees of Deutsche Bank, Exane BNP Paribas and Moore Capital Management, according to the newswires, with more arrests expected. The FSA described the operation as its largest ever against insider trading.

The FSA in London had earlier—in July 2008—rounded up eight individuals, including a subcontractor to J.P. Morgan Cazenove and a junior support staff at UBS. As it happens, this was hot on the heels of insider dealing charges being laid against MC, a former long-serving Cazenove partner, nicknamed "Streaky" because he was as thin as a slice of bacon, according to the *Daily Mail*. However, according to *Private Equity News*, a Dow Jones publication, it was because he used to streak across the floor as a schoolboy. Take your pick. Anyway, MC denied the charges that he misused confidential information relating to a series of proposed management buyouts and M&A deals involving HP Bulmer, Macdonald Hotels, British Biotech, Vernalis, Johnston, South Staffordshire and RAC. MC was eventually found guilty and sentenced to 21 months in prison. Interestingly, the FSA struck a plea bargain with his accomplice—a retired bookmaker and insurance broker—whom MC allegedly roped in to do the actual trading on his behalf in exchange for a third of the profits. As part of their agreement, the FSA merely fined the accomplice under its regulatory powers rather than pursuing a criminal case. Cazenove is the Queen's stockbroker, and I'm sure that Ma'am would not mind me pointing out that these charges related to 2003-2005, after MC had already left Cazenove.

Conclusions: The risks nowadays must surely outweigh the rewards in insider-trading cases—regulators always have the benefit of hindsight in being able to spot inexplicable price movements ahead of public announcements and to identify the people involved.

Serial insider trading cases are even more risky for the individuals involved. The more trades involved, the higher chance that one of the trades will be detected, and the more partners involved, the higher chance of being ratted on by one of them.

Furthermore, with some of the defendants in the SEC's case living and operating in Europe (Germany and Croatia), non-U.S.-based investors and analysts cannot take for granted immunity from U.S. regulations; the long arm of the SEC reaches far beyond the borders of

Gathering confidential information—*cont'd*

the U.S. Not only are exchanges around the world entering into cross-border mergers, but also regulators are increasing the level of cross-border cooperation like never before. And that's not to mention the ever-increasing power of local regulators on their own terms.

It is not just the tipper giving the inside information who runs the risk of breaching insider-trading rules, it is also the tippee who acts on the information. It's bad enough running the risk oneself, but to expose friends and family to insider trading must be even more irresponsible. Yes, friends and family members may agree to participate in insider-trading schemes out of greed, but analysts and other securities professionals shouldn't put temptation in their way to start with.

Going back to the subject of clinical trials for drugs, and expanding the themes of gathering confidential information and insider trading rings, here's a situation which some thought might constitute insider trading on a massive scale. The *Wall Street Journal* Health Blog generated some interesting discussion after Jacob Goldstein posted his article entitled "Biotech Stock Traders Sail Past Leaky Embargo" on May 18, 2007.

EXAMPLE

Receiving confidential information

Summary: For years, the American Society of Clinical Oncology (ASCO) distributed medical abstracts to thousands of doctors ahead of their annual meeting. In what came to be known as "the ASCO effect", stock prices would move, sometimes materially, ahead of the meeting. This raised suspicions among commentators that insider trading must have been going on. The practice stopped in May 2008, when ASCO distributed the abstracts simultaneously to doctors, the media and the investment community.

Details: In his *WSJ* health blog on May 18, 2007, Jacob Goldstein described how biotech stocks were starting to move based on information that wasn't due to be announced at the ASCO meeting for another two weeks. He reported that abstracts of studies to be presented at the conference had recently been released to more than 20,000 doctors, with instructions that the information should not be published or used for

Receiving confidential information—*cont'd*

trading. In addition to the original sources of the data (whether the biotech companies themselves or independent scientists), there seemed to be three other parties involved: i) ASCO, who passed confidential information to doctors, but with instructions as mentioned above; ii) doctors who received the information from ASCO, and either traded on the information or passed it onto investors; and iii) investors who received the information from the doctors, and traded on the information. Some bloggers who commented on the story aired their suspicions that insider trading must be going on—although, as the main story suggested, the legal issues become murkier as information gets passed along.

General considerations: Regulators and prosecutors in the U.S. can resort to the SEC's catch-all fraud rule, Rule 10b-5 of the 1934 Securities Exchange Act, as mentioned in the general example on dissemination of price-sensitive information above. However, intentional fraud or deceit needs to be proven (which may not necessarily be the case under the New York-specific Martin Act of 1921).

I'm not a lawyer, but in situations where information gets passed along and multiple parties are involved as in the ASCO situations, a prosecutor in the U.S. might need to consider both the "awareness" standard and the "misappropriation" theory in determining to what extent any insider trading has occurred and whether anyone is culpable.

According to the SEC, a trade "is on the basis of material nonpublic information if the trader was aware of the material, nonpublic information when the person made the purchase or sale". This is more specific than the mere "usage" of material, nonpublic information that might be sufficient to prove insider trading in other markets. Misappropriation applies when a person commits fraud "in connection with a securities transaction . . . when he misappropriates confidential information for securities trading purposes, in breach of a duty owed to the source of the information". According to the SEC, a duty of trust or confidence exists:

i. "whenever a person agrees to maintain information in confidence";
ii. "when two people have a history, pattern, or practice of sharing confidences such that the recipient of the information knows or reasonably should know that the person communicating the material nonpublic information expects that the recipient will maintain its confidentiality"; and
iii. in the case of certain family members.

Conclusions: Ultimately, from our perspective, whatever the intricacies of who sent what to whom and who did or didn't sign any confidentiality

Receiving confidential information—*cont'd*

agreement, if/while the information is deemed material and price-sensitive then, unless it has been reported in a widely circulated medium, analysts should not use it, base any recommendation on it or even pass it on. It would be risky to use as a defense the statement: "I don't know who does and who doesn't sign confidentiality agreements . . . I would assume that if they signed a confidentiality agreement they wouldn't talk to me." This was a statement made apparently by a UBS analyst, as reported by Luke Timmerman and David Heath in their exposé of the whole issue of drug-research leaks published in the *Seattle Times* on August 7, 2005.

An analyst wouldn't want to be the first to put any inside information (or rumor) into print, otherwise they may be an easy catch for any regulator or prosecutor who tries to establish the cause of any unexplained price movements in stocks before trial data are announced. Analysts should also be reminded that, as securities professionals, they are in the middle of regulators' radar screens and any suspicion of impropriety would prompt priority scrutiny. It is a presumption that analysts should know what's material and price-sensitive, especially if they change their forecasts on the back of such information.

Aside: Just to demonstrate that it's not all theory when it comes to analysts' involvement, we see from a NYSE decision in February 2006 that DTL, a former research analyst with Merrill Lynch, consented to censure, a two-month bar and a US$50,000 fine for disseminating nonpublic information about the results of clinical trials regarding a medical device (a cardiovascular stent). He neither admitted nor denied guilt.

Throughout this book I have tried to use case studies and examples to demonstrate principles, although I must reiterate that judgments and settlements rest on the specific facts involved in each case. No two cases are ever exactly the same. Here's an interesting case on the confidentiality theme, with what some may regard as a surprising outcome.

CASE STUDY

Receiving confidential information

Details: A judge in Texas dismissed the SEC's insider trading case against Mark Cuban, the billionaire owner of the Dallas Mavericks basketball

Receiving confidential information—*cont'd*

team, as reported by Bloomberg in July 2009. The SEC claimed that in June 2004, Cuban promised the CEO of Mamma.com[30] to keep confidential a planned private offering of company stock at below-market price. Cuban promptly sold his shares, thereby avoiding a loss of more than US$750,000. The judge said that the SEC didn't allege that Cuban agreed not to trade on the information, only to keep it confidential. Bloomberg quotes the judge as follows: "While the SEC adequately pleads that Cuban entered into a confidentiality agreement, it does not allege that he agreed, expressly or implicitly, to refrain from trading on or otherwise using for his own benefit the information." The SEC appealed the decision.

Conclusions: Unless this decision is successfully challenged or unless other cases make the situation clearer, some might presume, in the U.S. at least, that a duty not to trade is not necessarily implied in a confidentiality agreement. Similarities can be drawn with the Australian case study in Chapter 3, where the judge deemed that Citigroup did not breach any fiduciary duty when it traded on its own account in the shares of Patrick Corporation while advising Toll Holdings on a hostile takeover bid for Patrick. The reason was that a fiduciary duty on the part of Citi was specifically excluded from the firm's contract with Toll.

Notwithstanding the outcome of the Cuban case, I would urge all analysts and other securities professionals to steer on the side of caution, wherever in the world they are located. As we saw in the ASCO case study above, "misappropriation" is an important element in U.S. insider trading cases. However, in the U.K. and elsewhere, insider trading involves the use of material, price-sensitive information in a more broad-based way, whether it has been misappropriated or not. Securities professionals should refrain from using or passing inside information on. If, on occasion, they are obliged to bring someone "over the wall" and impart some confidential information to them, then they should ensure that the recipient not only agrees to keep the information confidential but also agrees not to trade on the information.

Rumors, speculation and M&A

The spreading of false or sensational rumors to move the market is an offense, under the securities regulations of most developed markets. Regulators are not too concerned with what people in the West might call "Chinese whispers", where stories get garbled the more they get told; they are more concerned with deliberate attempts to move the market through the starting and spreading of rumors.

Analysts should be able to draw rumors to their clients' attention, provided they quote the source (which should be a widely circulated medium such as Bloomberg/Thomson Reuters, a TV channel, a newspaper or the Internet) and give the respective parties a chance to represent themselves (by perhaps confirming or denying the rumor or declining to comment). By quoting a source, an analyst is seen to be reporting publicly available information, whereas without the support of a source an analyst risks being accused of spreading rumors to manipulate prices (for example, if the information turns out to be false) or trading on inside information (if the information turns out to be true).

Special care needs to be taken when an analyst discusses potential merger-and-acquisition (M&A) situations. As discussed elsewhere, the golden rule is that analysts must base their views on verifiable facts and reasonable assumptions, and be seen to be doing so. If they have some inside knowledge of a pending unannounced M&A deal and recommend purchase or sale of the shares of one or both of the companies, especially of the target of an acquisition, they could be seen to be putting the company/ies in play and could be charged with committing insider-dealing offenses. Don't forget that the regulator has the benefit of hindsight in being able to look back at the stocks' price histories to determine if there was any unusual price activity ahead of a deal announcement.

However, provided analysts don't have inside information, and base their analyses on facts and reasoning, then identifying potential M&A candidates could be regarded as good value-added research. In his Bloomberg article of June 20, 2007, Bob Drummond quotes Linda Thomsen, director of the SEC's enforcement division: "Timely pre-merger investments don't always turn out to be illicit. Through research into company financial statements and takeover trends, savvy investors may identify likely buyout targets without access to nonpublic information. There could be rumor or speculation that is not borne of material nonpublic information." Thomsen doesn't specifically refer to research analysts, but the same principle must apply since analysts are effectively merely agents acting on behalf of "savvy investors" in identifying likely buyout targets.

As a supervisory analyst, my suspicions would be aroused if an analyst were to appear to be picking a single name out of a hat and saying he expects the company to be bought out, with little in the way of explanation. If a sector has already been put into play, perhaps because of some M&A rumors reported in the press, analysts may be expected to provide their views. In such situations, an analyst could undertake a systematic, theoretical study of the sector, giving plausible reasons as to why each company might/might not be a suitable potential candidate for M&A consideration. Such a study could include a scenario analysis of potential synergies and economies of scale for the respective companies. Supporting factors could include the degree of market overlap, cost savings, the war chest of the potential acquiring party and the valuation of the potential target. Reference could be made to the valuations at which recent comparable mergers or acquisitions had been achieved in the same market and/or sector.

It would be especially important to make clear what, if anything, the managements and/or shareholders of the respective companies have said in public about their strategies and their willingness to merge, acquire or be taken over, and whether or not there has already been any relevant company-specific speculation or rumors reported in the press. An analyst who is the first to put a suggestion of potential M&A into print must be sure of his or her ground, as the case studies below demonstrate.

Furthermore, unless really convinced that a deal is pending, based on the piecing together of publicly available information (including official comments by the respective parties), an analyst should only really present potential M&A activity as an upside or downside risk to his valuation case. The fundamental call should normally be based on expected outcomes that have a high degree of likelihood based on publicly available information. If, however, the analyst is prepared to make a totally independent investment case based on a perceived M&A angle, and is prepared to run the risks of investigation as highlighted in the case study below (not to mention any loss of credibility if his call proves to be wrong), then he would need to make sure that all appropriate research disclosures are also made. These would include any interests in or business relationships with the company that he or his employer may have (see Chapter 3).

CASE STUDY

Identifying M&A candidates (putting companies into play)

Summary: TH, of UBS Securities at the time of the breach, consented to censure and was fined US$75,000 by the NYSE in May 2000 for presenting a rumor as a fact. UBS Securities also consented to censure and was fined US$60,000 for not having the appropriate supervisory structure. However, the NASD reversed its position against Jeffrey Putterman of Stephens Inc. in October 1997. (I have used Putterman's full name here on the assumption that he would want his vindication to be publicized as much as possible.) Since Jeffrey Putterman won and TH lost, a clear understanding of these cases should give analysts a good indication as to where to draw the line when discussing rumored M&As and speculating on their outcome.

Identifying M&A candidates (putting companies into play)—*cont'd*

Details: The question in the Putterman case was whether the analyst had conducted a reasonable investigation and had a reasonable basis on which to form an opinion that it was probable that Shoney's Inc. would merge with TPI Enterprises Inc. (which in the end it did—but three years later). The analyst came to his conclusion about the potential merger by piecing together various facts and rumors (that is the "mosaic theory"), and on appeal was found not to have breached NASD regulations.

TH was found to have breached the NYSE rule concerning the circulation of rumors. He stated as a matter of fact (rather than as a matter of rumor, which it evidently was) that Travelers Group would buy Bankers Trust New York Corp. (which in the end it didn't—it was bought by Deutsche Bank).

Conclusions: The Putterman case seems to confirm the principle that analysts can identify possible takeover targets, provided they can demonstrate that they reached their conclusion by analytical means based on "verifiable" facts rather than on rumors (and certainly not through any inside information), and that they present their findings as opinion, not fact. Indeed, the *FT* published an interesting article on December 14, 2006, by Peter Thal Larsen and David Wighton, on how prevalent the practice is now becoming. As an explanation for the recent surge in Barclays Bank shares, the authors cited traders who pointed to a research report by Merrill Lynch identifying the bank as a possible takeover target of Bank of America. And as major reasons for the rising trend in identifying M&A targets, the *FT* article cited the following:

  i. increasing demand from hedge funds for trading ideas;
 ii. greater freedom for analysts to act independently of bankers following the Spitzer reforms (the Global Research Analyst Settlements); and
iii. greater incentives for analysts to prove their worth, given the mounting pressure on research budgets.

The fact that the Putterman case was decided on appeal demonstrates that identifying possible takeover targets is a tricky area and one that must be treated with extreme caution. Furthermore, the case took more than two years to process, during which time Putterman and his employer suffered negative press, and the employer paid US$2.7 million to clients who had lost money by investing in TPI. It's not surprising that, according to the *Wall Street Journal*, Putterman vowed never to work in research analysis again.

Identifying M&A candidates (putting companies into play)—*cont'd*

If you quote the source of the unconfirmed report and give the subject party a chance to represent themselves, you're not circulating a rumor as such—you're reporting facts ("the newspaper said . . ." and "the company declined to comment . . ."). There's nothing wrong with dealing with facts. However, if an analyst circulates a rumor that hasn't been widely reported, he could be seen to be putting the company in play and trading on information that is not publicly available.

It's no excuse if an analyst phrases a reference to a rumored M&A without declaring it as a rumor on the basis that "everyone knows" (a principle which was also demonstrated in the U.K. market abuse case referred to in the selective distribution case study earlier in this chapter). It's not sufficient for an analyst to know that he is basing his view on good evidence; it's in his interest to be seen to be doing so by providing the evidence. By avoiding the appearance of impropriety, analysts will invariably save themselves a lot of trouble. In other words, they should defend themselves in their report, not in court.

Incidentally, if a company formally denies an M&A rumor, then an analyst would be hard pressed to make an M&A case as a base case. Since companies are obliged to be truthful in their public statements, an analyst could be seen to be implying that management was lying by denying a rumor, with the potential defamation ramifications that that may entail. Analysts therefore have to be very careful not to imply that the spokesman is a liar, but there is always the risk that he is! The Enron and WorldCom cases serve to remind us that managements can be blinded by greed and say or do things that aren't necessarily true or honest. In any case, there is also always the risk that management might change its decision, and pursue the opportunity anyway, even having initially denied any involvement or interest. Somehow analysts have to be able to present these risks to their readers as well. They could perhaps explain hypothetically what the rumored M&A deal could mean if it were ever to materialize, notwithstanding that the company has said that it's not in the works at the moment. (Also see the case study on Vivendi concerning false statements by issuers in the corporate governance section in Chapter 2.)

M&As are not the only situations when the rumor mill might be active. In the same way that some long-only investors might be tempted to talk up the market in a bull run (or anytime for that matter), so too some hedge funds have been accused of unfairly talking down particular stocks, especially during the credit crisis of 2007–2008. Some say, for example, that short sellers killed Bear Stearns. Lehman Brothers also blamed short-sellers for dramatic declines in its share price.

There are good reasons for allowing short selling, that is the speculative selling of shares that one doesn't own in the expectation of being able to settle later at a profit by buying them at a cheaper price (or else bearing the loss). Such speculation helps provide liquidity and efficiency to a market. Jenny Anderson of the *New York Times* quotes the financier Bernard Baruch in her article of April 30, 2008: "A market without bears would be like a nation without a free press."

The challenge for regulators is to distinguish between short sellers who sell shares for good fundamental reasons and those who try to realize profit from their short positions by spreading false rumors. Critics say that there's no shortage of information to help regulators in their job. Jim Cramer, a markets commentator for CNBC and TheStreet.com, has frequently aired explanations, evidently drawn from his previous experience as a hedge fund manager, as to how short sellers "torpedo" a stock by spreading rumors or by getting inexperienced "bozo" journalists to write negative articles about subject companies. The chairman of the SEC at the time, Christopher Cox, was reported by the press in April 2008 as saying that the SEC would "vigorously investigate and prosecute those who manipulate markets with this witch's brew of damaging rumors and short sales".

CASE STUDY

Short selling by hedge funds (abusive rumor-mongering)

Background: At the same time that the FSA in the U.K. launched an investigation into the trading of HBOS shares, Ireland's Financial Regulator launched a similar investigation into the trading of Anglo Irish Bank shares. This followed volatile share trading activity in both stocks on March 17, 2008—St. Patrick's Day as it happens.

Anglo Irish Bank evidently complained to its local regulator that rumors were being spread about the bank's funding and liquidity, to manipulate its share price. The bank had apparently raised a similar complaint the previous October. The *Irish Sunday Independent* on April 13, 2008, was pretty scathing in its article entitled "Wimps at Anglo cry 'foul'", saying that the bank's management didn't complain previously when there had been false rumors of a takeover of Anglo Irish Bank. The article highlighted that the reputable Lex column in the *FT* had identified both HBOS and Anglo Irish Bank as being vulnerable to a collapse in the commercial property

Short selling by hedge funds (abusive rumor-mongering)—*cont'd*

market in the U.K. and Ireland, and commented that no other Irish bank was so heavily into property.

The Irish Financial Regulator and the FSA initiated their investigations, requesting banks and brokers to provide trading details and communications concerning Anglo Irish Bank and HBOS.

Meanwhile, U.S. regulators were also being kept busy investigating claims that short sellers had been responsible for Bear Stearns' demise and the dramatic fall in Lehman Brothers' share price, which was down about 70 percent in the first half of 2008. At that point, the apparently unfounded rumor was doing the rounds that Lehman would be bought by Barclays at a steep discount.[31]

The U.S. regulators issued a news release at the end of March 2008 warning the market against spreading false rumors and other abusive market activity. They warned market participants that they should be especially aware that "intentionally spreading false rumors or engaging in collusive activity to impact the financial condition of an issuer will not be tolerated and will be vigorously and aggressively investigated". (Interestingly, the U.S. Justice Department even asked hedge funds such as SAC Capital and Greenlight Capital in early March 2010, amidst the Greek debt crisis, to retain their trading records relating to their euro trades. Suspected collusion within the currency markets may be beyond the realm of securities regulators, but it's not necessarily beyond the reach of the courts.)

In mid-July, the SEC issued an emergency order to help protect investors against naked short-selling in the securities of Fannie Mae, Freddie Mac and primary dealers at commercial and investment banks. This required short sellers who didn't already hold the securities to borrow or arrange to borrow them for delivery at settlement. Then, after these measures expired, even tighter measures were introduced in mid-September by both the U.S. and U.K. regulators, which would apply to all publicly-listed financial companies. Other regulators around the world introduced similar measures.

Regulators on both sides of the Atlantic widened their investigations by cooperating with each other to determine whether there were any unusual patterns or common elements.

Details: Specifically, Anglo Irish Bank took legal action against Mirabaud Securities in June 2008, relating to an alleged event dating back to February. They complained that an employee of Mirabaud had sent an e-mail that said: "Anglo-Irish, ML pull a US$2 billion credit line?

Short selling by hedge funds (abusive rumor-mongering)—*cont'd*

Rumor." However, this action evidently petered out, perhaps due to lack of evidence or an out-of-court settlement.

Separately, on April 24, 2008, the SEC in the U.S. settled with PB, a Wall Street trader formerly associated with Schottenfeld Group,[32] who had been charged with intentionally disseminating a false rumor concerning Blackstone's acquisition of Alliance Data Systems. The accusation was that six months after Blackstone had entered into an agreement to acquire ADS at US$81.75 per share, the trader spread a false rumor that ADS's board was meeting to consider a revised proposal from Blackstone to acquire ADS at the much lower price of US$70 per share. The SEC alleged that the rumor caused the stock's price to fall dramatically, and that the trader profited from shorting the stock. Without admitting or denying the allegations, the trader agreed to pay back US$26,129 in trading profits plus interest and to pay a civil penalty of US$130,000.

The FSA concluded its investigation into the trading in HBOS shares, and issued this statement on August 1, 2008: "Despite the likelihood that the rumors contributed to the fall in the share price, the FSA has not uncovered evidence that they were spread as part of a concerted attempt by individuals to profit by manipulating the share price." The chairman of HBOS, Lord Stevenson, reportedly told investors that the U.K. is "exceptionally bad at dealing with white-collar crime". It's a pity from this book's perspective that no wrongdoing was uncovered— readers might have been hoping for a hanging!

Conclusions: Analysts and brokers should be warned that just because the regulator doesn't find evidence in one instance doesn't mean that they won't find evidence next time.

Whether the Anglo Irish Bank action was a case of a company trying to find a smoking gun to explain why its stock fell or whether the stock was beaten down for good fundamental reasons might be arguable. Analysts always need to make sure they justify their recommendations, whether they are buys or sells, and would not want to be associated with a rumor that has been fabricated in order to move a stock's price.

As we saw in earlier insider trading and other market abuse cases, the returns garnered hardly compensate for the risks taken, not just given the financial penalties imposed but also the damage to one's reputation and future employment prospects, not to mention any jail time that might need to be served.

> ## Short selling by hedge funds (abusive rumor-mongering)—*cont'd*
>
> Readers should also see the comments about Greenlight Capital and HBOS's rights issue in the separate example entitled "Short-selling by hedge funds (pushing the envelope?)" in Chapter 2. They should also see the story about OCBC that follows that story, as well as the racketeering case study on Gradient Analytics in Chapter 3.

Incidentally, for those who wonder why a fall in a company's share price would necessarily affect a company's business and life expectancy, here's one explanation given in the SEC's emergency order referred to above: "During the week of March 10, 2008, rumors spread about liquidity problems at Bear Stearns, which eroded investor confidence in the firm. As Bear Stearns' stock price fell, its counterparties became concerned, and a crisis of confidence occurred late in the week. In particular, counterparties to Bear Stearns were unwilling to make secured funding available to Bear Stearns on customary terms." In the August 2008 issue of *Vanity Fair*, Bryan Burrough gives a good post-mortem of the Bear Stearns collapse—or murder as some saw it.

Separately, a former employee of Lehman Brothers was quoted in the *FT* of September 12, 2008, as saying: "Why would anybody, on the advisory side, do a deal with Lehman right now? No one is going to be the last guy to leave his money there and wait. It's a tsunami effect, it just builds upon itself." It's all about confidence.

And talking of not leaving money in a bank, on September 24, 2008, people queued up to take their money out of Bank of East Asia in Hong Kong. Apparently text messages were being buzzed around the community to the effect that the bank was going down. The chairman, David Li, issued a public statement to the effect that the bank had sufficient liquidity and that he would be buying the shares himself. Both the financial secretary of Hong Kong and the chief executive of the Hong Kong Monetary Authority, the banking regulator, also stepped in to calm the market by stressing that the rumors were unfounded. It just shows how easily and how quickly an unfounded rumor can spread among the public. As mentioned in the earlier example on media commentators, where we discussed bloggers and twitterers, it remains to be seen how effectively regulators will be able to police the spreading of rumors by members of the public armed with mobile phones and laptops.

Variations between local regulations: Analysts should always be conscious that variations exist between regulatory regimes. For example, as mentioned, in Hong Kong the SFC stresses that analysts must be satisfied that material, price-sensitive information has already been made available to the general public (that is, the person on the street, not just investment professionals) before they pass it onto sales and the company's client base; otherwise, they might infringe rules on selective disclosure. In Japan, the availability of information in just one widely available publication is not sufficient to satisfy the "publicly available" standard.

Defamation—libel and slander

The section on spreading false rumors leads us nicely into this section on defamation. Libel and slander are the two forms of defamation. Libel involves a defamatory comment that it is in a permanent form, whereas slander covers a defamatory comment that is in a more transient form, that is words that are spoken and heard by third parties but not recorded. Given the more permanent nature of analysts' comments (whether they appear in published research reports, in e-mail correspondence or in Bloomberg interviews), we will focus on libel.

Libel laws may vary between jurisdictions, and are a minefield in their own right. Charles J. Glasser, global media counsel for Bloomberg News, steers authors and publishers through this minefield in his book *International Libel and Privacy Handbook*. Glasser, in a broad definition, says that a libel claim usually requires that a publisher makes a statement to a third party that is not only false but also defamatory, that is that it exposes a subject's reputation to harm. However, he stresses that libel can also involve omission of facts. Someone can even be libelous by implication, for example with the use of hypothetical questions. Another useful book, with specific relevance to Hong Kong but also drawing from other jurisdictions, is *Hong Kong Media Law* by Doreen Weisenhaus.

As a supervisory analyst responsible for approving research reports prepared by securities analysts in different markets and for distribution to clients globally, I try to make sure analysts adhere to the common best practice of basing their views on publicly available information and reasonable assumptions, and acknowledging the sources of their information appropriately. Thus, they should be pretty well protected in most markets.

From the perspective of an approver of research who needs to catch libelous comments buried in the text, the risks of a libel suit are presumably much more skewed to sell—rather than buy—rated research. On the one hand an analyst is less likely to have a positive rating on a company, which in his view has a corporate governance or other issue that is serious enough to incite a defamatory comment. If the analyst is so incensed to make such a comment, he or she has probably also repeated it in the summary, making it that much easier to notice. On the other hand a company that is rated positively overall by an analyst might be less inclined to complain if the analyst has made a less-than-flattering remark. Analysts probably also have more protection when citing third-party comments from reputable sources such as global newswires and newspapers like Thomson Reuters, Bloomberg, *Financial Times* and *Wall Street Journal* (which have their own stringent recruitment, education and editorial processes), as opposed to amateur blogs and local rags.

Either way, if analysts are ever accused of libel, they should alert their compliance officers immediately or seek independent legal advice.

However well-established or factual a particular subject matter might be thought to be, analysts always have to be careful not to be seen to be prejudicial with apparently matter-of-fact statements such as "management has reneged on a contract" or "the company is bankrupt". For example, analysts need to distinguish between receivership and administration or between bankruptcy and bankruptcy protection. Giving each party a chance to represent itself is a basic tenet of most legal systems. Analysts should therefore qualify such statements by adding the source—"according to the company/press . . .", "management has conceded . . .", "the courts have ruled . . ." and so on. If it is just an allegation from one of the parties involved, analysts should add what management has to say on the subject: Do they concede that they have reneged, or are they resisting this accusation?

Analysts have to be sure of their facts and their sources, and need to substantiate any comments or claims they make. If a company is being sued for, say, breach of contract and, for whatever reason (including, for example, legal technicalities), is not found guilty, it could in turn sue the analyst for libel if the analyst had prejudicially decided they were guilty by making such apparently factual statements.

Similarly, care is needed in criticizing management, especially in a personal capacity by criticizing individual managers by name. People can be very sensitive and can react in very emotional or irrational ways. There's nearly always a positive way to bring readers' attention to some problem that management needs to resolve or some expertise they need to develop.

CASE STUDY

Defamation

Details: In August 2002, the *South China Morning Post* reported that the Haier Group, a mainland Chinese home-appliances company, had settled a libel suit against CY, an employee of a securities firm. CY was the author of a report that questioned the Haier Group's achievements and prospects, and that challenged the company to improve transparency.

Defamation—*cont'd*

CY published an apology, saying: "I had not interviewed Haier Group before publishing the report. Nor had I checked the relevant data and facts with Haier. Through further investigations, I admit that the report contained errors and inappropriate comments and has to some extent affected Haier Group's reputation." CY also had to remove his report from circulation.

Separately, in July 2002, the *SCMP* reported that UBS Warburg and one of its analysts, JZ, had agreed to pay HK$300,000 to end defamation proceedings by Greencool Technology Holdings. A UBS spokesman, however, said that the termination of the proceedings "doesn't represent an admission of liability on the part of UBS Warburg, or JZ, and was made to avoid further legal costs". (Greencool and its chairman were subsequently embroiled in their own scandals.)

There are other examples. In March and May of 2007 the *FT* ran a series of articles about the dispute between Softbank, the Japanese communications conglomerate, and CLSA. Until CLSA issued an apology over a critical report of the company, Softbank had been threatening legal action. As well as apologizing for not making it clear that the firm's auditors had endorsed a set of accounts that the analyst had brought into question, CLSA also apologized for the analyst's use of "Confidence Man" as a title for the research note.

The French case brought against Morgan Stanley by LVMH (details of which can be found in Chapter 3) sent shivers through the European analyst community. Notwithstanding that the French Court of Appeal in June 2006 overturned a lower court's decision that Morgan had been biased in its research against LVMH, the company was still found to have caused "moral and material damage" to LVMH. Could one say anything negative against a company anymore?

Conclusions: In the Haier case the analyst admitted wrongdoing, whereas in the Greencool case the analyst maintained his innocence. However, in both cases, the analysts suffered—whether from fines or negative publicity (although it's arguable whether the Greencool case diminished JZ's reputation in the minds of his clients since he was ranked as top analyst for China in *Asiamoney's* 2003 poll). These cases demonstrate yet again how important it is for analysts to be sure of their facts and to quote the source of their information. Analysts need to be able to substantiate any comments or claims they make.

The cases in the U.S. against Henry Blodget and Jack Grubman (see Chapter 3) focused on the overly positive comments made by superstar analysts in support of their recommendations. The Haier, Greencool,

Defamation—*cont'd*

Softbank and LVMH cases, as well as the various short-selling cases, demonstrate that analysts also need to be careful of overly negative comments. Analysts need to take extra care when criticizing companies or management, given the sensitivities involved. By criticizing management an analyst not only risks potential libel suits, legal costs/settlements and adverse publicity, but also risks being shut off from the information flow from that company (however unfair or wrong that may be in itself—also see the OCBC example under the section titled "Highlighting risks and volatility" in Chapter 2). There's invariably a positive/constructive way for analysts to get their message across without sacrificing their integrity or independence.

Once the press, regulators or law courts get involved in a case, you can be sure they'll be keen to find other skeletons in the analyst's closet, ranging perhaps from inaccurate data to more serious grounds for further accusations.

Intellectual property—copyright and plagiarism

As with libel, the whole issue of ownership of intellectual property is also a separate field in itself, and analysts would be well advised to seek compliance or independent legal advice if they suspect they may be at risk of breaching copyright laws or plagiarism ethics.

The differences between plagiarism and copyright can be subtle. Generally, plagiarism exists in the academic and research world as inappropriate behavior where someone uses someone else's idea without proper acknowledgment. Copyright theft is a legally recognized offense where someone steals a creative effort (maybe a song, written material or photograph), without acknowledgment or compensation.

EXAMPLE

Intellectual property

Summary: Plagiarism infringements are problems in all research fields, including the securities world. Cheating seems to be especially prevalent in business schools. This propensity to cheat may feed its way into the workplace where competition for jobs and business is keen.

Intellectual property—*cont'd*

Details: The *Financial Times* of September 21, 2006, cites a survey of graduate students in the U.S. and Canada that concluded that 56 percent of MBA students admitted to misdemeanors such as plagiarism and downloading essays from the Web. As if not to be outdone, U.K. university students were the subject of an *FT* article on October 18, 2006, entitled "Plagiarism is rife as bullet points stifle discovery". The newspaper reported that the national students' complaint watchdog said that PowerPoint presentations and handouts were discouraging students from thinking for themselves.

In the *FT* of May 19, 2008, Philip Delves Broughton discussed research that suggested that business students may be more inclined to cheat than students in other disciplines, possibly because their main purpose for continuing further education is to get a better job at the end of it rather than the pursuit of academic gratification.

Recent cases of plagiarism—for example, JB writing for the *New York Times* and the publishing of *Unwritten Rules of Management* by the CEO of Raytheon, provide high-profile examples of the potential consequences to reputations and careers when reporters, commentators, analysts and other authors purposely make up stories, lie about their sources or neglect to acknowledge their sources.

Conclusions: Research managers need to instill a sense of ethics within their teams. An article in the *Wall Street Journal* of August 16, 2006, on plagiarism in academic research quotes Elizabeth Heitman, a professor of ethics at Vanderbilt University Medical Center in the U.S., as saying: "We end up very often assuming people know the rules and don't tell them what the rules are until they get into trouble." This comment related specifically to medical research, but the same principle would no doubt apply to all fields of research, including securities research. Research managers need to educate analysts when they join the firm not just as to right and wrong forms of behavior but also to the consequences to them and their colleagues of inappropriate behavior.

Analysts should acknowledge their sources, and seek permission to use other people's material. If in doubt, seek legal advice. Ultimately, clients want to hear original ideas from analysts.

Aside: Analysts themselves are also at risk of having their work copied or stolen. In New York, Merrill Lynch, Morgan Stanley and Lehman Brothers sued theflyonthewall.com in June 2006 claiming that it had "pirated" their equity research. In one example quoted by Patricia Hurtado of Bloomberg News, Lehman published a research report on Genentech on March 1, 2005, which said: "We believe the company's guidance of US$0.95–US$1.00 is still fully achievable even if

---

Intellectual property—*cont'd*

fuel costs stay elevated." The Web site wrote on the same day about Genentech: "We believe the company's guidance of US$0.95–US $1.00 is still fully achievable even if fuel costs stay elevated." The Web site denied the accusations and filed a counterclaim, which was dismissed by the district court. Since then major banks and securities houses around the world have tightened up the distribution of their research.

Whether, technically speaking, an issue is one of copyright, plagiarism or even breach of contract is perhaps less relevant; analysts need to take care on all counts. We've already discussed at length the need for analysts to acknowledge the sources of their information. But permission to use the material may also be required.

Analysts must make sure they don't breach agreements with data-vendors or other information-providers by using and disseminating their material if it's not provided for under the contract.

Whenever analysts wish to reproduce photographs or other graphical material in their reports I would question whether they have secured permission to do so (as I have done for the Alex cartoons in this book).

Similarly, whereas it should be okay to quote from news publications, as I have also done in this book, reproducing the whole article or large sections might expose the analyst to risk. The risk would be heightened if a publisher can claim that it was losing revenue or was being otherwise disadvantaged as a result of the reproduction of its material.

Analysts often like to use famous book or song titles or catchphrases as titles or subtitles for their research reports. An ex-colleague of mine was particularly fond of Bob Dylan titles, I seem to remember. Generally speaking, titles and phrases aren't protected by copyright. For a start it would be difficult to argue that they constituted works of literature by themselves. Furthermore, many titles and phrases are already "in the public domain". The expiration of copyright protection would be a clear enough example of this, but it would also be difficult to argue ownership for any title or phrase that was already in normal usage. Take *The Usual Suspects* as an example. Even though this film title may have been a reference to a line in the film *Casablanca*, the phrase would have been used regularly enough by police forces around the world beforehand. (Even *Casablanca* as a title could not be regarded as an original work either since it's an existing place name, not to mention the common usage through the ages of "casa blanca" meaning "white house" in Spanish.) Some words created by authors get used so much that they even make it into dictionaries. Examples might include JK Rowling's "muggle" and JRR Tolkein's "hobbit", both of which are now in the Oxford English Dictionary.

The concept of "fair use" is another principle that might apply. Fair use of material for the purposes of criticism or commentary is deemed to be reasonable and in the public's interest. Interestingly, in May 2008 a judge in Manhattan ruled that the inclusion of the whole song "Imagine" by John Lennon in a documentary was acceptable based on the "fair use" doctrine.

Here's one particular subtitle I was pleased to come up with a few years ago for a Coca-Cola Amatil report where the Morgan Stanley analyst was identifying existing gaps in the company's market coverage: "There's not always Coca-Cola", as a play on the company's advertising slogan at the time that there's always Coca-Cola. One can of course overuse a catch-phrase as a title, and if I see "Show me the money" or "The Good, the Bad and the Ugly" one more time, I'll scream.

Certain titles or names might be protected by trademark, especially if they are associated with products or companies. Even then common sense dictates that someone else can have the same name. Using such names should be acceptable presuming there's no danger of the research report being seen to be posing any competitive threat to the product or company, thereby depriving the company of revenue. If you are directly referring to a name that normally has ©, ® or ™ attached to it, then one would be safer acknowledging this status.

If in doubt as to whether a title, name or phrase can be used, analysts should consult their legal and compliance department. In most cases they'll use "public domain" or "fair use" as justification, but sometimes they may also ask for some kind of acknowledgment to the original author to be added. In cases where there may be an element of doubt, they may ask you to seek the intellectual property holder's permission.

Lastly, I would suggest that it should be acceptable for analysts to use material from the Web sites of companies that they are writing about, provided the source is acknowledged. After all, the company is hardly likely to complain if the analyst helps to widen the company's audience by reproducing such material. The analyst should, of course, be satisfied that the material is factual and reasonable. I would suggest, however, that analysts should refrain from using the company's logo on their research since this may give the appearance that the company has endorsed the research, which may imply that the research is not independent.

Research integrity and consistency

The problem

Fundamental analysts, technical analysts, strategists and sales/traders on the sell-side are sometimes tempted to give investment opinions and recommendations, either explicit or implied, that may appear to be inconsistent with the firm's formal research recommendations. Such a variety of opinions, if left unchecked, might cause confusion among investors. Any inconsistency or cause for confusion or misinterpretation in the investment advice given might breach regulations and might provide clients, especially retail clients, with an excuse to assign blame if their investments go wrong.

The following sidebar involves a financial adviser rather than a research analyst. It doesn't involve conflicting advice given by different members of an investment firm. This bizarre story from Germany merely serves to demonstrate how some individual clients might react to losing their money. Anyone giving investment advice should beware!

SIDEBAR

Disgruntled clients

Details: Some pensioners gagged a financial adviser outside his home in Speyer, Western Germany, and bundled him into the trunk of an Audi A8. As reported by the *Daily Telegraph* on June 24, 2009, they then drove him 300 miles to a house in Bavaria, where they interrogated him about their savings. He replied that all their money was gone as a result of market conditions. (Cue Woody Allen's line that a stockbroker is someone who invests your money until it is all gone.)

The adviser was allegedly beaten with a Zimmer frame, was burned with cigarettes, had two ribs broken and was chained in a cellar like an animal, dressed only in his underwear. He told his abductors that he could pay them back if he could sell some securities. They accordingly let him send a fax to a bank in Switzerland. He included in the fax a coded message "call. po-lice", which was luckily picked up by the bank staff. Armed commandos stormed the house and released the adviser. A doctor accompanied the commandos, not just for the benefit of the captive but also for the captors, given their age and infirmities.

The pensioners, whom the police had nicknamed "the Geritol Gang" after an arthritis drug, were found guilty of kidnapping in March 2010. The 74-year-old ringleader was jailed for six years. You can't make this stuff up.

The principles

It's either "research" or it isn't: Under the principle of substance over form, anyone communicating what looks like new "research" could be deemed to be a research analyst, irrespective of their official title or role, and thus be subject to research regulations. Non-research personnel, such as sales and traders, would normally be expected to reiterate the research department's formal published recommendations.

Anyone making alternative analyses and giving alternative calls or recommendations, whether explicit or implied, could be deemed to be providing new "research". If so, then the material may need to be approved for fair distribution to clients simultaneously, with risk and other disclosures added as appropriate.

Buy means buy, sell means sell: The SEC in the U.S. states: "Definitions of ratings must be consistent with their plain meaning. Therefore, for example, a Hold rating should not mean or imply that an investor should sell a security." No doubt the rationale for including this example was to prevent a possible conflict of interest arising from an analyst publicly recommending clients buy the securities of a company with which the firm was involved in an investment banking deal, while disparaging it in private. However, the same principle would apply to all published research, irrespective of any banking relationships. Timeframes, valuation methods and associated risks for any recommendations and target prices must also be given.

Integrity of research: Brokerage firms would invariably want to maintain the integrity of their formal research recommendations. Clients should be able to trust that the firm, in giving investment advice, has undertaken thorough research into the companies it covers, and that recommendations "have a basis that can be substantiated as reasonable", as required by at least U.S. securities regulations.

In some firms, the internal investment/product-review committee or panel is a crucial part of the discipline imposed on analysts to help ensure that research opinions are robust. However, clients' confidence in the quality of the research could be undermined if brokers were to bandy about implied or explicit recommendations that may not be well-founded or that appear inconsistent with their formal recommendations.

Consistency of recommendations: Fundamental recommendations for individual stocks often represent the starting point or standard against which other strategies or trading suggestions made by the brokerage firm may be set, with any apparent inconsistencies explained. The research department's publishing system is unlikely to have been designed as a free-for-all bandwagon for contributors to air personal, unsupported opinions. That is not to say that there is no room for differences in opinions, but best practice would dictate that analysts should . . .

... be consistent or explain apparent inconsistencies

Recommendations and target prices: Any formal recommendation and target price should be highlighted, and both should be based on a stated time horizon. It should be made clear on what basis any target prices are set—for instance, whether they are based on absolute returns of a stated percentage from the current price or relative to an index such as the local market index or a privately compiled index such as MSCI.

Recommendations and target prices should be consistent with each other. A buy rating with a target price that seems more consistent with a sell rating under the firm's definitions can only cause confusion among investors and could provide them with ammunition against a broker if the recommended investment or trade goes sour.

Note: the rationale for new target valuations should always be given in the text; but even when target valuations are not being changed, a reminder of the basis and reason for the target valuation should still be given, to explain why the analyst thinks the target valuation is still appropriate. Analysts can also give in the text their "fair value" if this is different, provided they make clear what the timeframe is and what their valuation assumptions are.

As mentioned previously and as discussed more fully later, there may be occasions when analysts are reviewing their views, but clients would presumably not appreciate analysts who habitually hide behind this as an excuse for not being on top of their coverage. Analysts may be able to get away with the "under review" concession when writing news commentary in daily round-ups or in comparative valuation tables. However, it would be more difficult to justify its usage where the stock itself is being featured in a formal research report, or is included in a top-recommendation list. In such cases, clients deserve the analyst's up-to-date views, with consistency between the recommendation and the target price.

Consistency of methodology and assumptions: In some sectors at least, it might help make comparisons easier if analysts adopted an apples-to-apples approach when valuing companies, using the same valuation methodology across the board. Any departure from this policy and any variation in the valuation assumptions used between stocks in a sector should be explained.

I sometimes see examples in draft reports where analysts include potential new businesses or assets in their target price/valuation but not in their financial models. This seems inconsistent. If analysts can demonstrate a high degree of certainty that potential assets or businesses will be acquired or will become income-producing for the firm (for example, M&A agreements have been reached or advanced drug trials have been approved), they should include the assets and forecast earnings in their assumptions consistently—that is, in both their financial forecasts and their target valuation. If the potential acquisition is still a subject of speculation, then they should exclude them consistently. Either way, it should be clear to readers what is being assumed in both the financial models and the valuations, and what is not. And if potential earnings are being presumed, then the analyst should make clear what the risks would be to consolidated earnings and overall valuations if those expected contributions do not materialize. See the case study in Chapter 2 on M&A risks, where BHP Billiton abruptly pulled out of its takeover of Rio Tinto. Likewise, if analysts exclude potential assets from their forecasts and valuations, they can still draw to readers' attention the upside risks to their financial models and valuations if the assets eventually are acquired or become income-producing.

Analysts should also highlight and explain any apparent inconsistencies between their bottom-up stock calls and the top-down investment themes as promulgated by the strategists. Similarly, they should use any formal economic and commodity forecasts already published by the firm's economists and commodity analysts—for example, GDP growth rates, inflation rates, exchange rates and oil prices—or explain with good reason why any alternative forecasts or assumptions have been used. Again, sensitivity analyses can only help readers, and help satisfy the requirement to draw risks to their attention.

Pricing of reports: Analysts should avoid publishing information and/or views that are wrong or out-of-date. Valuations of peer stocks in comparable valuation tables should be priced on the same date for ease of comparison (unless analysts are including, in say a compilation report, already-published research, which need not necessarily be re-priced as long as the original publishing and pricing dates are clearly shown and that the research is still valid). However, if analysts have made any significant changes to their investment views since the pricing date or since the date of the published research, they should really present their most current thinking to their readers, with a footnote to explain any changes and any different pricing date.

The price on which the recommendation or valuation is based must be clearly shown, as required by U.S. securities regulations. This helps the client understand at what price the analyst's recommendation and valuation are good. The inclusion of the price protects the analyst and the brokerage firm from rapid movements in stock prices between the time the recommendation is made and the time the investor makes the trade. Otherwise, a situation might arise whereby, for example, the stock suddenly rises to beyond the point at which the analyst would still recommend the stock for purchase. The investor might then complain that the analyst had recommended him to buy the stock, to which the analyst would reply: "Yes, but not at that price."

Incidentally, I would also discourage analysts from giving future recommendations based on circumstances not yet known even if they make clear at what price the recommendation would be at. One simple example would be an analyst recommending to clients to sell the stock when the target price is reached. Circumstances may change in the meantime, and for all the analyst knows, at the time the target price is reached he may end up needing to raise his forecasts and either keep his rating or perhaps even raise it.

Analysts should also avoid referring to reports which they know to be in the production pipeline but which have not yet been formally approved and published, on the basis that, for whatever reason, they may end up not being approved and published. They certainly should avoid tipping-off sales and selected clients of any forthcoming investment conclusions and recommendations; otherwise, they run the risk of front-running.

Different time frames/trading suggestions: Analysts need to make clear what the time horizons are for their investment recommendations and views. Reference to the investment time horizon will also normally be made in the disclosures.

Analysts who give long-term targets to support their formal ratings on covered stocks should also be able to present short-term trading opportunities as separate research calls, provided that they clearly define recommendations and time frames, draw their readers' attention to risks and provide the appropriate disclosures. There should be no potential cause for confusion between the formal fundamental recommendation and the short-term trading call. In one draft research report I was asked to approve, an analyst was suggesting that investors should sell the stock as a short-term trade, but that longer-term investors should hold the stock. The analyst's formal recommendation was a buy; so, in one go, the analyst was apparently wanting to tell investors to buy, sell and hold the stock at the same time. Also of concern was that, since the formal recommendation and target price happened to be inconsistent with each other, this could have been seen as a signal that she was intending to change her formal recommendation from buy to hold. As mentioned earlier, such signals can mean different things to different readers, so care is needed.

For non-rated stocks, analysts should be able to objectively draw readers' attention to volatile activity in the market or possible short-term trading opportunities without giving substantive analysis. Other commentators—sales and traders, for example—should not be seen to be giving subjective alternative analyses and recommendations, for fear of being regarded by regulators as "research analysts" and therefore subject to research regulations. However, they can and would be expected to reiterate analysts' recommendations. They should also be able to objectively highlight trading opportunities that short-term traders could consider.

Informal recommendation terminology: Analysts should always highlight any formal recommendations and target prices. Unless these are formal recommendations with definitions made clear, quasi-recommendations such as buying on weakness or selling on strength might raise questions about what the current recommendation is. It might also be unclear how far the stock needs to move to trigger the recommended action. Something along the lines of "We recommend buy, especially on weakness" would, perhaps, avoid this particular issue. Reference to switching into an alternative stock might imply selling the subject stock, which may be at odds when the formal recommendation is to buy the stock. In such cases the call should probably be couched in terms of the analyst's preference for one stock over the other. In any case, the analysts should make clear that both switching and preference relate to relative trades, and make clear what securities they are advising clients to switch into, or overweight, instead. Similarly, analysts should make absolutely clear what they mean by top-slicing or taking profit, in cases where these may seem inconsistent with their formal recommendations. One possibility could be to say objectively: "Some investors might consider taking some profit."

Note: words such as "fair" or "reasonable" would normally be associated with a hold or neutral recommendation, rather than with a buy, accumulate, or outperform, whereas for the latter ratings, words like "attractive", "cheap", "undervalued" and "compelling" would be more appropriate. These qualifiers should always be given as representing the analyst's view. For a hold recommendation, I suppose one could say that current valuations "are not attractive" (that is, not attractive enough for investors to buy the stock). However, to avoid any misunderstanding that the analyst may also mean "not attractive enough even to hold the stock", I would reserve references to "not attractive" for sell-rated stocks and, instead, say that valuations seem "fair", "reasonable" or "justified" for hold-rated stocks.

And don't forget the UBS analyst who, according to the February 3, 2002 issue of the *Independent on Sunday*, was fired for trying to warn investors subliminally through the use of acronyms that he "Cannot Recommend A Purchase".

Sector/country weightings and universes

Sector and country weightings should really only be assigned by macro analysts, such as strategists, who are in a position to do so. They must make clear what context/universe the weightings are in. Thus, regional strategists can publish their own country and sector weightings, and individual country and sector heads can determine their own weightings within their own universes. For example, the country head in Korea could determine weightings for Korean sectors, and the regional banking sector head could determine weightings for the banking sector within the region covered. However, it would be difficult for individual country heads to determine their own weightings for their respective markets within a regional context, and for sector heads within individual countries to determine the weightings of their respective sectors within a regional-sector context.

Country strategists and the regional strategist should liaise with each other to ensure that index targets are consistent with regional weightings, or that any apparent inconsistencies are explained.

EXAMPLE

Consistency of views

For a period in 2001, Markus Rosgen, the Asian strategist at the time for ING Barings (subsequently taken over by Macquarie Bank) had an overweight for Hong Kong in his Asian model portfolio, and an underweight for South Korea. The Hong Kong strategist expected the Hang Seng Index to decline while, at the same time, the Korean strategist expected the KOSPI to rise slightly.

The rationale for this apparent inconsistency was that the banking analyst had a sell on HSBC, and Markus did not include the stock in his model portfolio. Hold-rated Hutchison Whampoa was included in the model portfolio, but underweighted. These two stocks were expected to drag the Hong Kong index down, given their relatively large market capitalizations.

The Hong Kong model portfolio, however, without HSBC and with an underweighted Hutch, offered better upside potential than the portfolio for Korea; hence the overweight for the former and the underweight for the latter in Markus's overall Asian model portfolio. It was, after all, a recommended portfolio, not an index-tracking fund.

When analysts say that a certain stock is their favorite, they must qualify this by making clear what universe they're referring to—for example, their sector (say financials) within the region (Asia), their sector within a specific market (South Korea), the market as a whole and so on. Analysts know their own sphere of coverage, but this may not be immediately evident to all readers. For example, an analyst might think that it's clear that his universe is restricted to a particular sector, but when a company report is included in a market-strategy monthly, readers might presume that such phrases as "favorite stock" should be taken in a market context.

Model portfolios, hedge funds and top picks: Sell-side strategists should define the investment parameters for their recommendation lists. They should only include in their respective lists, at least for top-recommendation or top-pick lists, stocks that are already included in the brokerage firm's overall coverage universe. This is because a recommendation is implied for any stocks included in a top-pick list. Such recommendations would fall under the purview of research regulations and would therefore need to be supported with valuation rationale, an assessment of the risks to the call and research disclosures.

CASE STUDY

Top picks (research requirements)

Details: Among FINRA's disciplinary actions, we see various examples of authors of stock-pick lists not being appropriately registered or not giving appropriate disclosures. For example, in the August 2009 round-up, an analyst in Atlanta consented to a US$10,000 fine and 30-day suspension for not having the required Series 86 or 87 licenses, which she needed for being "the principal author of or contributor to the Stock Pick sections of her member firm's newsletter". Furthermore, since she did not regard the stock pick section as constituting "research", she failed to disclose her ownership of securities featured as stock picks, and failed to explain her valuation methodology and the investment risks.

I would present here possible justification for inclusion of unrated stocks in model portfolios, although some may disagree with me. Where portfolios are meant to portray a balance of such criteria as risk, sector coverage and market capitalization, it may be that a sell-side strategist would be doing clients a disservice by excluding a particular stock that greatly contributed to the balancing of a portfolio or that represented the purest play in a particular sector. A market leader in a particular sector might be such a stock. Of course, the strategist would need to flag that the stock is not covered or rated, and that it was only being included for representation and balance purposes, and not as a recommendation *per se*. The analyst should probably flag what any consensus recommendation is for the stock.

(Some might argue that a consensus sell rating would hardly help in justifying its inclusion in the model portfolio, although others could cite the late Sir John Templeton's maxim that the time to buy is at the point of maximum pessimism.) And it may still be advisable to draw readers' attention to the analysts' and brokerage's interests and relationships with the subject companies so as not to risk breaching disclosure rules, even though you may not be making a recommendation as such. However plausible this justification may seem, as a rule I would not recommend the inclusion of unrated stocks in recommended portfolios. If a stock is worthy of inclusion in a portfolio it would presumably be worthy of coverage, so the safer—and more commercial—thing to do would be to hasten initiation of coverage of that stock.

Note: other lists that may include unrated stocks—for example, to portray stocks that are most highly correlated to a particular theme—should be seen to be merely an objective screening based on measurable criteria. These lists should not be seen to be subjective selections of stocks that the author thinks should outperform (unless they are formally covered with a positive recommendation or rating). Analysts should also beware that even the selection of such measurable criteria could be regarded as being subjective, especially if it could be demonstrated that the analyst's aim was to manipulate the results of the screening exercise in favor of a desired outcome. It should be clear which stocks are not rated, and that the valuations for unrated stocks are based on consensus estimates (with an acknowledgment to the data provider for permission to use the data). If a stock is dropped from the brokerage's coverage universe, it might seem reasonable for sell-side strategists to be able to keep it in the portfolio until there is a good reason for dropping it (the stock is no longer performing, for example). However, the fact that it has been dropped from coverage should be made clear in the footnotes. It should also be clear on whose estimates any valuations are based (which would presumably not be the research house's own estimates if the stock is no longer covered).

It makes sense for sell-side strategists to use weightings for stocks in their portfolios. Similarly, it makes sense for sell-side hedge-fund strategists to offer a hedging strategy with reference to long and short recommendations. However, they should draw readers' attention to situations where a recommendation for a security is evidently inconsistent with the respective analyst's fundamental recommendation, giving justification and making clear the time horizons.

A hold-rated stock might be difficult to justify in a top-picks list, at least while there are buy-rated stocks to choose from. It's one thing to include hold-rated stocks in model portfolios (for example, for sector, market cap or risk-representation purposes), but a sell-rated stock in a long portfolio, for example, would be harder to justify. In one example, though, a Hong Kong strategist justified the inclusion of a buy-rated, export-oriented stock among the shorts in his recommended long–short portfolio based on the

Asian strategist's relative call to overweight domestic non-tradables and underweight exporters. Similarly, it would be justifiable for a hedge strategist to recommend one stock as long and one as short, provided the analyst was expecting higher returns for the long-rated stock. If the hedge strategist makes the reverse call without reasonable justification, or offers a recommendation on a stock that is unrated by the firm's analysts, then he could be seen to be writing new "research", which would have to satisfy all the requirements of research outlined above.

Any apparent inconsistencies between portfolio stocks, top picks and new/fresh/hot-money buys and analysts' preferred stocks should be explained. For example, a sector head might rank stock A over stock B, but a strategist might only include stock B in his top-picks list. Sometimes a strategist, country head or sector head might think that a stock deserves a different recommendation from the one assigned by the analyst. Similarly, some strategists have presented one list of preferred stocks in a strategy report, only to show a different list in a top-picks list. Ideally they should be consistent; but if, for example, the lists are based on different time horizons, this must be made clear. Ideally, conclusion to such issues should be reached at the internal-product or investment-review committee meeting, so that a united front is presented to sales and clients.

Of course, sophisticated clients might appreciate being given a choice of independent views by superstar brokers, rather than just the "house" view. Morgan Stanley strategists and macro economists have been famous for giving such apparently divergent views, as the following examples demonstrate.

EXAMPLE

Consistency of views

The *New York Post* ran an article on October 7, 1997, entitled "Difference of Opinion Leads to War of Words at Morgan Stanley". It cited Barton Biggs as seeing a bull market and favoring stocks, with Stephen Roach calling a bear market and recommending bonds instead.

Then on January 7, 2000, Jake van der Kamp began his column in the *South China Morning Post* with "So Morgan Stanley looks like a house divided with one of its pundits recently forecasting 20,000 for the Hang Seng Index in a year's time and another 12,000." As an ex-strategist for the firm himself, he defended the practice of giving divergent views by saying, "It was the firm's attitude that it could not expect much from people it had taken on for their intellect if it chained them all to a house view."

Consistency of views—*cont'd*

Conclusions: Under the principle that one should be consistent or explain inconsistencies, I see no problem with such divergent views, at least when it comes to macro views, as long as strategists and economists draw to readers' attention any different views that colleagues may have published.

It may be difficult to do this with specific stock recommendations, however, given the need in some markets for disclosure of rating definitions and rating histories. Differences may be explained in terms of the time horizon used (short-term or long-term) or the type of analysis undertaken (fundamental or technical). In any case, at least some institutional clients say that they rely less on recommendations as such, but are more interested in the supporting analysis, information and data that an analyst can provide (see the "No recommendations" section below).

Technical analysis

There has been much debate as to how useful technical analysis really is in the securities industry. According to a Reuters article on July 19, 2006, Elizabeth Miller, a technical analyst with Redtower Research, contends that the Dow Jones stock-index collapse from the dotcom boom that peaked in 2000 followed a Fibonacci pattern. However, Professor Roy Batchelor and Dr. Richard Ramyar at the Cass Business School, City of London, have researched the peaks and troughs in the Dow Jones Industrial Average from 1915 to 2003 and have found no statistical evidence to support the use of Fibonacci patterns in predicting peaks and troughs.[33]

Meanwhile, proponents of behavioral finance would argue that markets are not necessarily rational or efficient, and that herd instinct has a role in determining market movements. After the financial crisis, the CFA Institute in Britain asked its members whether they trusted in "market efficiency". As reported by the *FT* on June 16, 2009, two-thirds of the professionals surveyed said they regarded behavioral finance as a useful addition to efficient market theories. However, only 14 percent thought that it could alone become the new paradigm.

As we discuss further in the appropriate valuation methodology section in Chapter 2, Andrew Milligan, head of global strategy at Standard Life, and his colleague Richard Batty examined ways investors could use valuation tools to enhance investor performance. They concluded from their research that, whereas valuations mainly matter in the longer term, in the shorter term of say a year, technical issues such as investor sentiment and positioning are more significant. They also concluded that other measures such as behavioral finance should be taken into consideration as well (see *FT* of October 16, 2007).

We will not dwell too closely on technical analysis here, and readers who wish to know more about this art or science (depending on your perspective) could do worse than read *Technical Analysis: The Complete Resource for Financial Market Technicians* by Charles Kirkpatrick and Julie Dahlquist.

Anyway, suffice it to say that the SEC in the U.S. states that "technical analysis concerning the demand and supply for a sector, index, or industry based on trading volume and price" would not constitute a research report "if it does not . . . recommend or rate individual securities".

Dedicated technical analysts may be able to satisfy the requirements for "research" for the individual securities they follow. Otherwise, technical comments on individual securities, unless made in support of an already-published fundamental recommendation for the same security, could be couched in objective terms. One example might be: "Breaching the five-year resistance line, as shown in the accompanying chart, could trigger a bullish signal." As with hedge and portfolio strategists, it can only help the reader to flag to them what the firm's fundamental research recommendations are for featured securities.

EXAMPLE

Useful qualifications (technical analysis)

- "... the technical analysis has generated trading buy/sell indicators/ signals on the following stocks" (that is, to ensure that the screen cannot be seen to represent the firm's fundamental recommendations);
- "... the stocks recommended by the technical analysts are not necessarily covered by the firm's fundamental-research analysts, and that the recommendations of those that are covered do not necessarily match the recommendations of the technical analysts";
- "past performance provides no guarantee of future performance" (an appropriate disclaimer for all securities research).

Coverage universe—initiations, terminations and transfers

Accountability principles

Brokerage firms need to make absolutely clear to their clients which companies are in their coverage universe, and which analyst is responsible for coverage of each company.

Analysts should not present themselves to the market as being experts in specific securities unless and until they can be seen to have undertaken thorough research on the companies concerned. Clients need to know the extent to which they can treat analysts' comments and recommendations seriously.

When analysts get clients into a trade, they have a duty to get them out again, or to give them notice that they will not be in a position to get them out again.

As with any research publication, supervisor and internal-review approvals would be required for all initiations, transfers and terminations of coverage. Full research disclosures would also be needed.

Initiation of coverage

When a new or existing analyst initiates coverage on any stock, this should be clearly shown at the beginning of the report.

Sufficient information for investors to make their investment decisions must be provided. This would no doubt include an introduction to the company (its business, capital structure, management, competition and so on), earnings drivers, valuation commentary (with, for example, DCF or DDM valuation, peer/historical comparisons and basis for target price), full financial forecasts and a discussion of risks including any perceived corporate governance issues. (See the earlier section on "Supervision and control of research" for questions that an internal-review panel might ask the analyst to address ahead of publication.)

Stock codes: It must also be clear which particular security the analyst is recommending. The use of Bloomberg or Thomson Reuters ticker codes and the full spelling of the company name would help effect this. Without the use of stock codes, a reader might mistakenly make an investment in a different class of shares from the one recommended (say, in preferred shares rather than ordinary shares) or even a different company altogether. The analyst may know which Mitsubishi or Samsung he is referring to, but it may not be so clear to some readers.

Transfer or re-initiation of coverage

An analyst who wishes to transfer coverage of a company to another analyst—for example, to a team member—should also make this clear to readers. The analyst taking over would need to take immediate responsibility for coverage and for the latest published views. If the new analyst is not prepared to take this responsibility, coverage should be suspended. The new analyst can then re-initiate coverage with his/her own recommendation, financial models and risk assessment for that company. As with initiations, analysts would need to provide sufficient information for investors to make their investment decisions.

Where circumstances allow, and provided clients are made aware of this, it might also be acceptable to stage the transfer by adding the transferee's name to the next research publication and then for the original analyst's name to be dropped off the following piece of research. In this way, continuity of coverage is effected (in much the same way as the axe at the Tower of London has apparently been there since 1687, notwithstanding that in the meantime the axe's head and handle have been changed alternately—at least that's what the tour guide told me). A transfer of coverage should not be regarded as a shortcut to initiating or re-initiating coverage, and analysts must still be able to demonstrate that they have undertaken in-depth research into the company concerned.

Any analysts to whom authorship is co-attributed must also share responsibility and be accountable for that research. Thus, during any staged transfer or, indeed, any situation where multiple names are shown as authors, both/all analysts must be happy with the arrangement and take full responsibility for any views and estimates shown. See the case study below as well as the comments on "Analyst Certification" in Chapter 3.

CASE STUDY

Co-authorship liability

Summary: The conflict of interest and reasonable basis charges against Jack Grubman, as part of the global settlements, are detailed in Chapter 3. What is also interesting is that Grubman's co-author on research relating to Winstar Communications Inc. did not escape either. The NASD announced on April 5, 2004, that CG, a former vice president and senior analyst at Salomon Smith Barney (SSB, which became part of Citigroup)[34] had settled charges relating to misleading research by agreeing, without admitting or denying the allegations, to a US$100,000 fine and a six-month suspension from the industry. She was prohibited for a further 18 months from having her name appear on research.

Details: Winstar Communications was one of SSB's banking clients. Private e-mail correspondence between CG and a client was used as evidence to support the charge that the research was misleading and had no reasonable basis to it. In response to the client's question as to why she and Grubman were using such a high free cash flow growth rate in their valuations, she answered: "There really is no good reason—except the unwillingness to change our Target Price for optics; although I would admit $50 per share is shall we say—extremely aggressive." The stock price at the time was US$20, but subsequently fell 99 percent to US$0.14 per share.

Co-authorship liability—*cont'd*

Conclusions: All analysts whose names appear on research need to take personal responsibility for that research. They need to be confident that conflicts of interest have been avoided or managed, and that the views and opinions are well supported, with risks to those views highlighted. Junior or supporting analysts need to have the courage of their own convictions, so to speak, and not be led astray by a superstar boss.

The case also serves to demonstrate once again that there's no such thing as a purely confidential e-mail. Any e-mail can find its way to clients, the press, regulators or the courts.

Termination of coverage

Terminations of coverage should be communicated to clients. The publication of termination should give reasons for the termination and state the final recommendation. A stock's performance that is contrary to the analyst's recommendation would not be a suitable reason for terminating coverage. However, if the market cap on a buy-rated stock had dropped so low that it was materially below the formal market-cap threshold for coverage stocks, given the brokerage's institutional investor profile, then that perhaps might be sufficient reason to drop coverage.

Other analysts, including strategists and country/sector heads, should not then give any investment opinions on the particular company involved, including the previous analyst's recommendation, target price, valuations or estimates. All such stocks must therefore be deleted from coverage-universe lists, including top-picks lists.

One possible exception to this rule could be for model portfolios, for reasons given earlier under "Sector/country weightings and universes". Stocks where coverage has been terminated can perhaps remain in model portfolios until there is a non-artificial commercial reason to drop the stock (for example, the stock is no longer performing), provided the firm draws to readers' attention that the stock is no longer covered by the firm's research analysts. In addition, if applicable, the firm should show whose estimates or valuations are being used.

Note: brokerage firms should regularly monitor their coverage and earnings databases to ensure that they do not show companies that are no longer actively covered by an existing analyst. This also applies to any lists of top picks—for example, in daily or country/sector products. This goes beyond having an analyst's name assigned passively to a company. If analysts cannot take full responsibility for the current recommendation, target price, valuations and estimates, and cannot stand up to scrutiny on any companies with which they are associated, then coverage should be dropped immediately, with appropriate notice given.

"Under review"

It is one thing flagging that earnings estimates are subject to upside or downside risk following earnings results or some macro or corporate news, but analysts should try to avoid specifically flagging that recommendations are "under review". This might at best show clients that the analyst is not on top of his coverage, from a commercial perspective, and at worst might give conflicting signals to clients. Although clients would receive the same information at the same time, some of them might act in anticipation of the change which, for whatever reason, may never come, whereas others might prudently wait for the change.

Sometimes during times of extreme volatility, recommendations and upsides/downsides to target prices or fair values might be inconsistent with each other (for example, a buy recommendation with negative returns to the target price, and vice versa). In such cases, a fundamental analyst's initial reaction might be to flag that he is reviewing his recommendation.

However, by the time he has undertaken his analysis, considering all the new information and any change in the market in the meantime, it may be that it is his target price or fair value that he changes, rather than his recommendation. (Where the analyst changes his target price or fair value he must, of course, provide good fundamental reasons for doing so, lest he is seen to be merely following the market as the stock's price goes up and down.)

It's important to let clients know if any views or recommendations are unsafe. To explain the apparent inconsistency, it should be sufficient for the analyst to say simply that he is reassessing his investment views, without specifying whether it will be the recommendation or the target price that he is expecting to change. This should provide sufficient warning to readers that they should not rely on the analyst's latest published views.

Note that if recommendations are flagged as "under review" in internal communications only, and sales or traders act in anticipation of the change, a regulator might use this as evidence of "front-running", with the charge that the analyst was tipping-off the firm's sales and traders.

Analysts must present their clearly thought-through views with recommendations and target prices that are consistent with each other. Discretion could apply in volatile situations where the price is dancing within a small margin around the recommendation threshold; but if there is a significant disconnect between a recommendation and target price, the analyst should be asked to change one or the other.

Publishing new research

As mentioned earlier, new research that is presented at morning sales meetings must already have been made available to clients by being published. To be fair to all clients and to avoid possible charges of front-running, analysts should not comment to sales or call individual clients on material that has not yet been published. They should be able to remind sales of their existing views and recommendations, but they should not present new unpublished "research". When published and made available fairly to clients at the same time through the firm's formal publishing systems, the publications can then be marketed separately to individual clients and internal constituents such as cash sales, prop traders and the structured products team. (For relevant case studies see the section earlier in this chapter entitled "Front-running and selective distribution of research".)

No recommendation?

The following thoughts may prove to be more academic than practical, depending on clients' needs and local regulations. One potential way of avoiding inconsistency between recommendation and target price would perhaps be to avoid assigning formal ratings/recommendations at all, but rather to focus just on valuations/target prices, or even just on the company's business and its earnings. From a commercial perspective, the sales team would still act as brokers in broking the research, but the research product itself would represent an independent analysis of the stock's valuation (much like an independent property-valuation report focuses on the valuation of the property rather than any recommendation to buy or sell).

This in effect would probably only represent a reversion to the original idea of stock analysis (before investment bankers tried to rope in the services of analysts). While such a system may not appeal to all clients, it might appeal to some, especially those less trustful of research analysts following the conflict-of-interest scandals of recent years.

Indeed, one of the Hong Kong SFC's major findings in its *Investor Survey on Investment Research Activities*, published in November 2003, was that both retail and institutional investors are more interested in factual details and analyses on specific stocks or industry sectors than in specific recommendations and target prices. According to the survey, 86 percent of respondents among institutional investors indicated interest in analysis on specific stocks, while only 36 percent indicated interest in a specific recommendation. This would imply that they tend to make their decisions based on facts and analyses rather than relying on analysts' recommendations.

Moreover, in his book *The Super Analysts*, Andrew Leeming asked Mark Mobius what he valued from sell-side analysts, commenting that some fund managers had told him that they didn't value stock calls or even valuation, but just wanted company and industry intelligence and data. Mobius replied that this was a fair comment, and said that at Templeton they liked to get information about a company and the industry, but didn't really value recommendations because of their time-sensitivity. Later in the book, Murdoch Murchison reiterated this view on behalf of Templeton. Stephen Horan, head of private wealth at the CFA Institute, is cited in the *SCMP* of April 4, 2008, as saying that investment professionals often ignore the recommendation or rating, opting instead to use the full report as one of many sources as they draw their conclusions.

In Hong Kong, Paragraph 16 of the SFC's Code of Conduct provides an interpretation of "research" by giving three criteria, any one of which needs to be satisfied for material to be classified as research (see the opening section of this chapter). The inclusion in a report of advice or recommendation based on investment analysis is one of the three, but is not a necessary prerequisite in itself. Up until a few years ago U.S. securities regulators included the word "recommendation" in the definition of "research report", with respect to communications with the public. The regulators' intention when they deleted the reference was no doubt to widen the net of what could be classified as "research", but it also suggests that formal recommendations are not now a prerequisite.

Furthermore, in defining "research analysts", U.S. regulations merely refer to "... the preparation of research reports, *or* making recommendations *or* offering opinions in public appearances *or* establishing a rating or price target" (my italics).

Note: the rules stipulate criteria that must be satisfied for recommendation/rating systems. For example, recommendations must have a reasonable basis, the market price at the time of the recommendation must be indicated, and the meanings of ratings must be disclosed. However, the definitions of "research reports" and "research analysts" suggest that recommendation/rating systems *per se* are not a requirement, at least not in the U.S.

(However, one caveat to this may apply under U.S. regulations. The SEC rules require disclosure to be made "for all ratings used" and that "definitions of ratings terms also must be consistent with their plain meaning". FINRA's interpretation of the disclosure rules is that "if a firm does not employ a rating system that uses the terms 'buy', 'hold/neutral' and 'sell', a member must determine, based on its own ratings system, into which of the three categories its ratings fall". Both the rules and the interpretation seem to apply where ratings of some description are used, but they do not say explicitly whether a rating system has to be used at all. In our scenario, where no recommendations or ratings are specified, the upside/downside to target valuations/prices might be regarded by the regulator as an implied rating system.)

By not having formal recommendations there would not be the problem of one size not fitting all, such as brokers have who choose either absolute recommendations (for example, buy/sell) or relative ratings or weightings (for example, outperform/underperform or overweight/underweight). Note that at least the relative performance ratings may not technically be "recommendations" as such, but could be regarded as "ratings".

Just giving upsides/downsides to target valuations/prices over a stated time frame would surely be the purest form of ranking stocks since it does not presume the investor's own investment parameters and risk profile. After all, whenever there is a trade, there is a buyer and a seller who both want to trade at that price. So a valuation level that means a buy to one investor may mean a sell to another.

Not using the lowest available recommendations—for example, the sometimes politically challenging sell rating—could pose a regulatory issue, but not if there was no recommendation system as such. In the April 2003 brokerage settlement in the U.S., one of the criticisms aimed at brokers was that analysts rarely, if ever, used the lowest recommendations/ratings. This was invariably highlighted as separate sections.[35] These criticisms were raised specifically in the context of investment banking deals, but the same criticism would presumably apply for general research.

Brokers could distinguish themselves from the competition by being seen more as independent valuers. The focus would be more on the different valuation/target aspects. Brokers who want to cater more to fund managers' different investment criteria could show more options; for example, both three-month and 12-month upsides/downsides to their target/fair valuations on an absolute basis, and three-month and 12-month upsides/downsides on a relative basis against the chosen index. The more targets/fair valuations shown, the more complicated it gets, of course.

Research strategists would still be able to present their recommended strategies or top-pick lists by, for example, showing portfolios with over-weighted and underweighted stocks. It's just that, under this scenario, analysts would not use buy, hold, and sell recommendations for individual company reports. A system of no recommendations or ratings would thus seem to bypass the inherent flaws found in all "one-size-fits-all" recom-mendation or rating systems and, judging by the earlier comment from Mark Mobius, would be of use to at least some clients. Note, however, that we're not talking here about bypassing "research" criteria and regulations. In other words, a report on a security without an explicit recommenda-tion would still be classified as a research report if it contained analy-sis and sufficient information to make an investment decision. As such, research disclosures would still need to be provided as appropriate to the jurisdiction(s) involved, and legal advice may be needed, as appropriate. I would also caution here that brokers and sales representatives, who distribute the research to clients, might be tempted to add their own informal recommendation, such as "buy" or "sell". If they then were to distribute these calls widely, rather than on a client-by-client basis, they could be seen to be touting themselves as research analysts, and unwittingly become subject to rules and procedures relating to "research". By adding their own one-size-fits-all recommendations they may need to provide rating histories and rating distributions as disclosures.

EXAMPLE

No recommendations

For about six months from mid-November 2004, HSBC did not assign specific recommendations, ratings or target prices to the stocks under its global research coverage. During that time, the company made the following statement at the back of its equity-research reports to define the basis for its financial analysis:

"HSBC does not seek to value companies in order to provide a target price or recommendation. Instead, the principal aim of HSBC's sector and company research is to show how a particular theme or idea may affect the future earnings or cash flow of a company. To this aim, we provide earnings and cash-flow forecasts, including an illustrative discounted cashflow analysis, and present standard valuation metrics to help clients in their investment decisions."

So, for this period, HSBC research analysts did not try to reach a specific fair value or target price for their covered stocks. Similarly, they did not try to determine the extent to which any discount or premium to a stock's current price was warranted, or proffer a one-size-fits-all recommendation or rating. HSBC's sales team merely discussed the research theme with its clients on an individual basis, and tailored investment advice to suit the client's specific investment criteria (according to the client's value or growth preference, time horizon and risk profile, for example).

Stock ratings were subsequently introduced. According to the Lex column in the May 23, 2005, issue of the *FT*, the bank partly blamed regulators "who want analysts' preferences to be clear" for having to backtrack on its analysis rationale. Research disclosures were changed to give definitions for the new overweight, neutral and underweight ratings. In essence, the methods of valuing stocks on a fundamental basis did not change. HSBC still offers various valuations of a company based on various metrics, and shows the risks to those valuations using sensitivity models. Incidentally, HSBC also introduced short-term trading ideas, with a 0–3-month time horizon.

No recommendations—*cont'd*

Conclusion: Given the inherent flaws found in all "one-size-fits-all" recommendation or rating systems, I think such a theoretical model of no recommendations still has merit and would be of use to clients, at least institutional ones. It remains to be seen whether other brokers can successfully manage to introduce and maintain such a system without being penalized by regulators or otherwise dissuaded.[36]

Endnotes

1. FINRA is the consolidated entity of the National Association of Securities Dealers (NASD) and the member regulation, enforcement and arbitration functions of the New York Stock Exchange (NYSE).
2. See Rule 15a-6 of the Securities Exchange Act 1934.
3. See the SEC's proposed rule entitled "Exemption of Certain Foreign Brokers or Dealers", dated June 27, 2008.
4. Alternative recommendations could, of course, only be given if the appropriate research coverage criteria have been met by the analyst or colleague (see "The realm of research" following), and acknowledgment would need to be given to any colleagues covering these securities or instruments.
5. Some regulators might not necessarily require sales, traders and other professionals who may from time to time provide communications to clients that might constitute "research" to be formally registered or qualified as research analysts. However, they would expect such professionals to make sure other research requirements are met, for example, that the research is objective, that it is distributed fairly and that risk and other disclosures are provided. For example, this was one of the new exemptions that FINRA of the U.S. proposed in its Regulatory Notice #08-55, dated October 2008.
6. See www.sec.gov and www.finra.org.
7. Following the merger between the Bond Market Association and the Securities Industry Association into the Securities Industry and Financial Markets Association, these voluntary principles can now be found at www.sifma.org/research/pdf/Guiding_Principles_for_Research.pdf.
8. See www.ec.europa.eu/internal_market/securities.
9. See www.sfc.hk.
10. See SFO sections 245 & 285 Part XIII-civil & Part XIV-criminal.
11. See www.iosco.org.
12. See http://www.iosco.org/library/pubdocs/pdf/IOSCOPD301.pdf.
13. The full article, "The impact of the 2004 research analyst rules on hedge fund research reports", is reproduced in the *Journal of Financial Regulation and Compliance*, Vol. 14 No. 2, 2006, and is available at www.emeraldinsight.com.
14. Interesting journalism-related cases are featured in a research paper by Damian Tambini of Polis and the London School of Economics entitled "What is financial journalism for? Ethics and responsibility in a time of crisis and change".

15. FINRA in the U.S. introduced guidelines in January 2010 to help broker-dealers deal with blogs and communications on social networking sites such as Facebook, Twitter and LinkedIn. Ultimately, if the comments constitute research, then disclosures, supervision, record-keeping and so on would be required.

16. The fine represented the notional profit that the insider trader could have made had he sold all his shares at the time when the information became public. The defense counsel argued for a lighter fine on the basis that DJ's overall profit was only HK$2 million, since he sold half of his stake at a loss later on—in the depths of the financial crisis. Mr. DJ appealed the decision.

17. One of the new measures proposed in FINRA's Regulatory Notice #08-55 dated October 2008 was that firms may provide different research products and services to certain classes of customers, provided the firm discloses its research dissemination practices to all customers.

18. One example of a market where proprietary trading restrictions are imposed is Korea. Basically, prop traders cannot trade in a counter for at least 24 hours (that is a full business day) after the firm publishes a research report that includes a material change to investment opinion, that is a change of rating or target price.

19. According to the SEC, a trade "is on the basis of material nonpublic information if the trader was aware of the material, nonpublic information when the person made the purchase or sale". Furthermore, a person commits fraud "when he misappropriates confidential information for securities trading purposes, in breach of a duty owed to the source of the information".

20. Victoria Kim and Brooke Masters of the *FT* analyzed data compiled by Measuredmarkets, and reported on August 6, 2007, that almost 60 percent of the 27 big deals announced in North America for the year to date were preceded by unexplained spikes in trading in the stock of the target company. Furthermore, on average since 2003, the percentage of large deals that were preceded by abnormal share trading had been 49 percent, skewed heavily toward sectors such as casinos and hotels (80 percent of large deals) and banking (52 percent). A similar study by Measuredmarkets for the *New York Times* the previous year concluded that "the securities of 41 percent of the companies receiving buyout bids exhibited abnormal and suspicious trading in the days and weeks before those deals became public".

21. The FSA reported that suspicious trades occurred ahead of 29.3 percent of public takeovers in 2008, up from 28.7 percent in 2007.

22. The SEC revised charges and added new ones in November 2009 against Galleon, New Castle Funds, Spherix Capital, S2 Capital, Far & Lee, Schottenfeld and several individuals. The SEC alleged that the defendants in the two overlapping insider trading cases reaped over US$50 million. The cases centered on Raj Rajaratnam of Galleon and an ex-Schottenfeld trader nicknamed "Octopussy" (given how far and wide his information tentacles supposedly reached). Inside information was allegedly gleaned from insiders at companies themselves (relating to Polycom, Intel and IBM), a ratings analyst at Moody's, a lawyer at Ropes & Gray and a director at McKinsey. Some of the individuals pleaded guilty and others not guilty. Schottenfeld agreed at the end of March 2010 to pay US$1.2 million to settle one set of charges.

23. Adopted in May 2002, an IOSCO MOU provides for improved enforcement-related cooperation and the exchange of information among regulators. Cross-border

cooperation was a major theme at the 32nd Annual IOSCO Conference held in Mumbai, India in April 2007 (see www.iosco.org).

24. Rule 10b-5 of the 1934 Securities Exchange Act is the catch-all anti-fraud measure in the U.S. There's also the Insider Trading Sanctions Act of 1984, which allows for a penalty of up to three times the illegal profits garnered from the insider trading, or the New York-specific Martin Act. Criminal sanctions introduced in Hong Kong in 2003 allow for fines of up to HK$10 million and imprisonment of up to 10 years. In the U.K. insider trading carries a maximum jail sentence of seven years.

25. This is a reference to an earlier case where the FSA gained convictions against a brokerage intern and his dentist father.

26. Full details of the case can be found at www.idt.gov.hk.

27. The sin stocks were chosen from these industries: alcohol consumption, adult services, gaming, tobacco, weapons and biotech alterations.

28. *Investing with Anthony Bolton* (Harriman House, 2006).

29. Those that signed the Global Research Analyst Settlement in 2003—see the Conflicts of interest (global settlements) case study in Chapter 3.

30. Mamma.com changed its name to Copernic in 2007.

31. Eventually, alas, Lehman Brothers couldn't survive the negative press any longer and filed for bankruptcy protection in mid-September 2008. Barclays did indeed pick up parts of Lehman's business, with other operations being bought by Nomura. This was at more or less the same time that HBOS in the U.K. was bought for a song by Lloyds TSB in a takeover that under normal circumstances might not have been approved under anti-trust measures. Lloyds TSB was then renamed Lloyds Banking Group. Anglo Irish Bank was nationalized in January 2009.

32. Also see endnote 22 in this chapter about Schottenfeld's alleged involvement in the Galleon insider trading cases.

33. See "Magic numbers in the Dow" at www.cass.city.ac.uk.

34. Citi began divesting its Smith Barney interests in January 2009 to Morgan Stanley.

35. For example, see sections 62–64 of the NYSE transcript of the Hearing Panel decision 03-69 for Morgan Stanley.

36. One type of research where ratings or recommendations (or even target prices) would invariably not be permitted is so-called pre-deal research. Given the nature of the exercise and the risks involved, analysts would merely analyze the business as a whole rather than its securities. For more details see the section on pre-deal research in Chapter 3.

Chapter 2

Reasonable Basis, Valuations and Risk

Key points ▮▮▮➤

- Analysts need to answer two fundamental questions that investors ask: Why should I invest or trade in this security? What are my risks?
- Analysts should not just say what their target price is, but explain why they think it's appropriate and achievable, with full valuation methodology given and with historic or peer comparisons, as necessary.
- Any material changes to views, estimates or target price arising since the previous report should be highlighted.
- The more upside or downside expected, the more readers will expect analysts to draw their attention to the associated risks.
- Analysts need to eke out differentiating factors for their investment calls. Risks to the investment case, corporate governance issues and dividend distribution are always important, but become even more so during bear or volatile markets.
- Issues that might affect the valuations of one company's securities might affect the valuations of the securities of other covered companies as well, such as corporate customers, suppliers or competitors. Clients would expect analysts to look at all angles.
- Analysts must remember that it's their name on their reports, so they must be comfortable with their recommendations and target prices, and take responsibility for them.

It's common sense that investors need analysts to justify their recommendations before they make an investment. Many regulators require analysts to have a "reasonable basis" for their investment views. To help satisfy this requirement, fundamental analysts should be able to demonstrate a thorough knowledge of the companies they cover and the industries they are in, and provide reasons and valuation support for any recommendations and target prices.

As mentioned in the Introduction, this book is about regulatory and best-practice issues—which, in effect, represent the main risks that analysts face—and does not attempt to teach analysts the analytical skills they need to do their job, such as valuing securities, for which plenty of resource material already exists. The classic *Security Analysis*, written by Benjamin Graham and David Dodd, remains the standard by which all other books on securities research, including—dare I say—the one you're reading now, are judged. The following comments on valuations and the risks to those valuations merely represent general points that I, as a supervisory analyst, would keep my eyes open for when reading draft research reports. I trust the case studies and examples help demonstrate the issues.

Consistency of recommendations

Individual recommendations and target prices should be consistent with each other, with the time horizon made clear. In the U.S., the SEC highlights that the meaning of recommendations must be made clear and that, for example, a "hold" cannot mean "sell". Since "switch" implies selling one of the stocks, analysts should probably use a word like "prefer", and reserve "switch" only for when the applicable stock is rated sell.

If "switch" is to be used for a buy- or hold-rated stock, an explanation should be given to define the circumstances under which analysts can recommend investors sell stocks that are otherwise rated buy or hold. Such circumstances might include short-term, relative-value pair/hedge trades, where the difference in performance between the two stocks represents the upside/downside, rather than the absolute performance of one or the other. Whatever definition is used should be clearly made in the disclosures to the research report.

Short-term trading opportunities should be presented as separate items of "research", with their own rating definitions, timeframes and disclosures included. Otherwise, they could perhaps be identified in the body of the text as short-term risks for investors to be aware of rather than as formal recommendations for suggested action. There should be no potential for confusion with the formal fundamental recommendation.

Calls such as "buy on weakness" and "sell on strength" beg the question what the recommendation is at the current price, and how weak or strong the stock's price movement needs to be to trigger the trade.

Explanation for inconsistencies

One of the basic principles in publishing research is that analysts must be consistent or explain apparent inconsistencies. The use of "under review" might give clients the impression that analysts are not on top of their coverage. From time to time, however, analysts may need to explain why a recommendation and target price are not consistent with each other, perhaps during short periods of extreme price volatility or when an analyst is waiting for further details from the company.

So as not to risk being seen to be tipping-off sales of forthcoming recommendation changes, or to be giving potentially misleading signals to clients, I would suggest that analysts do not specify that they are reviewing their recommendation *per se* (since it may end up being the fair value or target price that ends up needing to be changed for some valid reason), just that they are generally reassessing their investment views. This offers some protection against appearing to be giving contradictory investment advice. It stands to reason that in such cases, until analysts have had a chance to complete their analysis, they should refrain from giving any conclusions or making any investment implications.

Any "under review" or "reassessing views" qualification should not be taken as a long-term excuse for analysts not to be on top of their coverage. The latest published recommendation and target price should be shown in any case, for reference and transparency purposes.

Following the market

One thing that I see now and again as a supervisory analyst is where an analyst maintains a rating—for example, neutral or hold—but keeps changing the target price to stay in line with the stock's price. So, by sitting on the fence and having his target price always within a narrow band around the current share price, the analyst can always claim that his neutral rating is appropriate. Of course, the analyst always has to justify any change of target price. Anyway, by following the market up and then following it down again, the analyst loses the investment opportunity for his clients. Analysts only add value for clients when they can be seen to be leading the market, not following it. Again I would refer to Byron Wien, especially his comment that anticipating change is worth a lot more than analyzing change.[1]

Valuation support

To get to a stage of being able to value a company, an analyst needs to have a pretty firm grasp of the company's business, its financial health and its earning ability (see again pages 4–9). The analyst needs to determine the true picture, and whether or not the company's accounts reflect this.

Forensic analysis of accounts

Analysts are not auditors, and do not have an auditor's access to a company's internal records or information. However, analysts do owe their firms' clients a duty of care[2] and would do well to question anything they think looks suspicious in a subject company's accounts and statements.

They should highlight the items in a company's financial accounts that they think are most subject to interpretation or where the board and the auditor are most likely to disagree. Furthermore, as we'll see from a couple of examples shown below, analysts cannot always rely on auditors to do a thorough job of uncovering or revealing fraudulent or irregular accounting.

Examples of suspicious accounting treatment might include the smoothing, accelerating or delaying of earnings by booking income at times other than when it is earned or received, or by booking expenses at times other than when they are incurred or paid. Company managers might be tempted to manipulate sales or earnings to meet financial targets or to maximize share valuations (perhaps ahead of a sale of shares), while manipulating interest costs may help raise the company's creditworthiness and bond ratings. Analysts would also need to determine any off-balance-sheet liabilities the company may have (as in Enron's case) and, for example, how stock options are treated and when they are issued and exercised (as in the case involving the COO of Monster Worldwide).

There are all sorts of ways a company can try and manipulate their numbers. Let's look at what two of the best-known companies in the world have allegedly been up to in recent years.

CASE STUDY

Channel-stuffing and other activities

Details: Coca-Cola agreed in July 2008 to settle a long-running U.S. shareholder suit to the tune of US$137.5 million. Investors alleged back in October 2000 that the company had artificially increased sales through a practice called channel-stuffing, by forcing Japanese bottlers to buy excess concentrated syrup. The *WSJ* of July 8, 2008, noted that this followed a similar settlement with the SEC in April 2005. In both cases the company agreed to settle without admitting or denying the allegations.

Separately, in his book *Fooling Some of the People All of the Time: A Long Short Story*, David Einhorn of Greenlight Capital, a hedge fund, argued how in 1998 Coca-Cola's earnings multiple of around 50 times earnings was unjustified because its earnings were of poor quality since they included gains from the disposal of bottling operations. Einhorn said that he didn't have the guts to short Coca-Cola, but says he should have. He presumed that he couldn't possibly have a unique insight into such a large well-covered stock.

Another large, well-covered stock—General Electric—paid US$50 million in August 2009 to settle an SEC complaint that it had misled investors through various instances of accounting fraud. On four

Channel-stuffing and other activities—*cont'd*

separate occasions in 2002 and 2003, according to the SEC, high-level GE accounting executives or other finance personnel approved accounting that was not in compliance with Generally Accepted Accounting Principles (GAAP). In one instance the improper accounting had allowed GE to avoid missing analysts' final EPS (earnings per share) expectations. The company made the settlement without admitting or denying the SEC's allegations.

Conclusions: Even companies as apparently well-run as Coca-Cola and General Electric can get caught up in controversial accounting issues. Analysts need to be on the ball in identifying potential controversy and gauging the consequences of any protracted litigation.

(See also the story about Coca-Cola's Dasani bottled water in the corporate governance example on social responsibility later in this chapter. There's also more on David Einhorn in the "Short-selling by hedge funds" example coming up in the "Highlighting risks and volatility" section.)

Analysts who cover multiple companies within the same industry should be in a relatively good position to spot evidence of cross-industry shenanigans. The following case study looks at price-fixing and other antitrust issues.

CASE STUDY

Cross-industry antitrust issues

Details: LG Display of South Korea, Sharp of Japan and Chunghwa Picture Tubes of Taiwan pleaded guilty and paid fines totaling US$585 million in November 2008 for fixing the price of liquid crystal display panels. These three were followed just over a year later by three more companies, namely Epson Imaging Devices, a unit of Hitachi and Chi Mei Optoelectronics, raising the total fines paid to over US$860 million. LG Display's share of these fines was US$400 million, and Chi Mei's was US$220 million, according to the newswires.

At the time, LG Display's fine represented the second largest criminal fine that the antitrust division of the U.S. Justice Department had imposed, after the US$500 million fine meted out to F. Hoffmann-La

Cross-industry antitrust issues—*cont'd*

Roche in 1999 for leading a price-fixing cartel in vitamin supplements. (The Justice Department seems to be on a roll now. Pfizer reached a whopping US$2.3 billion settlement in October 2009 for drug misbranding. This included a record criminal fine of US$1.2 billion and a civil penalty of US$1 billion, according to Bloomberg.)

The share prices of the first three LCD panel-makers to be fined fell by between 7 percent and 11 percent on the day the fines in the U.S. were announced. Chi Mei's fell 3 percent on the day its fine was announced.

On a smaller scale, six chipmakers including NEC, Renesas Technology, Micron Technology and Hynix Technology agreed to pay a total of US$25 million in January 2010, as reported by Bloomberg, to settle claims that they conspired to fix prices of static random access memory (SRAM) chips.

One major danger for global companies is that they can face multiple suits around the world. Intel was fined €1.06 billion by the European Union in May 2009 for abusing its dominant market position. This was the largest single penalty to be imposed on a company for antitrust breaches in Europe, according to the *FT*. The original complaint had been filed by Intel's main competitor, Advanced Micro Devices, and related to conditional rebates made to computer makers like Acer and Dell. The conditions apparently were that they had to use Intel's processors rather than AMD's. Intel appealed the decision.

Intel then agreed in November 2009 to pay AMD US$1.25 billion to settle all its antitrust disputes with that company. AMD's shares surged on the news, whereas Intel's price hardly budged—possibly because the settlement had already been fully discounted or perhaps because of the sheer scale advantage that the company would still enjoy in its market as the world's biggest chipmaker.

Conclusions: Analysts would of course need to gauge how exposed a company that is fined in one location would be to similar fines in other countries, and how its reputation may suffer.

Astute analysts should also wonder how other companies might be affected. For example, the Justice Department cited Dell, Apple and Motorola as companies which had been affected by the LCD panel price-fixing conspiracy since they had purchased screens from the panel-makers. These companies could have grounds for private lawsuits. Sure enough, Dell filed a lawsuit against five companies including Sharp and Hitachi in March 2010, alleging that it had been overcharged over several years in respect to a certain category of their LCD purchases.

Michael Gordon, the global head of institutional investment at Fidelity International, contributed an article to the November 6, 2008, issue of the *FT* entitled, "Analysts must pay more heed to company cash flows". His message was that analysts had been focusing on companies' P&L accounts and whether or not earnings beat estimates, but with the economic slump looming they would need to pay as much attention to cash flow, the balance sheet and the effect that different forms of financing have on a company's common stock.

In an earlier market cycle, as reported in the February 3, 2002, issue of the *Independent on Sunday*, Richard Dale, joint head of equity research for Citigroup, gave a presentation on a similar theme to the firm's analysts: "There is a generation of analysts who have grown up in the bull market . . . and never had to look at a balance sheet. That is where the real story is, and they have to learn what alarm bells sound like." The presentation was entitled "Time for forensic analysis".

A degree of forensic analysis never goes amiss at any time. Indeed, RiskMetrics, an independent research firm based in New York, specifically focuses on companies that its analysts think are heading for a fall. As reported by Steve Johnson in the *FT* on November 19, 2008, the firm claims to have identified, for example, the challenges facing Northern Rock a few months ahead of the crisis. The *FT* cites Niels Aalen, managing director of international operations at RiskMetrics: "We look for any deterioration of the business model via forensic analysis . . . We are exclusively focused on getting down to the weeds of the accounts."

Of course this approach of spotting firms with accounting issues is not without its own hazards, as Gradient Analytics experienced. See the case study in Chapter 3 on potential or apparent conflicts of interest for independent research firms, in which Gradient was accused of colluding with hedge funds to drive stock prices down.

In addition to scrutinizing the numbers, analysts need to take a close look at the notes and disclosures to the accounts. They need to compare them from period to period to see what words have been added or deleted, or how definitions may have changed over time. Analysts might also need to compare translations of disclosures—is the company giving one version to local investors and another version to international investors?

EXAMPLE

Disclosures and notes

Summary: New Century Financial was the first major financial company to fail during the subprime-driven credit crisis in 2007. According to an independent report commissioned by the U.S. Justice Department, the company engaged in "significant improper and imprudent practices".

Disclosures and notes—*cont'd*

Details: According to an article by Vikas Bajaj in the *International Herald Tribune* on March 28, 2008, the investigators did not find sufficient evidence to conclude that New Century engaged in earnings management or manipulation, although its accounting irregularities almost always resulted in increased earnings. The commissioned report contended that profits were the basis for significant executive bonuses and helped persuade Wall Street that the company was in fine health when in fact its business was coming apart. The investigators also criticized KPMG for not being skeptical enough in auditing the accounts of New Century Financial.

Marc Siegel, head of accounting and governance research at RiskMetrics, cites a specific example of a note to New Century's accounts to the effect that the allowance for losses on loans held for investment at June 2006 was US$209.9 million. Then on September 2006, the statement was changed slightly to show the allowance for losses on mortgage loans held for investment and real estate owned was US$239.4 million. On the face of it the number had increased. However, disaggregating the reserves revealed that it was an increase in the real estate owned valuation allowance that was masking a decrease in the loan loss allowance under the original definition—these had fallen by 9 percent to US$191.6 million.

Conclusions: As mentioned earlier, analysts are not auditors and do not have access to internal records and information, but neither should they necessarily rely totally on auditors to uncover or reveal fraudulent or irregular accounting. Investors rely on an analyst's analysis and recommendation. Analysts should therefore be extra diligent in uncovering the true state of a company's finances. They should also be watchful that whatever accounting treatment firms use, they are consistent from period to period and not just as it suits them.

Later on in this chapter, where we discuss the need for analysts to highlight risks to their views, we discuss various aspects of corporate governance at companies. The old *"falsus in uno, falsus in omnibus"* adage would apply. If the analyst catches management doing or saying anything suspicious or inconsistent, then they should suspect everything that management says or does, and consequently dig that much more deeply into the company's accounts and statements.

Aside: Here's an embarrassing story from New Zealand. NZX, the national stock exchange, asked NZ Farming Systems Uruguay in August 2009 to explain a note to the annual financial statements relating to depreciation that read, "Fudge this to equal depn in

---

Disclosures and notes—*cont'd*

FA note 11″. The comment had been left in the accounts inadvertently when they were formally filed at the exchange. I can't wait for the film to come out—*Fudge This*, the alternative sequel to *Analyze This*, starring Robert De Niro and Billy Crystal.

In addition to publications by RiskMetrics, there are some good books on the subject of identifying fraud and other accounting irregularities. Three bestsellers are *Accounting for Growth* by Terry Smith, *Financial Shenanigans* by Howard Schilit and *The Financial Numbers Game: Detecting Creative Accounting Practices* by Charles Mulford and Eugene Comiskey.

Pro-forma accounting and use of selective data

Analysts should make sure they present to readers a complete picture of a company's financial position, and not ignore data that do not fit with the analysts' theses. Neither should analysts blindly accept a company's reason for focusing on other measures of earnings (*pro-forma*, core, operating, recurring, underlying, parent or whatever), unless they are comfortable that it really does represent a more appropriate methodology. They should draw readers' attention to any earnings numbers or P/E valuations that they quote or focus on which are not based on standard net earnings per share. Analysts should always make clear what adjustments have been made to any "adjusted" earnings, and include the standard net numbers anyway for readers to consider.

Reasonableness of valuations

If/when giving fair or target valuations, analysts should say how and why they think their underlying estimates differ from those of consensus, and why they think their own valuations are realistic and achievable. For example, a stock analyst might refer to a DCF (discounted cash flow), DDM (dividend discount model), EVA (economic value added), NAV (net asset value) or SOP (sum of parts) calculation. Comparisons can be made against the stock's historic valuation multiples or peer valuations (for example, using one-/three-/five-year peak/low/average P/E, EV/EBITDA or P/B for the stock, market or sector). Consideration can be given as to whether the P/B is justified by the expected growth in ROE, whether the P/E is justified by the expected growth in net earnings or how competitive the expected dividend yield is compared with yields from alternative investments given the risks attached.

When analysts give valuations they must make clear what their underlying assumptions are; for example, the discount rate used for calculating the net present value of future returns (whether the returns are represented by earnings, cash flows or dividends). Analysts should also be able to justify the choice of peers used for any comparable market-based valuations given, and why any obvious examples, such as industry leaders, may have been omitted. Analysts must make clear what valuation years are being used and, if they are prospective, whose estimates they are based on.

Highlight valuation changes

Analysts should always make clear if their fair value or target price for a stock is being maintained or changed. If the latter, they should say what element of the valuation has changed (for example, forecasts, discount rate or—in the case of price-based valuations for comparison purposes—the multiple, the forecast year and so on). Readers need to see to what extent a change in recommendation is being made as a result of a change in the analyst's target valuation or multiple, as opposed to a change in the market price. Giving the history of recommendations and target prices is a requirement in some markets.

The appropriate valuation methodology

Most fundamental equity valuation techniques attempt to ascertain a net present value of future streams of income from the company (whether in terms of cash flow, net earnings or dividends). Supply and demand factors are also relevant. However, the "horses for courses" maxim applies, since different earnings and valuation drivers apply for different industries. Some companies, such as utilities, tend to produce pretty regular and dependable income streams, whereas in other industries a lot of money needs to be invested in research and development, and capital expenditure needs to be invested in assets and equipment, with varying degrees of likelihood of returns. Examples include metals-mining or oil-drilling, where future business growth is determined by the likelihood of new supplies of the raw commodity being found (categorized, for example, in terms of probable and provable reserves). Airlines and telecom companies, with expensive assets bought or leased at different times, are often valued on a like-for-like cash-earnings-generating basis, stripping out interest, tax, depreciation and amortization. Ultimately, the challenge for any analyst is to determine how long new investments might take to bear fruit, how big the fruit will be and what the risks will be along the way.

Incidentally, Andrew Milligan, head of global strategy at Standard Life, wrote an interesting article in the *FT* on October 16, 2007, arguing why valuation tools are powerful but dangerous. He and his colleague, Richard Batty, found from their research that in the long term, say 12 to 24 years, valuation mainly matters as a driver of equity, whereas in the short term, say one year, technical issues such as investor sentiment and positioning are more significant. They determined that across the big markets dividend yield, P/B and P/E were the most significant drivers. They also determined that, rather than returning to long-term averages, valuations merely return to recent trends. Fashion and simplicity matter in terms of which valuation technique is regarded as superior at any one time. Given that many valuation approaches come down to forecasting changes in the equity risk premium, which is one of the more sophisticated aspects of financial theory, they were not surprised that some investors look for simpler solutions. They concluded that valuations matter as one part of a wider toolkit including other measures such as behavioral finance, analysis of margins and understanding the long-term drivers of the inflation cycle. Analysts need to appreciate how relevant or important their valuations are to investors, especially given their investment timeframes.

One thing I've learned from my own trading experience is that for every dollar that's pushing a currency, commodity or security one way fundamentally, there's more or less another dollar speculating or hedging against that direction—thereby providing liquidity (and volatility) for the market. Ultimately, individual buyers and sellers have different investment or trading purposes, different investment time frames and different risk-tolerance levels. When buyers and sellers collectively meet in the market place it's like a tug-of-war match, with the market price being subject at times to a relatively even match between buyers and sellers, and at other times to periods of dominance of one side and weakness or even collapse of the other. Yes, it's difficult for the price to avoid the pull of fundamentals indefinitely, but technical, behavioral and momentum factors, whether driven by hedgers or speculators, can be serious forces in the meantime. As John Maynard Keynes famously remarked, "The market can stay irrational longer than you can stay solvent." Tell me about it.

Unrealistic expectations or questionable bases for valuation

During the credit crisis there was much controversy over fair-value or mark-to-market accounting, and how this practice of valuing marketable securities may have contributed to the crisis. Newt Gingrich, the former speaker of the U.S. House of Representatives, said in a Bloomberg interview in October 2008: "Historians will look back some day and say that the government drove companies into bankruptcy by creating artificial losses."

What became clear in the crisis is that the market had little idea, if any, as to how structured products such as collateralized debt/mortgage obligations (CDOs and CMOs) were constituted, what their real underlying valuations were and who bore the ultimate liabilities.

Market clearing prices became the ultimate basis for valuation. However, marking-to-market proved to be an academic exercise at times when there was no market demand for these securities. If there's no market for a security, instrument or product at any particular time, given the absence not just of fundamental investors but also of speculators, arbitrageurs and even market-makers, does that really mean that its fundamental fair value is zero, or is it just a temporary anomaly?

Of course historic cost accounting also has its critics. What seems fair to say is that neither method is particularly meaningful when asset prices are spiking irrationally, whether at the top or at the bottom.

The Internet bubble that burst in 2000 provided another classic example, albeit in hindsight not quite such a dramatic one as the financial crisis of 2007–2009, of how the markets can fall prey to unrealistic expectations and unreasonable valuations. The market's behavior was characterized as "irrational exuberance" by the then chairman of the U.S. Federal Reserve, Alan Greenspan. There was talk of a "paradigm shift" in the productivity of the world's economies, brought on by globalization and technological advances, which to some justified the ever-increasing valuations for stocks.

For example, staid old utility companies suddenly found themselves with the infrastructure needed for exciting new technologies. How were they to be valued—as defensive utilities or fast-growing technology companies? Other technology startups promised nothing except a good idea. Analysts came up with ever-imaginative valuation methodologies to justify current valuations and target prices for specific stocks, such as the number of eyeball hits on Internet web pages.

Greed and fear had evidently taken hold of the collective psyche of the market—greed to make more money and fear of being left behind. The individual analysts who were criticized for ramping up share prices should not, however, be expected to shoulder the blame on their own—the insatiable demand by some retail investors and the sensationalizing of the stories by some less-reputable newspapers evidently contributed to the hype.

EXAMPLE

Excessive valuations

Details: Internet bookseller Amazon.com was one of the more high-profile companies to be brought to market during the Internet bubble. By July 8, 1998, the *Wall Street Journal* was questioning how much higher the stock's valuation could go. Despite not having actually generated any profits at that stage, the company was already valued at about twice as much as the combined value of Barnes & Noble and Borders Group, the two largest booksellers with real bookshops.

The article said that the methods being used to value Internet stocks ranged from estimating revenues and profits much further out in the future than was customary, to extrapolations based on current marketing expenditures, to the number of Web site users. The article cited Morgan Stanley's Mary Meeker (dubbed "Queen of the Net" by Barron's) as saying that the new valuation zone for technology companies warranted new valuation approaches. In a later issue, on July 17, 2000, the *WSJ* recounts that in December 1998, when Amazon.com was trading at US$240, Henry Blodget made a forecast that the share would hit US$400 within 12 months. It passed this target within four weeks on its way to a high of over US$600. By the time of the July 17 article, the stock was back to trading at a third of this.

PCCW provides a good example of optimism-fuelled valuations for Internet companies in Asia. The *WSJ* of February 18, 2000, quotes the stock's price as HK$25.80 at the time, up more than 15 times in less than a year. The company was in discussion to buy Cable & Wireless HKT Ltd. (which in the end it did).

The *WSJ* article cites a target price for PCCW by Lehman Brothers of HK$35 per share within 12 months as equating to a market capitalization of almost US$46 billion, just shy of General Motors' value at the time. According to the article, the head of Lehman's Asian Internet coverage explained the difference between the HK$10 per share SOP valuation and the HK$35 target price by saying that such fundamental analysis is largely irrelevant when it comes to valuing Internet

Excessive valuations—*cont'd*

companies. He further argued to the effect that the premium valuation was accounted for by the deal-making abilities of the company's chairman, Richard Li. David Webb, a local investor and financial commentator, remarked that he doubted the market would be willing to pay that much even for Bill Gates, the co-founder and chairman of Microsoft. PCCW shares subsequently fell by more than 90 percent from their February highs.

A Reuters article of November 4, 1999, provides further quotes from Internet analysts at the time, again demonstrating how nebulous valuation methodologies had become for Internet stocks. According to the article, the head of Asia Pacific Internet research at Merrill Lynch told a news briefing: "I don't think they [Internet valuations] can be quantified"; and an Internet analyst at Goldman Sachs said: "Qualitative measures are going to be more important than quantitative measures because of the nascent stage of this industry."

Postscript: At least Amazon.com and PCCW survived, while some other Internet companies didn't. After the bubble burst in 2000, Mary Meeker maintained her confidence in leading technology companies (see the *WSJ* of October 23, 2000) and continued with her successful career at Morgan Stanley. Henry Blodget was eventually fined and barred from the industry (see the case studies on conflicts of interest in Chapter 3).

Highlighting risks and volatility

The foregoing discussion on excessive valuations leads us nicely into a discussion on drawing readers' attention to investment risks. Under securities regulations, analysts are invariably required to draw investment risks to investors' attention. Note that in some markets a distinction may be drawn between securities or investment analysts (who write research for clients generally, or at least one specific institutional client in the case of buy-side analysts) and financial or investment advisers (who provide investment advice tailored to individual retail clients' needs). However, in other markets there may not be such a clear distinction. For example, securities firms and investment advisory firms in Japan are grouped together with other investment organizations as "financial investment firms", although they are required to categorize clients either as "professional investors" or "general investors" (see the Japan example of "Regulations tightening up around the world" in Chapter 1). Also remember the view espoused by Elisse B. Walter of the SEC that all types of finance professionals should be held to a fiduciary standard. The chairman of the SEC, Mary Schapiro, has also stated that the rules governing brokerages and investment advisers should be "virtually identical".

While analysts and advisers are required by regulations (and indeed moral principles) to highlight risks, it also makes good commercial sense to do so. You would presumably want risk and volatility to be drawn to your attention if you were the investor, and would no doubt only deal with brokers who satisfied this requirement. If analysts don't give their investors what they want, someone else will.

Furthermore, I would argue that it's in the analysts' own interests to make as full use as possible of the risk section of their research report, as opposed merely to paying lip service by providing the minimum amount of risk information required. A comprehensive risk section can help the analyst later if events turn out contrary to expectations. If the analyst had included, for example, a sensitivity analysis showing how sensitive his earnings forecasts might be to different assumptions, then he can keep on referring to that table as the risks become more realistic or likely (rather than having to remain silent until he publishes a new research report for fair distribution to all clients). And if the analyst had warned of these risks, then he can't be accused of being entirely wrong if events unfold to prove his base case wrong.

The more the expected upside/downside to the target price, the more readers will expect analysts to draw their attention to the volatility of the security and risks in achieving the target. The less sophisticated the investor is with regard to investments, the more the analyst/adviser is expected not just to disclose the risks involved but also to explain them fully, especially with respect to geared investments or structured products. It may seem to go against the grain when you're trying to sell an idea to sales and clients to then draw attention to the downside risks to that idea. However, analysts must draw investors' attention to associated risk.

Appropriateness of sell ratings

The challenge when recommending a buy on a security is to make sure the reasons to buy are more compelling than the reasons to sell. But analysts are obliged to give a fair presentation of both. If, in the analyst's own mind, the downside risks outweigh potential upside returns, then perhaps he should rate the security as a sell rather than as a buy. Analysts should not be afraid to rate a security a sell; even if the fundamentals of the business look sound, the stock (or bond) can still be regarded as overvalued.

Analysts of course should still be sensitive when making a sell recommendation. Markets are all about confidence, and whereas it's absolutely appropriate to rate a stock a sell when an analyst thinks valuations have overshot, care is needed. Analysts owe it to their clients to give them the appropriate investment recommendation, but should avoid careless remarks that are more sensational than objective. Analysts should take care not to push a company over the edge that might otherwise have survived.

EXAMPLE

Short-selling by hedge funds (pushing the envelope?)

Summary: There has been much controversy over the short-selling practices of hedge funds, with some blaming such investors for the demise of Bear Stearns and Lehman Brothers. In the rumor section in Chapter 1, we looked at rumor-driven short-selling cases involving Anglo Irish Bank and Alliance Data Systems, including discussion of Bear Stearns and Lehman Brothers. Here are two more stories on a similar theme, but where perhaps any accusations of abuse may be tempered or countered.

Details: Louise Story (an appropriate name for a journalist) commented in the *New York Times* of June 4, 2008: "Critics say David Einhorn is needlessly fanning fears about the precarious health of the financial industry at the very moment executives are struggling to stabilize their ailing companies. Many on Wall Street still wonder if hedge funds like Greenlight helped bring down Bear Stearns and spread false rumors about the bank, a possibility the Securities and Exchange Commission is investigating." I don't usually spell out the names of individuals being criticized, but Einhorn is evidently someone who has been seeking the limelight in his crusade against what he believes are bad companies. He makes his case for shorting stocks in *Fooling Some of the People All of the Time: A Long Short Story*. The book is about Einhorn's long-running battle to draw to regulators' attention various perceived shortcomings (if you'll excuse the pun) at Allied Capital, a business development company. Einhorn started shorting the company's shares in 2002.

Short-selling by hedge funds (pushing the envelope?)—*cont'd*

Separately, my former colleague Andrew Inglis-Taylor drew to my attention the article in the *Daily Telegraph* of June 17, 2008, entitled, "FSA angered by Deutsche Bank's 'crass' short selling advice". In response to rights issues being launched by Royal Bank of Scotland and HBOS, Deutsche advised clients to buy the rights and short the stock. The article said that although the action recommended in the note was not illegal, the FSA privately scolded the bank.

Conclusions: As usual, analysts need to justify and balance their views and ratings. In the dotcom bubble analysts were accused of not justifying their buy recommendations or drawing the downside risks to the readers' attention. In a bear market, as the one spawned by the credit crisis, analysts also need to justify their sell recommendations and should still not forget to balance their views by providing upside risks.

Aside I: The Deutsche note may have been one of the catalysts for the introduction of new measures by the U.K. regulator requiring investors to disclose significant short positions in a company that is raising funds through a rights issue.

Meanwhile, the *WSJ* highlighted on July 14, 2008, how companies in the U.S. are quietly changing their by-laws to make investors disclose more about their transactions including their share-borrowing and lending and hedging positions, so as to make activist shareholders' motivations more transparent. The columnist, Phred Dvorak, commented that an activist seeking a board seat while betting against the stock would not have the same interests as other shareholders.

Aside II: Jonathan Weil of Bloomberg published a hilarious article on October 8, 2008, entitled, "SEC's Witch Hunt Nabs a Munchkin". At a time when the world was experiencing the worst financial crisis in living memory, the SEC issued a press release charging a certain KR and his hedge fund, Lion Gate Capital, with allegedly gaining a mere US$207,291 from illegal short-selling in some stocks during 2005 and 2006. The allegation was that the individual used shares purchased during initial public offerings to cover short sales made during the restricted period before the pricing of the offerings. The Bloomberg author challenged the readers if they'd ever even heard of the stocks in question.[3]

One can imagine the *Late Show* host David Letterman breathing a sigh of relief that, even though Osama bin Laden was still at large,

Short-selling by hedge funds (pushing the envelope?)—*cont'd*

and despite the fact that those responsible for bringing down Lehman Brothers and Bear Stearns were still walking the streets, the authorities nevertheless had managed to catch Public Enemy No. 1—this one-man-band hedge fund manager from Beverly Hills. The Madoff, Stanford and Rajaratnam scandals were yet to unfold, not to mention the Goldman Sachs fraud allegations. Within a year, without admitting or denying the allegations, KR and Lion Gate had agreed to pay US$100,000 in disgorgement and prejudgment interest as well as a civil penalty of US$50,000.

The next case is also interesting. The analyst claimed to have used good research in identifying companies at risk of failing.

CASE STUDY

Management's reaction to negative research (legal action)

Details: BankAtlantic sued an analyst at Ladenburg Thalmann and the firm itself for defamation and negligence, as reported by Dow Jones on July 22, 2008. The allegation was that the analyst, using flawed methodology, had identified BankAtlantic as being a firm that might be about to fail. The stock price fell sharply before rebounding when the bank issued a press release to the effect that it remained well-capitalized. BankAtlantic claimed that using holding company data to determine the financial state of the insured subsidiaries was nonsensical, and that the bank itself was adequately capitalized. The analyst said that he stood by his methodology, and said that companies shouldn't be able to muzzle independent analysts with threats of litigation.

The case took another twist when the analyst left Ladenburg Thalmann for a competing firm. Ladenburg threatened to sue the analyst if he didn't cough up US$1 million to help settle the case with BankAtlantic, as reported by the *New York Post* on February 26, 2009.

Note that Ladenburg Thalmann consented to a censure and fine of US$200,000, as reported in FINRA's round-up of disciplinary actions for June 2009. The firm did not admit or deny various findings including one relating to the approval of research. (This was immediately after the

Management's reaction to negative research (legal action)—*cont'd*

firm was fined US$275,000 on charges relating to commissions. In that case the firm also had to repay US$1.2 million to customers.)

Conclusions: However the BankAtlantic case turns out, analysts always need to be sure of their facts and arguments, and should make sure their research is approved by their own research management.

Aside: The *Economist* published a story on February 5, 2009, detailing how some research firms had been criticized for their negative views. One anecdote concerned an analyst who had received this threatening phone call from a *sushi* restaurant owner after he'd issued a "sell" recommendation: "I have many sharp knives. Stay away from dark alleys."

Analysts should also see the defamation case studies relating to Haier and Greencool in Chapter 1. They should also consider the case study in Chapter 3 concerning independent research firms, specifically Gradient Analytics, which was accused of colluding with hedge funds in driving stock prices down. In that case firms learn that suing their critics can backfire. The more mundane problem of course is that company management may take a sell rating too personally and exclude the analyst from the information flow, as the following example demonstrates.

EXAMPLE

Management's reaction to negative research (restricting information)

Details: The October 26, 2007, issue of the *FT* reports how Oversea-Chinese Banking Corp. (OCBC), one of the big Singapore banks, had decided not to invite Morgan Stanley's Singapore analyst, Matthew Wilson, to its briefings with senior executives. None of the parties commented, but OCBC had earlier told Reuters: "Whether we invite any particular investor, analyst, fund manager, or journalist to any of our various briefing events is at our discretion."

Ironically, the *FT* noted that Wilson had recently written a research report that raised questions regarding the bank's attitude to corporate governance. Furthermore, the *FT* commented that Wilson

Management's reaction to negative research (restricting information)—*cont'd*

had never given a "buy" recommendation for OCBC since he began covering the bank in 2004.

Conclusions: It may be okay from our perspective for a company to exclude an analyst from its briefings, provided the company doesn't pass on any material, price-sensitive information, or, if they do, that they make it available simultaneously to the rest of the market, for example through a webcam recording. However, questions regarding corporate governance might be raised if they purposely exclude analysts from briefings as a form of punishment.

The *FT* made no comment as to whether clients trusted Wilson's views more given his tenacity, but that must surely be a possibility.

Mis-selling and not highlighting risks

Analysts have ample opportunity in the text to say what their assumptions are based on and to highlight the risks to those assumptions. It's not enough to bury references to risk in the middle of the text of a long report. At the very least, the summary of a report should include a paragraph on risk, with fuller details given in the text. Initiations of coverage and changes of rating reports should, as a matter of course, highlight risks to the investment case.

Below we look at various cases related to the credit crisis in the U.S. and around the world as well as some cases not related to the crisis. Many involve mis-selling by brokers and financial advisers, but they all serve as lessons for securities analysts as well.

CASE STUDY

Highlighting investment risks (credit crisis of 2007/08, U.S.)

Introduction: Alleged mis-selling of auction-rate securities evidently proved to be a widespread problem in the U.S. Joanna Chung, writing for the *FT* of June 30, 2008, quotes Karen Tyler, President of the North American Securities Administrators Association (NASAA), as

Highlighting investment risks
(credit crisis of 2007/08, U.S.)—*cont'd*

saying that investors who were sold these auction-rate securities made a common complaint—that they thought they were being sold liquid, safe, cash-equivalent investments.[4]

Another major complaint was that the banks did not disclose adequately the fact that the liquidity of the securities relied heavily on the bank's support during the auctions when there was insufficient demand. Investors were left holding the baby when this support dried up in February 2008. Some investors claimed they didn't need the securities or instruments being sold to them.

One complaint was that the investment bank selling the investments had positions that were in conflict with the investors' interests, and that they didn't advise investors appropriately when the quality of their investments started to deteriorate.

Of direct interest to us is the charge against Merrill Lynch that it had co-opted its research analysts to help place the securities with customers (and we explore this further in the conflict of interest case study on auction-rate securities in Chapter 3).

These complaints formed the basis for settlements reached between global investment banks[5] and U.S. regulators during the latter half of 2008, whereby the banks agreed to pay fines and/or make good losses incurred by individual investors, small businesses and charities, and to provide liquidity to help larger businesses and institutional customers.

Details: In its first criminal investigations relating to the auction-rate securities market, the U.S. Justice Department alleged that two former Credit Suisse brokers, EB and JT, lied to investors by telling them that the securities they were selling them were backed by student loans, whereas they were backed by risky CDOs with a subprime mortgage element. After being on the run in Spain for three months JT eventually returned to the U.S. and pleaded guilty to conspiracy. EB was convicted of securities fraud and conspiracy. He was sentenced to five years in prison and fined US$5 million. Interestingly, the judge acknowledged that the pair had operated in a culture of corruption and lack of regulation and supervision in the securities industry.

The *WSJ* also reported how UBS had been accused by securities regulators in Massachusetts of misleading investors about the risks involved in the auction-rate securities market. Allegedly UBS

Highlighting investment risks
(credit crisis of 2007/08, U.S.)—*cont'd*

described the investments as "cash alternatives", increased its efforts to sell the securities after realizing the market was in trouble, and "actively managed" the interest rates to set them high enough to keep the market functioning. However, when dealers stopped supporting the market, investors could not get their money out. The article quotes William Galvin, the state's top securities regulator, as saying: "The game was fixed; only the customers were in the dark." The *WSJ* later reported that the bank had suspended its head of fixed income in the U.S. (who was also the bank's global head of municipal securities).

Merrill's penalty and the terms of its settlement with the SEC took into account the usual complaints; that the firm had misrepresented these securities as safe and liquid cash-equivalents, and that it had not adequately disclosed that their liquidity was based on Merrill Lynch supporting the auctions when there was insufficient demand. The settlement also apparently took into account evidence of conflicted research, which we look at in Chapter 3.

Citigroup had apparently taped over some tapes that Andrew Cuomo had requested. They said that taping over the conversations had been "inadvertent". According to the *IHT*, Citigroup then said that they had mistakenly kept 10 tapes that had been requested. Sounds like Citigate to me (begging the pardon of any organizations actually called Citigate).

Conclusions: Aside from any contractual or regulatory obligations they may have to their clients, analysts, brokers and advisers surely owe their clients a duty of care, as discussed previously. They should adequately explain investment risks to clients. Of course they shouldn't lie. The level of risk disclosure may be dependent on the relative sophistication of the client, with retail clients perhaps needing a little more hand-holding than institutional clients. (But even this assumption needs to be treated with caution in light of the SEC's fraud allegations against Goldman Sachs, whose CDO clients were institutional investors.) The long and short of it is that investment risks must always be disclosed.

In the valuation section earlier I suggested that analysts and investors should not rely on auditors, but should scrutinize accounts and disclosures themselves, accepting of course that analysts do not have the same level of access to company data and information. Similarly, it has become clear that analysts should not rely on credit ratings either. The market price of triple-A rated securities can fall further—much further—than one or two percent. There is no such thing as a risk-free[6] security or investment.

SIDEBAR

Highlighting investment risks (credit crisis of 2007/08, global)

The *Economist* issue of August 9–15, 2008, includes a candid, albeit anonymous, article entitled "Confession of a risk manager" in which a senior risk manager of a large investment bank explains what went wrong in the credit crisis. In the article, the author said that at the beginning of 2007 he and his colleagues could not really see where the risks lay, and that indeed it was the most benign risk environment they had seen in 20 years. Various causes and effects relating to the crisis are discussed, including banks' misplaced trust in the rating agencies. There was also apparent confusion as to whether traded credit products such as CDOs were the responsibility of the market risk department or the credit risk department.

The overriding excuse for the risk management failures, however, seemed to be that decision-making at banks has always been biased in favor of risk-taking and making business and against risk-avoidance and the prospect of losing business. Collective common sense evidently went out the window during the credit crisis. Let's see whether this bias shifts going forward.

The Corrigan report[7] entitled "Containing Systemic Risk: The Road to Reform", published by Counterparty Risk Management Policy Group III in August 2008, is an interesting examination of the 2007/08 credit crisis with recommendations for reform.

Cases were being played out all around the world, as we can see from the following examples.

CASE STUDY

Highlighting investment risks (credit crisis of 2007/08, global)

Australia: The *FT* reported on December 21, 2007, that Wingecarribee Shire Council was suing Lehman Brothers (formerly Grange Securities) over the sale of CDOs. Wingecarribee claims that Lehman did not act in the council's best interests and engaged in misleading and deceptive conduct.

Highlighting investment risks (credit crisis of 2007/08, global)—*cont'd*

One perceived conflict of interest was that the firm was offering independent financial advice while selling financial products. A spokesman for Lehman denied these claims.

The *FT* reported that Satyajit Das, a risk consultant, said the CDOs were extremely complex and it was highly unlikely the councils were able to weigh independently the risks or value of the securities. Lehman argued that the councils were "sophisticated wholesale investors who have responsibility for their own investment decisions and due diligence".

From September 2008 Nomura, which took over the Asian operations of Lehman Brothers, inherited the case. Good luck, Nomura! Other aggrieved councils were also considering a class-action suit.

Norway: The *New York Times* published a story on December 2, 2007, explaining how some municipalities in Norway were suffering a similar fate. The article focused on a town called Narvik in the Arctic Circle. The towns were facing losses from investments sold to them by a local Norwegian brokerage firm called Terra Securities. The products had been created by Citigroup. The towns alleged that they had been duped by Terra's brokers, who did not warn them of the risks associated with these investments. The Financial Supervisory Authority of Norway, Norway's financial regulator, sided with the municipalities and revoked Terra's license, which prompted the firm to file for bankruptcy. Narvik and six other municipalities went on to sue Citigroup for US$200 million in a New York federal court in August 2007. They accused the bank of egregious fraud and of concealing the risks associated with the fund-linked notes that had been marketed as "conservative investments", according to the *FT*. The bank's motion to dismiss the case was denied in February 2010.

Japan: Reuters reported in late October 2008 how the social welfare council in Higashimatsuyama, Japan, had switched more than a quarter of its investment funds from government bonds into Lehman's corporate bonds in the hope of boosting returns. The loss of US$1 million meant less money to fund day care centers and helpers for the elderly.

Hong Kong (and Singapore): Thousands of retail investors complained in the wake of the credit crisis that they had been misled by banks and brokers into buying so-called "minibonds", issued by Lehman Brothers. The individuals were evidently under the misapprehension that, with the word "bonds" embedded in the name, these investments would be relatively low-risk. However, unlike minidresses (which are still dresses,

Highlighting investment risks (credit crisis of 2007/08, global)—*cont'd*

however short they are), these were not actually bonds but credit-linked notes. Even the terminology had become blurred, with any distinction between different types of investments being lost on the public.

The SFC reached an agreement with 16 banks in July 2009.[8] According to the *SCMP*, the HK$6.3 billion that these banks agreed to repay to 29,000 people would likely be the world's largest compensation package for retail investors. Bank of China (Hong Kong), the biggest distributor of Lehman's minibonds, accounted for about half of this amount. The settlement effectively meant that 90 percent of investors would get 70 percent of their money back.

Another product that prompted complaints, due to investors' lack of understanding of the risks involved, was called the "accumulator" (or "I kill you later", as the product soon came to be nicknamed). These were contracts that investors entered into to buy securities (or currencies or commodities) at a fixed price at regular intervals. The appeal would be that the price would normally be set at a discount to the market price at the time that the contract was entered into. That's all well and good in a rising market, but when market prices started to fall, the losses started to mount. The products were invariably marketed to high net worth individuals and companies, which perhaps gave these investors a sense of exclusivity. J.P. Morgan Private Bank was commended in the October 2008 issue of *Asia Risk* for steering clients away from equity accumulators.

Here are some more examples from before the credit crisis where analysts and brokers evidently failed to draw risks to clients' attention.

CASE STUDY

Highlighting investment risks (general)

Details: One of the two analysts who received multimillion dollar fines in the Global Research Analyst Settlements of 2003–2006 was Jack Grubman of Salomon Smith Barney (which became part of Citigroup and is now part of Morgan Stanley). He was fined US$15 million and barred from working in the industry. In Chapter 3, we examine the wider

Highlighting investment risks (general)—*cont'd*

conflicts of interest issues that he was embroiled in. As for not drawing risks to readers' attention, we see this from the NASD settlement papers: "From January 25, 2001 through April 17, 2001, Grubman authored research reports that recommended the purchase of Winstar stock with a Buy rating and a Target Price of US$50 per share. During this time, Winstar's stock price fell more than 99 percent—from approximately US$20 per share on January 24, 2001 to US$0.14 per share on April 17, 2001. The reports omitted material facts and failed to disclose risks of investing in Winstar."

Interestingly, Grubman's co-author of the research reports on Winstar Communications, Ms. CG, was also fined. In her case it was a much smaller fine of US$100,000, but it serves as its own lesson for co-authors and associate analysts. It's not just the superstars that get caught and fined. A trawl through FINRA's disciplinary actions nets regular instances of US$10,000–US$80,000 fines being meted out to smaller companies and individuals for approving or preparing research reports that did not contain any disclosure regarding "the risks associated in the subject company" or "the risks to achieving price targets".

The *FT* reported on June 7, 2007, that Citigroup had agreed to pay US$15 million (including a US$3 million fine) to settle an investigation by the NASD into allegations that its Smith Barney brokers misled hundreds of BellSouth employees during retirement seminars from 1994 to 2002, telling them at one point that the Dow Jones Industrial Average would hit 20,000 by 2006. The NASD alleged that the brokers led the employees, many of them unsophisticated investors, to have unrealistic expectations, and that Citigroup's managers failed to check the marketing materials and supervise the team. This may be one of the reasons that prompted FINRA to announce in September 2007 that they were initiating measures to ensure that securities firms use appropriate sales practices in their dealing with seniors and individuals approaching retirement.

In its press release of February 9, 2006, the NYSE announced that it had fined Bear Stearns US$1.5 million for various offenses, including improper communications during an IPO roadshow in 2003. The NYSE press release stated: "Neither the analyst's introduction nor any of his comments during the question and answer period included any discussions of risks associated with an investment in the company." The interesting point gleaned from a *Wall Street Journal* article the following day was that the firm was fined not for conflict of interest issues (the SEC's rules on conflicts of interest, including the

> ## Highlighting investment risks (general)—*cont'd*
>
> prohibition of analysts from participating in sponsored road shows, had yet to come into effect) but, rather, for what the newspaper termed "stock-touting".
>
> **Conclusions:** The same conclusions as reached in the previous case studies on the subprime credit crisis apply—draw risks to readers' attention, and be especially sensitive to the needs of retail clients.

Evaluating risks and catalysts

The following comments are not meant to represent a comprehensive study of the different types of risk; they are just general pointers for analysts to consider when discussing risks to their investment calls.

Risk comes in all sorts of guises, from systematic or market/macro risk to specific/company risk, and can be upside as well as downside (or even sideways). Regular macro risks include not just socio-political and regulatory risks, but also changes to economic and financial variables such as GDP growth rates, inflation rates, foreign-exchange rates, interest rates and commodity prices, including oil prices.

Everyone, analysts and investors alike, have their own ideas about risks. Often analysts just talk about risks in terms of well-established risks, risks that are already known or risks that can somehow be measured (for example, the beta of a stock, given its historic volatility compared with the market). However, analysts should not just be backward-looking in analyzing risks in a quasi-academic or formulaic way but also forward-looking as well; they should try to anticipate new real-world risks that might arise under the changing environment. Nassim Nicholas Taleb, author of *The Black Swan*, says that historical analysis is an inadequate way to judge risk. He specifically criticizes the traditional Black–Scholes option-pricing model for being too backward-looking. To demonstrate this he uses the analogy that before black swans were discovered in Australia it was incorrectly assumed that all swans were white.

As mentioned in the Preface, each era brings new crises and scandals. Sometimes the market gets caught out, but a good analyst should try and anticipate different eventualities. Analysts should also appreciate the real nature of the risks that they are dealing with. They need to have a good understanding of the dynamics of these risks in the particular markets they cover, and how they may affect the securities of the companies they cover. For example, as Steve Vickers and Andrés Gentry of FTI-International Risk point out, in some emerging markets where central banks may not be independent and where currencies may not be fully convertible, monetary policy and international trade may be driven more by political motives than by economic need.

In any case, analysts owe it to investors to explain the assumptions on which their current recommendations, valuations and forecasts are based, and how they think these would be affected by any dramatic or unexpected movements in their assumptions. They should draw investors' attention to how their forecasts would be affected by changes to these and other variables under various scenarios. Sensitivity tables help in this regard.

Catalysts and consensus

In practical terms, many analysts and investors think less in terms of the risks to their investment case and more in terms of the catalysts needed to reach a target price: in other words, what needs to happen for a target price to be reached, and what would happen to the share price if those catalysts did not occur. Analysts might also ask themselves what the chance is that a stock on which they have a buy or sell recommendation is fairly valued after all and that consensus expectations will prove to be right, or at least less wrong than the analyst's own expectations. By the way, an analyst who quotes consensus estimates needs to acknowledge which data provider is providing the forecasts, provided of course that the analyst has the permission to use and publish those forecasts.

Market liquidity and contagion risks

However rationally markets might behave during normal times, they can become quite irrational when greed and fear take over, typically at the peak of a bull market or the trough of a bear market. When one market rallies or falters, there's often a knock-on effect on other markets, as funds are attracted to or flee from those markets deemed to be associated, whether by risk level, asset class or whatever. The way the Asian crisis was sparked by financial problems in one country, namely Thailand, in 1997 and the way global markets sold off a decade later in response to fears over subprime mortgages in the U.S. provide good examples, not to mention the inflating and bursting of the dotcom bubble in between. In such instances, explaining market movements lies more in understanding human behavior than in cold calculation of valuations. Nevertheless, analysts need to be aware of these risks and warn investors of them.

Foreign exchange and interest rate risks

Analysts should not forget that when they say how a certain percentage change in, say, a currency's exchange rate or an interest rate would affect their earnings forecasts, they need to make clear what exchange or interest rate the base assumption is based on. Equity analysts should really base their currency and interest rate assumptions on the forecasts made by their in-house economists or currency specialists, or else use the spot, forward or futures rates; they should probably not tout themselves out to the market as being currency or interest rate experts by coming up with their own different rates.

Not only do analysts need to identify the risks that a company might not be able to service its own debt, especially in a rising interest rate environment, but they also need to determine the extent to which a company, for example a bank, is exposed to non-performing loans (NPLs) and subprime debtors.

But in any case, given that a company's income, costs, assets and liabilities may all be affected by currency and interest rate risks to varying degrees (for example, a company might export its goods in U.S. dollars, but pay its costs in local currency, and may have debt in both or other currencies), it may be useful to provide sensitivity analyses showing how the analyst's base forecasts might change under different assumptions. The extent to which the company hedges its currency and interest rate exposure with the use of financial instruments such as forwards, futures and options should also be considered.

Of course, investors themselves may have an additional currency risk to consider—the currency used to make the investment, if different from their base currency.

EXAMPLE

Currency risks

Summary: The strength of the yen at the end of the calendar year 2008 was cited as one reason why many Japanese manufacturers were expecting huge losses for the financial year ending March 2009 and why they had to lay off thousands of employees. Job cuts announced by Japanese manufacturers worldwide in early 2009 included: 20,000 each at Nissan and NEC, 15,000 at Panasonic and 10,000 at Pioneer.

Sales were weak anyway during 2008, given the severe economic conditions globally. However, in many cases the added yen effect was not so much an export-sales phenomenon (after all, many Japanese manufacturing companies actually make the products in many of the countries where they sell them); it was more an accounting translation effect at the bottom line.

Details: As one example of a major Japanese trading company warning the previous year how the yen might affect sales, this is what Mitsubishi

Currency risks—*cont'd*

Corporation said in its notes to its consolidated accounts for the year ending March 2008:

> ". . . because dividends received from overseas businesses and equity in earnings of overseas consolidated subsidiaries and equity-method affiliates are relatively high in proportion to our net income, and because most of these earnings are denominated in foreign currencies, which are converted to yen solely for reporting purposes, an appreciation in the yen relative to foreign currencies has a negative impact on consolidated net income. In terms of sensitivity, a one yen change relative to the U.S. dollar would have an approximate 2.7 billion yen effect on consolidated net income."

Conclusions: Analysts need to understand a company's sensitivity to foreign currency movements and what measures the company takes to hedge against adverse currency movements.

Foreign exchange movements are notoriously difficult to forecast. (Forex markets are large, liquid and volatile, and for many participants profit is not a primary motivator.) Analysts shouldn't really base a fundamental stock recommendation on expected currency movements; they should base their valuation and call on the company's fundamental business, with potential foreign exchange movements merely representing an upside or downside risk.

Here's a situation where a company made a wrong-way bet on a currency, with some added disclosure issues to make matters worse.

CASE STUDY

Currency risks

Summary: CITIC Pacific's share price plunged over 50 percent in a matter of days after the company revealed on October 20, 2008, that it had lost HK$15.5 billion from currency trades. (This figure was later raised to HK$18.6 billion, causing a further sharp drop in the stock price.) As reported by *China Daily*, the company had bet that the Australian dollar would rise against the U.S. dollar, but it instead fell 30 percent from its high in July. Investors in Hong Kong were not amused.

Currency risks—*cont'd*

Details: What irked investors more, however, was the six-week delay in reporting the original loss and an official statement that the directors were not aware of any material adverse change in the financial or trading position of the group. Some investors who had recently invested in the stock demanded their money back claiming that they wouldn't have made the investment if they had known about the trading loss. One investor cited by *China Daily* said that he'd chosen CITIC because of its stable financial fundamentals.

CITIC Group, the investment arm of China's State Council, subsequently bailed out its Hong Kong affiliate by injecting funds and taking responsibility for the forex contracts. (This then resulted in a downgrade by Moody's of its credit rating for the group, although by the end of July 2009, after a speedy rebound in the Australian dollar, it looked like the contracts were back in the black again.)

The finance director and financial controller at CITIC Pacific were the first two heads to roll. As the scandal escalated into a full-scale police investigation, the chairman (dubbed the "last red capitalist") and managing director both resigned.

Conclusion: As we also see later on in the corporate governance risks section, analysts need to have a clear understanding of a company's derivatives, currency trading and hedging strategies. They should also be comfortable that management has instituted sufficient risk management procedures, and has a good track record of communicating with the market on a fair and timely basis.

Earnings risks

An overriding principle of businesses, at least those with shares listed on stock exchanges, is investing capital to make profits for shareholders. Such business or investment decisions range from spending capital on projects, assets/land, people, information/knowledge, securities in other businesses and even the securities of their own business (share buybacks), to decisions on whether to reinvest the profits generated or distribute them back to shareholders in the form of dividends. The reinvestment or distribution decision determines whether the return to investors comes immediately or in the future. The long and short of it is that any investment carries the fundamental risk that the investment won't generate as much capital growth or income as expected, or as quickly as expected. Indeed it might not generate any returns at all. (Don't I know it.)

Brand theft risk

One way that potential earnings can be lost is through intellectual property theft, as the following example demonstrates.

EXAMPLE

Brand theft

Summary: It's bad enough when someone copies your product, but how about if pirates copy the whole company? That's what happened to NEC in China, as reported by David Lague for the *New York Times* on May 1, 2006.

Details: Pirates had evidently set up a parallel NEC brand with links to 50 factories in China, Hong Kong and Taiwan. According to Steve Vickers of International Risk,[9] hired by NEC to investigate the fraud, evidence showed that the counterfeiters had their own NEC business cards, commissioned product research and development in the company's name, signed production and supply orders, issued official-looking warranty documents and collected royalties from the factories. Some of the factories had erected fake NEC signs, and the products were shipped in authentic-looking NEC packaging. The investigations further found that the fake goods were being sold around the world, in some cases alongside genuine NEC products in retails outlets.

As Vickers said, this was not just a case of a series of intellectual property infringements, but one where a highly-organized group had attempted to hijack the entire brand.

Separately, a court in Shenzhen, China, convicted 11 people of counterfeiting Microsoft software on a grand scale, as reported by Cui Xiaohuo of *China Daily* on January 2, 2009. The counterfeit software, priced at about a tenth of Microsoft's official price, was discovered in 36 countries and in 11 different languages. The group earned an estimated US$2 billion from their activities. The production techniques were apparently so advanced that the bogus software not only contained legitimate computer code written by Microsoft but also had touches of the criminals' own coding as well.

Conclusion: Notwithstanding the cynical attitude that Alex might have to buying Chinese-made branded goods (see the cartoon below), analysts need to gauge how protected a company's brand is in their markets, and what the risks are that copycats could be stealing business away from the company.

Here's another interesting story about what might effectively amount to brand theft (or at least brand-usurping) on a large scale and on a systemic basis, and in a developed market too.

CASE STUDY

Brand usurping

Background: India's top five drug-makers by sales—Ranbaxy Laboratories, Dr. Reddy's Laboratories, Cipla, Sun Pharmaceutical Industries and Glenmark Pharmaceuticals—together sell more than US$14 billion worth of generic drugs annually in the U.S. and have a combined 25 percent share of that market, as reported by Uday Khandeparkar for the *Wall Street Journal* on February 2, 2009. This market share is the most that is derived from any single country.

Khandeparkar goes on to say that the highest profits come from "at-risk" launches of generic drugs before lawsuits brought by the patent-holder are resolved.

Details: Such cases can take years, by which time the generic drug-makers could have made more than enough profit to pay the fines—or of course they might not have made enough profits in time. The generic drug-makers also gamble that the patent-holder would prefer a settlement as early as possible, before the price of the drug plunges, rather than a protracted lawsuit.

One recent long-running case was when Pfizer sued Ranbaxy in 2002 over its patents for Lipitor, a cholesterol drug, which is also the world's best-selling drug. Pfizer won the case initially. However, on appeal Pfizer's original patent was found to be flawed. The two companies reached a settlement whereby Ranbaxy would keep generic versions of Lipitor off the U.S. market until December 2011.

Brand usurping—*cont'd*

Generic drug-makers can end up on the losing side. Barr Pharmaceuticals, a U.S. generic drug-maker, ended up paying US$80 million in September 2005 to Organon as a settlement after launching a generic version of Organon's Mircette birth-control pill. Barr's initial victory in the district court was overturned on appeal. The company had other successes though. For example, in August 2009 Bayer lost its appeal over its patent for the Yasmin birth-control pill, leaving the generic market open for Barr (which by then had been acquired by Teva).

Conclusions: Analysts need to weigh the chances of the generic drug-makers' gambles paying off, and highlight the downside risk to investors. The ultimate Damoclean sword hanging over drug-makers, whether licensed or generic, is the prospect of having to pay damages on a massive scale.

There may also be a political angle to consider. President Obama has made efforts to increase the availability of cheaper generic drugs for U.S. citizens. Rightly or wrongly this may have an effect on which way marginal cases might go. (As seen from cases like Stoneridge versus Scientific-Atlanta[10] and the BAE Systems arms deal,[11] politics can appear to have an influence over the legal system, even in democratic countries.)

Aside: The brand or patent issue can of course arise in any industry. For example, Samsung Electronics agreed in January 2010 to pay US$900 million to end a dispute with Rambus over computer memory patents. Rambus' shares soared 14 percent on the news, as reported by Bloomberg.

Cashflow and liquidity risks

Intertwined with earnings and the above financial risks is the risk that a company doesn't have the wherewithal to pay its debts and liabilities as they become due. One can be asset-rich, and even earnings-generative, but still cash-poor. In March 2008 the market evidently became concerned about Bear Stearns' liquidity, and shorted the stock (see the earlier case studies on short-selling by hedge funds). The company's creditors and counterparties had evidently lost confidence and pulled the plug on its funding.

Valuation risks

The concept of capitalization (assigning a value to a security or asset) in effect means assigning a net present value to expected future benefits or returns. Crucial to any discounted cash flow (DCF) or dividend discount model (DDM) calculations is determining not only the appropriate levels of returns expected (whether in the form of net earnings, cash earnings or dividends) but also the most appropriate discount rate to apply. Pricing risk appropriately (that is, quantifying the risk premium over the so-called risk-free rate) is what analysts and the markets attempt to do; indeed, overpricing or under-pricing risk is a major risk in itself.

Some analysts often just say that their target price is based on DCF or DDM, whereas it would be more meaningful to let investors know or remind them what their underlying assumptions are; for example, in terms of the risk-adjusted discount rate, weighted average cost of capital (WACC) and beta used, and why they think such assumptions are appropriate. Thus, if clients have different assumptions, they can make their own adjustments to the analysts' figures accordingly. Again, sensitivity analyses showing how the DCF or DDM valuation might change under different assumptions can only help the reader in this process.

Valuation multiples, such as P/E, EV/EBITDA and dividend yields, compared against the stock's historical valuations or against those of its peers would help in gauging whether the valuations are currently relatively high or relatively low, and therefore help in assessing the risk of achieving any given target valuation. Other comparisons such as a company's P/E to its earnings growth rate or P/B to ROE growth are similarly helpful.

Two measures that John Authers of the *FT* likes particularly are: i) the q ratio (or Tobin's q ratio),[12] which compares a company's stock market value to the replacement value of its assets; and ii) the cyclically adjusted P/E ratio, which compares its current stock price to its average earnings over say 10 years.

It should, of course, be clear whose estimates are being used for any comparable valuations provided, and the prices on which the valuations are based.

Modeling and miscalculation risks

By the way, one risk that is quite common but which analysts would not like to admit to or highlight as a risk (because they assume they are right to start with), is the risk of error when they do their sums. From time to time, *errata* messages have to be published because of miscalculations, double-counting or incorrect use of formulae, or even flaws in well-established formulae that need to be reworked. These can be material enough to affect earnings estimates, valuations, target prices and recommendations.

After the fall from grace in 1998 of Long-Term Capital Management (LTCM), whose partners included the illustrious Drs. Merton and Scholes, financial modelers around the world scurried back to re-examine their formulae. For more on arguments as to how historic evaluation of risk is inadequate, analysts might like to read *The Black Swan* by Nassim Nicholas Taleb.

EXAMPLE

Modeling risks

Summary: Although referring specifically to computerized trading systems rather than analysts' models, Gillian Tett and Anuj Gangahar summed the problem up nicely in their *FT* article of August 15, 2007: "Several 'once in a millennium' events last week cost billions and point to flaws in the design of many algorithmic trading platforms."

Details: The dramatic U-turn by Moody's in March 2007, as reported in the March 16 issue of *Euroweek*, a Euromoney publication, regarding a new rating methodology for banks that was criticized by the market for being flawed, was a high-profile event demonstrating how analysts can go round in circles with their calculations. Another example was exposed by Sam Jones, Gillian Tett and Paul Davies in the *FT* on May 21, 2008. They described how senior executives of Moody's had known early in 2007 that certain triple-A-rated products called "constant proportion debt obligations" (CPDOs) should have been rated up to four notches lower after a coding error was corrected. However, the ratings were downgraded only in January 2008 amid the general market decline.

Outcome: In response to the *FT*'s exposé of the CPDO fiasco, Moody's said they were conducting a thorough review of the matter. Meanwhile, Moody's shares plunged 15 percent on the day. Within two months the London-based head of Moody's global structured finance business was on his way out.

The global subprime-driven credit crisis started to unfold in 2007 when it became clear that no one really knew the worth of CDOs and CMOs (collateralized debt/mortgage obligations) that had been packaged, sold, repackaged and resold, and no one really knew where liabilities ended. This is a problem when products get structured so intricately that they become too complicated to understand or value appropriately. In his Bloomberg article of September 24, 2008, Elliot Blair Smith quotes Joseph Stiglitz, the Nobel laureate economist at Columbia University in New York, as saying that the rating agencies were the ones that performed the alchemy that converted CDOs from F-rated to A-rated.

CASE STUDY

Mispricing risks

Details: One case arising from the subprime crisis that was reported in the *New York Times* on June 1, 2008, involves a dispute between UBS and Paramax Capital, a relatively small hedge fund, over a credit default swap. UBS had evidently negotiated with Paramax to sell the swap to them as a hedge to cover CDOs of about US$1.3 billion. The CDOs were rated AAA by Standard & Poor's and Moody's, and the effective insurance premium was apparently 0.155 percent (or US$2 million). Apparently Paramax expressed concerns about its potential liability, but UBS made efforts to allay these fears. The securities were after all triple-A-rated. The hedge fund's fears were realized when the price of the CDOs started falling. As part of the deal Paramax needed to stump up more capital as the price declined. And as the price declined, the margin calls kept coming. The details make my head hurt. Anyway, the newswires reported on October 28, 2008, that the two parties had reached an amicable settlement.

Another case concerns Credit Suisse, which was fined £5.6 million in the U.K. by the FSA for systems and controls failings. The firm benefited from an early settlement discount. The underlying problem was its misvaluing of certain asset-backed securities. According to the FSA's Web site, Credit Suisse announced in February 2008 that it had identified mismarking and pricing errors by a small number of traders and that it was repricing certain asset-backed securities. The repricing involved a write-down of revenues by US$2.65 billion. Margaret Cole, director of enforcement, said that the sudden and unexpected announcement had the potential to undermine market confidence.

In a separate type of situation, the *FT* reported on February 5, 2008, how Natixis, a French bank, was suing Terra Firma, a private equity firm, for allegedly using a flawed financial model to overstate boxclever's net present value during a £750 million refinancing in 2002. Terra Firma defended the executives involved, saying that they would have had no motive for concealing an obvious modeling flaw that could destroy their careers and the firm's reputation. Within a couple of months Natixis and Terra Firma had entered into a confidential settlement, as reported by the *FT* on April 2.

David Oakley wrote an article in the July 21, 2008, issue of the *FT* showing how credit default swap prices in the Eurozone differed significantly from country to country. Perhaps no surprise there, given the different credit risks for each market. However, interestingly, the article showed how prices for protection had dramatically increased over the previous six weeks.

Mispricing risks—*cont'd*

During this period, for example, the cost of insuring Germany's sovereign debt against default had jumped by €1,000 (or 20 percent) to €6,000 to cover €10 m of debt, and had risen a lot more for the Mediterranean countries (for example, more like 45 percent in the case of Greece—a portent of the sovereign debt crisis that was yet to fully unfold). It had become evident that credit default risk had been priced too cheaply.

Conclusions: Analysts and anyone involved in valuing securities or instruments must flag to their clients (or client in the case of buy-side analysts) any risks to their calculations and valuations at the outset. Invariably analysts will have a gut feeling as to whether they are being relatively conservative or relatively aggressive in their assumptions, and they'll also know how their estimates compare with those published by their competitors. They can also endear themselves to their clients by highlighting different valuation methodologies for their consideration.

If an analyst does discover some material flaw in their methodology or find that their assumptions are not as robust as originally thought, then they really need to raise the alarm immediately, rather than dig their heels in deeper as the problem escalates, as the creators of the Barings, SocGen, Madoff and Satyam losses evidently did. If it can be proved that the analysts knew that their models were flawed, then they might find themselves at the sharp end of a lawsuit.

Information risk

Some risk can be measured or adjusted against benchmarks; for example, yields of so-called risk-free assets such as U.S. Treasuries (see endnote 6). Other uncertainties may not be so easy to measure. One such risk is that regarding the quality of information. One of the main and recurrent themes of this book is that analysts should make clear what the source of their information is, which helps in determining how reliable it is. This helps investors weigh their risks in reaching their investment decisions. Stock exchange filings, press releases, XBRL (eXtensible Business Reporting Language) or equivalent interactive data, management comments at one-on-one company meetings, confirmed and unconfirmed press reports, blogs, comments on social networking sites, consensus estimates and analysts' views, estimates and analyses all have their place in the information-gathering exercise. However, some of that information may be more reliable than others, and some may be more discounted by the market than others. Investors need to have all this information (within the extent of regulations; that is, excluding material, price-sensitive inside information or rumors designed to affect market conditions), and need to know how reliable it is in order to make their investment decisions.

M&A risks

Other risks include those that relate to the capital and corporate structure of a company (including the ownership structure and the level of free float) and the potential for restructuring (including M&A and share overhangs). For a discussion on highlighting M&A risks, please see the section in Chapter 1 on rumors, speculation and M&A, and the accompanying case study on identifying M&A candidates. Let's now look at the example below showing how analysts may need to reverse their assumptions rapidly when a previously assumed merger or acquisition fails to materialize. I suppose this case highlights various risks such as economic, M&A, corporate governance and management execution risks.

EXAMPLE

M&A risks

Summary: The surprise pulling out by BHP Billiton from its hostile takeover of Rio Tinto at the end of November 2008 shows how abruptly analysts' assumptions might need to be changed. BHP's CEO had only recently confirmed that he was still pushing ahead with the deal, despite the deteriorating global economic conditions, and that credit facilities remained in place.

Details: Adele Ferguson highlights some of the costs to the deal in the December 1, 2008, edition of the *Australian*: "All up BHP will write off $450 million in costs related to the bid, but the real cost is far higher when you consider the hours spent by management, the plunging share price and the opportunity cost of not doing other deals or share buybacks. There is also the incalculable damage BHP has done to its relationships with customers in the region. They were very concerned that the deal would create a monopoly in the iron ore trade."

The journalist questioned whether the key players in the failed bid had been fair to their shareholders in terms of adequate disclosure.

Analysts had to get their calculators out yet again six months later when BHP and Rio Tinto announced an iron-ore joint venture. This was when Rio rejected Chinalco's bid to increase its shareholding, opting instead for a rights issue and the joint venture with BHP.

M&A risks—*cont'd*

Conclusions: Analysts need to react quickly when previous assumptions change, but they also need to proactively keep investors warned of any possible repercussions if events don't transpire as expected. There may also be implications for other covered companies in the sector or market.

Corporate governance risks

Given the growing importance of corporate governance, I've dedicated a separate section to this issue, as follows. Anyone who still needs to be convinced that good corporate governance and stock market performance are correlated should read *Corporate Governance and Equity Prices* by Paul A. Gompers of Harvard, Joy L. Ishii of Stanford and Andrew Metrick of Yale University.[13] They found that an investment strategy that bought firms in the lowest decile of their "Governance Index" of 1,500 firms (that is those where shareholder rights were strongest) and sold firms in the highest decile of the index (weakest rights) would have earned abnormal returns of 8.5 percent per year during the sample period. They concluded that firms with stronger shareholder rights had higher firm value, higher profits, higher sales growth, lower capital expenditures and made fewer corporate acquisitions.

So, valuing companies is not just about juggling numbers from the financial statements; it's also about understanding people and how companies are managed.

Gauging corporate governance risks

The scandals at major companies such as Enron, WorldCom, Ahold and Parmalat in 1999–01 brought the whole issue of corporate governance to the fore. In those cases creative accounting and off-balance-sheet items were the focus of attention. The credit crisis and instances of so-called "rogue trading" in 2007–08 reminded the public that risk management at many major listed companies was still flawed. That credit crisis mushroomed into a full-blown global financial crisis where confidence in the capitalist system broke down. Rebuilding trust will be a long and slow process, and individual companies will need to regain that trust.

The starting point for analysts is to appreciate how systemic corporate governance risks are in the country in which the covered company is based and in the countries that it operates in or markets its products or services to. Various organizations and publishers compile such lists every year, based on various criteria. The World Bank, for example, ranks countries depending on how easy it is to do business in each country.

Analysts will then need to gain a thorough understanding of individual companies and their managements, and gauge what the risks are for investors. Governance Metrics International (GMI), which bills itself as the world's first corporate governance ratings agency, measures companies by the following corporate governance criteria:

- Board accountability;
- Financial disclosure and internal controls;
- Shareholder rights;
- Executive compensation; and
- Market for control and ownership base; and
- Corporate behavior and corporate social responsibility (CSR) issues.

Asiamoney, a Euromoney Institutional Investor company, annually compiles a list of Asian companies that the regional business community rates in terms of disclosure and transparency. Some brokerage firms, notably Deutsche Bank and CLSA, regularly rank companies by assessing how they score in terms of corporate governance and their levels of risk management. For example, Amar Gill, who compiles such rankings of Asian companies for CLSA, says that usually companies score better when they don't have a controlling shareholder. According to the *SCMP* of October 12, 2007, he says: "When there isn't a controlling shareholder, senior management don't feel their primary responsibility is to the controlling shareholder and other shareholders come second."

At the other extreme, I suppose, a shareholder base that is too wide can also pose problems. Small individual shareholders can be apathetic. Without opposition from a meaningfully large body of proactive shareholders, managements can become entrenched and potentially can do more or less what they want. Knight Vinke, with less than 1 percent of HSBC's shares, challenged the banking giant in September 2007 to review its strategy and address governance concerns. It wasn't until June 2009 that the activist hedge fund eventually got the public support of HSBC's largest shareholder, Legal & General. But even L&G's stake was only just over 3 percent. Interestingly, shareholders managed in February 2010 to get HSBC to abandon its plans to increase the CEO's salary by just over a third.

One very useful Web site for analysts (and investors for that matter) to check out is that of the International Finance Corporation,[14] the private sector arm of the World Bank. It lays out the steps the IFC's officers take in order to ascertain the level of corporate governance of the companies and organizations they are considering investing in. These steps include the first impressions that the officer has when meeting the client, a self-assessment by the client and an in-depth review of the board of directors, control processes, transparency and disclosure levels, and shareholder rights.

Ultimately, analysts must get a good feel for whether the companies they are analyzing are being run well or badly, and whether in respect to each company, management takes into consideration the interests of all stakeholders, that is not just its shareholders but also its creditors, employees, customers, trading partners and the community at-large. Only then can they attempt to add a premium or discount to their valuations. At the very least they should highlight any perceived corporate governance issues as risks. Investors' interest in good corporate governance might be even more acute during bear or volatile markets, when clearer differentiation between good and bad companies might be called for.

Below we look at examples of corporate governance issues such as social responsibility, executive compensation, equal treatment of shareholders, related-party transactions, independent non-executive directors and risk management.

Social responsibility

Good corporate governance in effect means that a company's management needs to be accountable and to balance all its stakeholders' interests fairly. As mentioned, these stakeholders include not just the majority shareholder(s), but also minority shareholders as well as employees, creditors, customers and trading partners. Indeed management should assume wider social and environmental responsibilities too.

(Note that I include social responsibility—that is the way a company treats the mass consumption market or society at-large—as a corporate governance issue. After all, as taxpayers and polluters, listed companies have a direct relationship with the community. I am not talking here about any ethical objections that some might have concerning a company's products, such as tobacco or arms, provided that the company is legally allowed to make or sell the product in the markets where they operate. For a discussion on the separate matter of socially responsible investing see the separate section in Chapter 1, which includes a case study on *Shari'ah* law.)

EXAMPLE

Corporate governance (social responsibility—rankings)

Details: The *Sydney Morning Herald* reported on October 30, 2007, the names of major companies identified as falling short on ethical standards at the first Consumers International World Congress, held in Sydney.

Corporate governance (social responsibility—rankings)—*cont'd*

The "winner" was:

Takeda Pharmaceuticals, which was judged "most unethical" for advertising in the US its "back-to-school" Rozerem sleeping pills for children, without including health warnings.

Runners-up included:

Coca-Cola, which was forced to take its bottled water Dasani off shelves in Britain after an analysis found the product was sourced from local tap water;

Kellogg's, for its use of cartoon characters and product tie-ins for its sugar-dense cereals marketed to children worldwide; and

Mattel, for blocking investigations and shifting blame after more than 21 million toys were recalled worldwide over concerns about lead-based paint.

With regard to the Mattel case, Richard Lloyd, the director general of Consumers International said: "This is a classic case of avoiding accountability and shifting responsibility on a global scale." (Compare this with Toyota's global recall in January 2010 of nearly 8 million cars for problems linked to sudden acceleration. The company received criticism for the way it handled the recall, and it was such a big recall that it will inevitably tarnish the company's reputation and affect its sales going forward. It just remains to be seen whether the company president's apology was early enough and sincere enough for the market to regain its confidence in the brand.)[15]

Zurich-based Ecofact lists the most environmentally and socially controversial companies, ranking them by the amount of negative press and criticism that they generate. Shijiazhuang Sanlu, China Petroleum (Sinopec), Samsung Group, Siemens and ArcelorMittal were top of the list in 2008. Sanlu achieved notoriety for its involvement in the Chinese melamine scandal (more on which below), and was declared bankrupt in December 2008. In terms of financial institutions, Barclays, Citigroup, Société Général, Bank of America and Deutsche Bank headed the list.

Conclusions: Failure by a company to take account of the interests of any one of its stakeholders might indicate management's attitude toward all its stakeholders—*"falsus in uno, falsus in omnibus"*, and all that. Excusing my use of Latin, please also see the example in Chapter 5 on the use of plain English when managements (and analysts for that matter) communicate with shareholders. Analysts need to determine whether there's a systemic problem within the company's corporate

Corporate governance (social responsibility—rankings)—*cont'd*

culture or whether the problem is a one-off one, perhaps at a departmental or individual level.

Ultimately, negative press and product recalls directly affect a company's profits and market value.[16] But even without such direct consequences, analysts should reward or penalize a company by applying a premium or discount to their security valuation, depending on their assessment of a company's corporate governance standards, or at least highlight any corporate governance issues that may represent risks to the investment case. Companies are often faced with crises, but it's the way that management deals with them and the level of confidence that they instill in the market that's perhaps more important.

During bull markets when investments are going well, such considerations may not be the most pressing on investors' minds. However, analysts should be aware that, as markets turn or become more volatile, investors may seek scapegoats for any losses incurred. An analyst who has failed to highlight investment risks might be an easy target. During prolonged bear markets, analysts will need to eke out differentiating factors such as corporate governance issues and dividend yield with respect to the securities they recommend.

Aside: Coca-Cola is evidently not the only company to have been found out for selling tap water. Pepsi's Aquafina is also tap water and had to be labeled as such as of 2007. In addition, the Lai See column in the September 5, 2008, edition of the *SCMP*, compiled by Ben Kwok, relates how Tingyi Holdings' subsidiary Kangshifu had to apologize for suggesting through its marketing images that its bottled water came from a beautiful mountain lake, when it was sourced from local tap water.

I would note that it takes a lot to keep a good brand name down:

SIDEBAR

Durability of brand names

Details: Siemens, Volkswagen, Bayer and even Hugo Boss are still thriving decades after their association with the Nazis. UBS and Credit Suisse entered into a settlement in 2000 to compensate victims of the Holocaust, but they are still—financial crisis

Corporate governance (social responsibility—rankings)—*cont'd*

notwithstanding—globally recognized names, as is Barclays despite its association with the Apartheid regime in South Africa.

Conclusions: Hugo Boss apparently made the SS uniforms, which by all accounts were pretty smart even if the thugs wearing them weren't. The market can be very forgiving if a company makes a good product. As mentioned in the social responsibility example above, it remains to be seen whether or not Toyota can regain the market's confidence. Likewise for Goldman Sachs and BP, following their respective crises during 2010.

Few things are more socially irresponsible than tampering with the product that the mass consumer buys.

EXAMPLE

Corporate governance (social responsibility— the mass-consumer market)

Details: In September 2008, it was discovered that melamine in infant milk formula was causing thousands of infants to become sick in China, culminating in some deaths. Melamine is normally used in the manufacture of plastics and fertilizers. However, because of its nitrogen content, some unscrupulous producers and merchants had evidently been adding it to foods to suggest a higher level of protein than there really was.

We've already mentioned Shijiazhuang Sanlu, which was at the forefront of the melamine scandal. Many milk-based products of Hong Kong-listed Mengniu Dairy and of Yili Industrial, a sponsor of the Beijing Olympics, were removed from supermarket shelves in China and Hong Kong. Even Cadbury, the international confectionary company, voluntarily took some brands of chocolate off the shelves. (Having been fined £1 million plus costs in the U.K. in 2007 for selling chocolate tainted with salmonella, the company wasn't taking any chances this time.) In Indonesia, the confectioner Mars was shocked to hear that

Corporate governance (social responsibility— the mass-consumer market)—*cont'd*

authorities had destroyed batches of M&Ms and Snickers, despite the fact that tests elsewhere had found that Mars products made in China were safe for consumption.

In an earlier scandal in the U.S., melamine was found to have been included in pet food imported from China.

Conclusions: In some cases it may be difficult to prove at what stage and by whom the chemical was added to the product, but in any case there had evidently been a lapse of quality control on a large scale.

As an example of how analysts can react to negative news and scandals, apparently all sell-side analysts as at September 22, 2008, covering Mengniu's shares had downgraded their recommendation to underweight or equivalent as well as their share price targets. The next day the stock fell from HK$20 to HK$8.15. Up until the scandal the stock had been trading at a premium to the Hang Seng China Enterprises Index. Not so thereafter.

Analysts who are ahead of the curve and who identify companies that are at risk before scandals break will inevitably appeal to clients more than those analysts who merely follow the market. To achieve this, they really do need to get in among the weeds of a company and find out what's really going on. They need to understand what safety measures are in force at the companies they cover, and how effective they are. The food chain is always a potential terrorist target as well.

Of course it's not always a rogues' gallery. Companies can get credit for good corporate governance, as the following example demonstrates.

EXAMPLE

Corporate governance (social responsibility— corporate governance excellence)

Details: The *SCMP* ran a special report on December 5, 2007, identifying the winners of the first *Hong Kong Corporate Governance Excellence Awards*. This was jointly organized by the Chamber of Hong Kong

Corporate governance (social responsibility—corporate governance excellence)—*cont'd*

Listed Companies and the Center for Corporate Governance and Financial Policy of the Hong Kong Baptist University, with sponsorship by Citigroup. The criteria by which short-listed candidates were judged were effective internal controls and risk management processes and internal and external audit processes that minimize fraud, corruption and other malpractices. The overall winner was China Life Insurance, with other category winners including NWS Holdings, Shui On Land, Industrial and Commercial Bank of China, and China Construction Bank.

Separately, Google was top of Millward Brown Optimor's Brandz table, a ranking of global brands, as featured in the *FT* on April 21, 2008. However, the *FT* reported on December 4, 2007, that One World Trust, a non-governmental group, listed Google at the bottom of its "openness and accountability" league with the comment that the company needed to "sharply improve transparency toward customers and staff".

Wal-Mart put itself forward as a beacon of social responsibility at the depths of the credit crisis. As Michael Skapinker reported in the *FT* on October 28, 2008, Wal-Mart's CEO, Lee Scott, told a meeting of 1,000 Chinese suppliers in Beijing: "I firmly believe that a company that cheats on overtime and on the age of its labor, that dumps its scraps and its chemicals in our rivers, that does not pay its taxes or honor its contracts, will ultimately cheat on the quality of its products." This was at a time when other businesses were more worried about their very survival.

Wal-Mart is also one of the founding members of the Business Ethics Leadership Alliance, organized by the Ethisphere Institute to raise standards of ethics across the business community. The members agree to uphold four core values: legal compliance, transparency, conflict identification and accountability.

As with many large organizations, Wal-Mart has also had its fair share of negative press. For example, the company agreed it would pay up to US$54.25 million to settle a class-action lawsuit that alleged that it had cut workers' break time and allowed employees to work off the clock in Minnesota, as reported by Associated Press on December 10, 2008. The company also paid US$11 million in 2005 to settle allegations that it had used contractors who employed illegal immigrants to work as cleaners in its stores. Indeed, Wal-Mart ranked number one in Ecofact's list of most environmental and socially controversial companies in North America for 2008.

Corporate governance (social responsibility—corporate governance excellence)—*cont'd*

Conclusion: Analysts must not only weigh the positive and negative aspects of a company's corporate behavior, but they also need to judge how well or badly companies respond to issues, scandals and criticism. Only then can they determine any corporate-governance-related premium or discount that should be applied to their valuations. At the very least analysts should warn clients of any perceived corporate governance risks, provided they have good grounds for doing so.

Executive remuneration

Executive remuneration or compensation is another subject that raises the public's hackles, and gets politicians riled. Notwithstanding apologists such as Jeffrey Friedman of the University of Texas who argued in the September 24, 2009, issue of the *WSJ* that executive compensation was not a cause of the financial crisis, bankers were widely denounced for their greed and risk-taking. Some executives who received million-dollar bonuses received death threats. One much publicized threat called for all the AIG executives and even their families to be "executed with piano wire around their necks".

Among the more heated discussions in reaching the US$700 billion Troubled Asset Relief Program (TARP), announced by the U.S. government in early October 2008, were proposed measures to limit senior executives' compensation and so-called "golden parachutes" in respect to troubled financial institutions. In February 2009 the newly-elected U.S. president, Barack Obama, set US$500,000 as the limit on pay for senior executives at organizations that receive exceptional government assistance. Similarly, in April 2009 the Ministry of Finance in China set a pay limit for senior executives at state-controlled financial firms for 2009. Total pay including bonus could be no more than 90 percent of the 2008 level, according to Xinhua News Agency.

The then U.K. prime minister, Gordon Brown, criticized the bonus system saying that it gave incentive to bankers to take huge risks and that changes were needed. European authorities are keen to ensure that going forward executive compensation should satisfy three broad principles: that all rewards and benefits should be transparent; that any variable pay should be linked to performance; and that excessive and irresponsible risk-taking should be discouraged. The Netherlands Bankers' Association was among the first to institute a broad-based code of conduct for bankers when they recommended that bonuses for senior executives should be restricted to one year's salary.

How to address the issue was hotly debated at the G20 Summit in Pittsburgh in September 2009. By mid-December the SEC in the U.S. had passed new rules requiring companies to disclose their compensation policies and practices if these policies and practices "create risks that are reasonably likely to have a material adverse effect on the company". Meanwhile, the U.K imposed a temporary supertax of 50 percent on 2009-related discretionary bonuses of over £25,000. The fact that this tax would be payable by the banks rather than by the bankers generated some criticism because it would be the shareholders who'd effectively be paying for it.

EXAMPLE

Corporate governance (executive remuneration)

Background: One wonders how the chief executives of major banks like Citigroup and Merrill Lynch could walk away with millions of dollars in March 2008, when the shareholders of the banks that they had been running had lost much of their investments.

Details: The *Daily Mail* in the U.K. reported on September 22, 2008, that PricewaterhouseCoopers, the administrators in the Lehman bankruptcy proceedings, discovered that £4.4 billion had been transferred from London to New York just before Lehman filed for bankruptcy. Of this amount US$2.5 billion was being set aside as a bonus pool for senior New York-based Lehman managers, while London employees were not guaranteed any pay after that month. Did these U.S. managers include the same senior managers whose decisions helped drive the company into bankruptcy?

As reported by the *WSJ* on February 13, 2009, New York attorney general, Andrew Cuomo, wrote to Barney Frank, chairman of the House Financial Services Committee, accusing Merrill Lynch of secretly accelerating the payment of US$3.6 billion in bonuses just before reporting a loss for the fourth quarter of 2008. Four executives shared US$121 million of the bonus pool. Nearly 700 individuals earned US$1 million apiece. This was in the depths of the financial crisis, after Merrill had received assistance from the TARP fund. Bank of America, which acquired Merrill Lynch, eventually settled with the SEC in February 2010, and agreed to pay US$150 million as a penalty (raised from US$33 million on new evidence). District Judge Jed Rakoff, who had rejected the first settlement, had queried why the SEC thought the company—that is the shareholders—should pay a

Corporate governance (executive remuneration)—*cont'd*

fine for something that the executives and lawyers had done. After all, the shareholders were the victims to start with. The judge reluctantly agreed to the settlement between Bank of America and the SEC, saying it was "half-baked justice at best". Meanwhile, Cuomo filed a civil fraud case against not just Bank of America but also its former CEO and CFO. The charges were that the defendants failed to disclose to shareholders: i) how great the losses were at Merrill Lynch; and ii) how much Merrill was planning to pay in bonuses. The fact that the defendants then used these losses as leverage to secure bailout funds did not go unnoticed.

Conclusions: Whether in future any broader-based and longer-term regulations are introduced in any markets specifically to control or limit executive pay, over and above any stipulations associated with relief programs or one-off tax impositions, remains to be seen. One of the basic tenets of capitalism is that everyone is not equal, and that incentives are needed to attract the best talent. From a commercial perspective at least, policy-makers will need to take care not to drive the best away. Higher tax rates tend to do that. (I'd also note that temporary taxes sometimes become permanent. Income tax in Great Britain—which hadn't formally merged with the Kingdom of Ireland yet to form the United Kingdom—was originally introduced in 1799 as a temporary measure to pay for the war against Napoleon!)

Some companies have started to respond to the challenge in their own way. For example, Morgan Stanley and Citigroup said they would claw back bonuses if results don't match the expected performance on which the bonuses were based. (But then both these banks, as well as UBS and J.P. Morgan, announced, in mid-2009, that base salaries for the senior executives would be raised, apparently in an effort to reduce the importance of their annual bonuses.) The top two executives of Barclays went a step further in February 2010 when they announced that they'd waive their 2009 bonuses altogether. The CEOs of RBS and Lloyds did likewise, while the CEO of HSBC promised to donate his to charity. I was unemployed by then, so I didn't get a bonus either.

No doubt shareholders will be more active in future in rejecting what they regard as overly generous pay and incentive schemes. At Royal Dutch Shell's AGM in May 2009, for instance, more than half of the voting shareholders voted against the proposed remuneration package for senior executives. Apparently only about 2 percent of

Corporate governance (executive remuneration)—*cont'd*

shareholders abstained from voting. And we saw earlier how HSBC had to abandon its plans to increase the CEO's salary due to shareholder pressure.

Ultimately, analysts need to be able to gauge for each company that they cover the extent to which executive remuneration, performance and shareholder value are aligned. They should also be able to detect whether a company is trying to skirt these principles through ingenious scams, as in the following Alex cartoon.

EXAMPLE

Corporate governance (executive remuneration)

Summary: Lee Kha Loon, then head of the CFA Center for Financial Market Integrity for the Asia Pacific region,[17] and a colleague of his at the time, Abe de Ramos, published in February 2008 a comprehensive and timely study on executive compensation disclosures in Asia, entitled "It Pays to Disclose". In the report they note that share-based compensation is almost universally accepted as the most powerful tool for aligning managers' and shareholders' interests, but comment that guidelines on disclosure in Asia are not up to international best practice standards.

Details: The CFA authors make various conclusions. Among these, they advise investors to make sure that management incentives are aligned with their long-term interests, and that investors should get their voices heard through proxy voting and in general meetings. Specifically, they

Corporate governance (executive remuneration)—*cont'd*

suggest that institutional investors should ask management the following questions:

- What percentage of management remuneration is performance-related?
- What are the performance criteria and incentives?
- How are share-based compensation schemes designed?
- Did the remuneration committee review and approve the remuneration policy covering both fixed and variable pay components?
- What are the identities of the highest paid employees, and what is the amount of their compensation?
- What is the total executive compensation as a percentage of profits?

Separately, as a response to the credit crisis of 2007–08, the Corrigan report—a report representing the conclusions of the major players in the global securities industry—recognized the need for management incentives to be better aligned with risk-taking and risk-tolerance.[18] The report concludes that compensation for senior executives should be based heavily on the performance of the firm as a whole, and should be heavily stock-based. Furthermore, the vesting period should be extended further out to smooth out the effects of any short-term surges in profits and losses that might arise in high-risk business lines.

My old friend Glenn Darwin drew to my attention an example of individual initiative to raise the standards of corporate governance in the U.S. The billionaire investor Carl Icahn called on his fellow Americans in October 2008 to join his "United Shareholders of America" campaign, to kick back against the mismanagement of American companies.[19] Icahn identified various egregious examples of American board behavior, including these compensation-related examples:

- Board compensation committees that approve ever-higher pay packages to top-level executives allowing them to walk off with millions of dollars even when the companies later fail due to bad management decisions.
- Boards that cozy up to managements so they can enjoy US$300,000 annual salaries and perks like the use of the corporate jets and golf junkets in return for a few hours of work each month to rubber-stamp management proposals.
- Boards that approve millions of dollars in signing bonuses that can't be taken back when a CEO leaves after a short period, even when the company collapses.

Corporate governance (executive remuneration)—*cont'd*

In a specific criticism of Lehman Brothers' board, Icahn queried why they had approved US$20 million in payouts for two executives who were fired just before the company's bankruptcy filing.

Conclusions: From our perspective, analysts represent investors and should make sure they have satisfied themselves on the above issues before making any investment recommendations to their clients.

Astute analysts might want to dig more deeply into insiders' shareholdings, and enquire how the shares have been funded. Analysts might also seek to determine whether or not directors have lent their shares out, perhaps to hedge funds that need to cover their short positions.

EXAMPLE

Corporate governance (executive remuneration—disclosures)

Details: The founder of ABC Learning Centres (a global childcare operator based in Australia) and three other directors of the company sold about A$50 million worth of shares in February 2008 following margin calls that they had received with respect to their shareholdings. This triggered a further selloff by some hedge funds. This raised questions as to why disclosures of the directors' margin loans had not been made beforehand, given how material they were to the value of the shares. This prompted a rare joint statement by the Australian Securities Exchange (ASX) and the Australian Securities and Investments Commission (ASIC) reminding directors and companies of their disclosure duties. By the end of the year ABC Learning Centres had gone into receivership.

Separately in the U.K. the FSA clarified in January 2009 its stance on the disclosure of shares used as collateral for personal loans. Persons discharging managerial responsibilities, such as directors and connected persons, should disclose such transactions to their companies, which in turn should make disclosure to the market. This followed an instance where a director of Carphone Warehouse resigned after not disclosing to the company about using his shares to get a

Corporate governance (executive remuneration—disclosures)—*cont'd*

loan. However, the FSA did acknowledge that the EU Market Abuse Directive, on which the FSA rules were based, had not been very clear on the subject. There was also an unfortunate incident, as reported by the *FT* in January 2009, where a Barclays director had used almost all of his 900,000 shares as collateral for a loan just before Barclays' share price collapsed.

The Securities and Exchange Board of India introduced measures in January 2009, following the Satyam scandal (see the case study later on in this chapter), requiring stock promoters to disclose to their companies the number of shares that they pledge as collateral for loans, and then for the companies to disclose this information to the stock exchange. This immediately prompted disclosures by nearly 500 companies, including many of India's large family-controlled groups of companies, such as the Tata, Reliance and UB groups, as reported by the *FT*.

Conclusion: Analysts really do need to scratch below the surface to find out not just who is getting what in terms of stock-related compensation, but also what they're doing with their shares. This has risk implications as to potential changes to ownership and control of companies.

SIDEBAR

Corporate governance (executive remuneration—disclosures)

Australia again provided the setting for another case demonstrating the perils of margin loans and stock-lending, especially during the volatile credit crisis, when a local stockbrokerage called Opes Prime went into administration. As explained by the *Sydney Morning Herald* of April 5, 2008, in most margin loans, investors borrow against the value of their existing shares to buy more shares, but they retain ownership of the whole stake. In the case of Opes, however, the loans were made on condition that investors signed over ownership of all their shares as security. The investors' shares were spread across more than 600 companies. The leverage that Opes could achieve was astounding, and this over-leverage evidently contributed to its downfall.

Corporate governance (executive remuneration—disclosures)—*cont'd*

When Opes went under, its lenders ANZ, Merrill Lynch and Dresdner Kleinwort, became owners of all the investors' shares in these 600 or so companies. The investors were left as unsecured creditors to Opes. The legal status of investors was tested in May when Beconwood Securities, an Opes client, tried to claim back its securities. Australia's Federal Court ruled that, under their contract with Opes, clients no longer retained any legal title to their securities. Ouch!

In an ironic way that was typical of other subprime-related stories, ANZ, by lending funds to Opes, ended up owning shares in other companies that they wouldn't have lent money to directly. Heads at ANZ rolled as a consequence. A class action suit was initiated in the U.S. by investors claiming that ANZ misled them by not disclosing to them the extent of their risk exposure to Opes Prime, but this was eventually dropped.

One particular fallout story that was reported by John Burton in the *FT* was that of Singapore-based Jade Technologies. The president and largest shareholder of Jade, a Singapore entrepreneur, had to abort a planned takeover of the company when most of his Jade shares, which had been pledged to Opes Prime, were seized by Opes' creditors. The report stated that the Jade shares were seized by the creditors on March 27, but that this wasn't disclosed in a public notice to the Singapore Exchange until April 9, after the reporting deadline. One of the creditors, Merrill Lynch, apparently sold the shares on April 1 to investors who believed that the takeover bid would soon be completed at a higher price. This led to questions about whether Jade or Merrill were responsible for the late disclosure, and whether OCBC, the financial advisor on the deal, had conducted sufficient due diligence. On June 11, 2008, the Monetary Authority of Singapore handed the investigation over to the Commercial Affairs Department. A few months later, both OCBC and the entrepreneur were censured by the Securities Industry Council for their involvement. Merrill was found to have breached takeover rules, but not in a serious enough way to warrant any punishment.

Executive insider trading

By the nature of their jobs, senior executives are always in the know about material, price-sensitive information. They have a duty to disclose such information to the market fairly, and not use that information for their own advantage before disclosing it to the market. They need to make sure that there's no impropriety or even the appearance of impropriety whenever they buy or sell their company shares, including the buying and exercising of share options.

Temptation, however, is never far away. Insider trading by company directors is always a corporate governance risk that analysts need to be aware of. The level of trading activity in a company's shares ahead of major announcements might give analysts an idea as to how leak-proof the board is.

CASE STUDY

Corporate governance (executive insider trading)

Summary: The European aerospace company EADS "came under fierce attack from minority shareholders . . . over its standards of corporate governance", according to an *FT* article on October 23, 2007. By April 2008, Peggy Hollinger and Gerrit Wiesmann were reporting for the *FT* that the French stock market regulator had concluded that top executives and core shareholders of EADS were aware as early as June 2005 that profits in its main subsidiary, Airbus, would decline over the medium to long term. The regulator alleged that these insiders sold shares in EADS ahead of making the material information available to the public.

Details: At issue was the sale of stakes by at least 15 present and past directors of EADS and its Airbus subsidiary and by two core shareholders between November 2005 and April 2006 ahead of an announcement in June 2006 regarding a six-month delay in the delivery of the company's new A380 Airbus. The selling by the insiders had already put pressure on the share price, but following the announcement the shares plunged a further 26 percent. According to France's Autorité des Marchés Financiers, the total profit gleaned amounted to €20 million. All the accused denied any wrongdoing.

It was not until late December 2009 that the AMF's enforcement committee concluded that EADS had indeed told shareholders about the delay in a timely manner. The information given to the executives was not deemed to be detailed enough for a "reasonable investor" to anticipate a significant drop in the share price. In which case, one might wonder why the executives sold their shares?

In an Indonesian case that bears some similarity with the EADS case, the local regulator Bapepam fined nine former executives of PT

Corporate governance (executive insider trading)—*cont'd*

Perusahaan Gas Negara (PGN) a total of IDR3.2 billion in December 2007 for insider trading. According to Dow Jones, Bapepam found that the former company officials had traded in the company's shares prior to letting the market know about a delay in a pipeline project. Earlier some of these executives and the company itself were fined for not disclosing key information to shareholders early enough. Apparently Bapepam had obtained proof that the PGN executives had withheld the information from the shareholders for at least 35 days.

Conclusions: Even in cases where they are not proven guilty, defendants spend so much time defending themselves that they have little time to run the company properly. Analysts need to weigh the possible outcomes of such cases, and the potential impact on or risks to the companies' businesses and the securities' valuations. This is not always easy to do, and analysts must take care not to be prejudicial, for example, perhaps by determining that the defendants are guilty before the regulators or courts make their decision. In the meantime, whatever the outcome, the loss of confidence by customers, suppliers, trading partners and investors can be seriously damaging.

Aside: Insider trading doesn't have to involve direct trading by the directors and executives themselves. In a high-profile settlement in January 2008, the Hong Kong-based chairman of Bank of East Asia, who was also a member of Hong Kong's Legislative Council and Executive Council, agreed without admitting or denying liability to an SEC fine of US$8.1 million. This was to settle charges that he had alerted a close friend to News Corporation's intention to acquire Dow Jones. As a board member of Dow Jones, he had privileged information about the deal. The same principle would apply to any research analyst who alerted clients or friends about any material and price-sensitive information.

Equal treatment of shareholders

It's all very well buying shares cheaply in a company that on the face of it makes a good product and generates high sales, but the investment becomes less attractive if the interests of minority shareholders are regularly ignored and information is kept from them. Mergers and acquisitions often provide opportunities for analysts to gauge to what extent a company's management treats all its shareholders equally, although as we can see from the following example there may be situations where the outcome is a little surprising.

CASE STUDY

Corporate governance (equal treatment of shareholders)

Background: The *Economist* issue of February 16-22, 2008, quotes Takao Kitabata, the vice-minister of Japan's Ministry of Economy, Trade and Industry (METI), as saying: ". . . shareholders in general do not have the ability to run a company. They are fickle and irresponsible. They only take on a limited responsibility, but they greedily demand high dividend payments." This statement may not represent an official stance, but it does reveal a lot about prevailing attitudes in Japan. The *Economist* goes on to say that companies in Japan are social institutions with a duty to provide stable employment and consider the needs of employees and the community at-large, not just shareholders.

Details: Lee Kha Loon and Abe de Ramos of the CFA Institute drew to my attention the Bull-Dog Sauce poison pill case in Japan. This case serves as a warning to analysts that they can't presume a court would necessarily treat all shareholders of a certain class equally.

In June 2007, Steel Partners, a U.S. hedge fund, launched an unsolicited takeover bid of the 89.48 percent shares of Bull-Dog Sauce Co. Ltd. that it did not already own. (At this stage Steel Partners claimed to have the largest individual shareholding. However, given the interests and relationships of the other shareholders, the investor was evidently regarded as the activist "outsider".) Bull-Dog's board sought to prevent the takeover by issuing three warrants for every share in Bull-Dog. These warrants would be convertible into shares for all the holders other than Steel Partners, who would receive cash on conversion instead. Steel Partners sought an injunction on the basis that this arrangement was unfair to them. In July 2007, the district court denied the injunction, and the following month the Supreme Court rejected Steel Partners' appeal. The courts determined that Steel Partners was an "abusive" acquirer. They also determined that the cash compensation was a fair economic compensation.

The Bull-Dog case seemed to galvanize other acquisition targets in Japan to adopt a similar defensive strategy, at least against foreign activists such as Steel Partners. The *WSJ* reported on February 5, 2008, that Sapporo Holdings had sought advice on how to deal with Steel Partners' bid to increase its stake in the company from 17.52 percent to 66.6 percent. The consultants determined that Sapporo's corporate value and shareholder interests would be damaged by the proposed takeover by Steel. Sapporo duly rejected Steel's advances.

Corporate governance (equal treatment of shareholders)—*cont'd*

In a variation on the Japanese poison pill theme, Michiyo Nakamoto reported in the *FT* on February 25, 2008, how some Japanese companies were raising money from group members through loans that were combined with warrants. One example cited was Sumitomo Realty, which raised ¥120 billion through a subordinated loan from Sumitomo Mitsui Banking Corp., with warrants attached. The prospect of the warrants being exercised by the friendly party could be a deterrent against future unwanted bidders. Some investors feared that this may indicate a revival of the old *zaibatsu* industrial conglomerate system.

Conclusions: Although equal treatment of shareholders of a certain class of shares is a basic principle, discriminatory treatment might be exercised in certain companies and markets, for example to protect a company's enterprise value and the interests of shareholders and other stakeholders such as employees and customers. So, it seems that in some markets all common shareholders are equal, but perhaps some are more equal than others. Was George Orwell perhaps satirizing capitalism as well as communism in *Animal Farm*?

Ultimately, all companies—in Japan and elsewhere—need to realize that treating shareholders fairly, maximizing shareholder value and other aspects of good corporate governance provide the best defense against hostile takeover attempts.

For more on Japanese corporate governance issues, see the example on national interest later in this section.

Notwithstanding the above cases, I would say that cracks are starting to appear in corporate Japan's protectionist armor. At the end of May 2008, foreign shareholders led by Steel Partners at least managed to oust the president and top management of Aderans, a Japanese wig-maker. Furthermore, importantly, the Ministry of Economic, Trade and Industry (METI) conducted a study of 15 companies in which Steel Partners had a stake of at least 10 percent. As reported by Michiyo Nakamoto in the *FT* on June 26, 2008, METI concluded that hedge funds and buyout funds provide much-needed risk capital and financial skills. At least Yoshinori Komiya, director of the industrial finance division at METI, is encouraging more funds to invest in Japan.

Furthermore, lest Western readers adopt a holier-than-thou attitude, let's look at some examples from the U.S. and Europe.

EXAMPLE

Corporate governance (equal treatment of shareholders)

The May 22, 2008, issue of the *Economist* quotes a representative of Exxon Mobil, America's largest public company at the time, as saying that its board "is better placed than shareholders to determine its leadership structure". This was in response to the Rockefellers' endorsement of a resolution to split the role of chairman and chief executive at Exxon Mobil.

Separately, Citigroup introduced a "tax benefits preservation plan" in June 2009 to discourage investors from buying stakes greater than 5 percent. But hey, guess what? The poison pill would not apply to the U.S. government, which was poised to become the biggest shareholder on conversion of the preferred stock that they received for bailing out the company during the financial crisis.

Paul Betts and Andrew Hill commented in the *FT* on February 12, 2008, that a takeover of Société Générale, the French bank, which had to launch an emergency rights issue at a heavy discount in the wake of its trading losses, would not be easy. This was because the company had previously decided to cap the voting rights of any shareholder at 15 percent. An investor might have 50 percent of the equity, but unless it has 50.01 percent, its voice would only count for 15 percent. Similarly, the statutes of Iberdrola, a large Spanish utility, have limited the voting rights of individual shareholders in that company to 10 percent.

India was the setting for the following interesting situation, involving related-party transactions.

CASE STUDY

Corporate governance (related-party transactions)

Summary: Satyam Computer Services, a major Indian outsourcing firm, enraged shareholders including Franklin Templeton when it announced suddenly that it would spend US$1.6 billion to buy out Maytas Properties and Maytas Infra, both controlled by the chairman's family. (Note how

Corporate governance (related-party transactions)—*cont'd*

any connection between Maytas and Satyam was cunningly disguised by having their names as the mirror image of each other.) It was not the first time that this had happened within the Satyam group. Eyebrows were raised in 1999 when Satyam Infoway paid what seemed like much too high a price for IndiaWorld.

Unbeknown to the shareholders, there was worse news to come.

Details: As reported by the *FT* on December 22, 2008, the transaction would have exhausted the group's net cash position and left it with net debt of US$400 million. In an *FT* article two weeks later, we see that the deal valued Maytas Properties at US$1.3 billion, whereas its net worth was only US$225 million. Following a teleconference call with domestic and foreign fund managers, the chairman backed down.

Indeed on January 7, 2009, the chairman stepped down altogether after confessing that he'd been cooking the books over a number of years. In a letter to shareholders he stated that the gap between reported sales and actual sales had grown so large that it could not be filled. Over the years the hole in the balance sheet enlarged. The Maytas deal was "the last attempt to fill the fictitious assets with real ones". The hole amounted to about US$1 billion, that is a billion dollars of supposed cash, which wasn't there. By buying Maytas Properties for US$1.3 billion, this "cash" would have been replaced by a real asset (albeit an overvalued one). In what must be one of the quotes of the year, the chairman said in his resignation letter: "It was like riding a tiger, not knowing how to get off without being eaten." The company's share price fell nearly 80 percent on the day. The BSE Sensex fell 7 percent.

Investors were left scratching their heads as to how the auditors at the Indian affiliate of PricewaterhouseCoopers could have missed this. Other companies audited by PwC were tarred by the same brush, in the market's mind, and Indian corporate governance generally was called into question. Credit, however, should go to the Indian companies who responded to this event by going to the other extreme in terms of disclosure. Infosys Technologies, one of Satyam's leading competitors, published details of its cash holdings in its various bank accounts.

Aside: The irony is that in Sanskrit "satyam" means "truth". The World Council for Corporate Governance stripped Satyam of the prestigious Golden Peacock award for good corporate governance that it had bestowed on the company the previous year. News also started to emerge that some insiders had been selling their shares in the weeks

Corporate governance (related-party transactions)—*cont'd*

before the scandal broke. There were even allegations that the chairman had invented a phantom workforce of 10,000 employees, so that he could siphon off their wages.

By the way, one has to feel a little sorry for the ABN AMRO analyst who upgraded his recommendation on Satyam to buy on the very morning the chairman issued his resignation statement. As mentioned, the stock fell nearly 80 percent that day.

Conclusions: Notwithstanding disclosure requirements in most markets (whether through stock exchange listing rules, securities regulations or accounting standards), there's no substitute for diligent research into a company and its management for investors to gain a better understanding of how well a company is being run. They, or analysts on their behalf, need to assess the risks that they might be disadvantaged in any way as minority shareholders, including through related-party transactions.

Analysts need to scrutinize their covered companies' transactions to identify any that might not be at arm's length. A management that deals with connected parties at prices or rates that appear less favorable to the company and more favorable to the connected parties may well be destructive in terms of shareholder value, and stands to lose the confidence of minority shareholders. Such behavior may indicate more serious underlying problems, as in the Satyam case.

Here are some recommendations that the CFA Institute makes about related-party transactions.

EXAMPLE

Corporate governance (equal treatment of shareholders—related-party transactions)

Summary: In research published by the CFA Institute,[20] the authors identified various instances of related-party transactions in Asia. The authors made some recommendations, some of which are addressed to regulators and lawmakers and some aimed at corporate managements.

Corporate governance (equal treatment of shareholders—related-party transactions)—*cont'd*

Conclusions: Of particular interest to readers of this book is the recommendation to investors that they should try to engage controlling shareholders. They should be critical of transactions when they are put up for vote. They should not be defeatist by voting with their feet. One example cited by the authors is Lazard Korea Corporate Governance Fund, which has consistently, and at times successfully, taken Korean *chaebol* managers to task.[21]

Also of interest is the authors' comment that, whereas related-party transactions are usually associated with the abuse of independent shareholders' rights, auditors consider them (or should consider them) as potential warnings of fraudulent financial reporting. Significant transactions occurring toward the end of a reporting period should raise an auditor's suspicions.

Here's an interesting story from Hong Kong that straddles the issues of shareholder equality and related parties.

SIDEBAR

Corporate governance (vote manipulation)

Summary: Trading in the shares of Hong Kong-listed PCCW was suspended on February 2, 2009. This followed an anonymous tip to David Webb, an independently-funded, self-styled watchdog of the Hong Kong stock market, regarding suspected vote-manipulation ahead of a buyout offer of the telecoms company by the group's two largest shareholders. The matter went to court.

Details: Evidence seemed to suggest that hundreds of insurance agents representing Fortis Insurance (Asia)[22] were being offered 1,000 shares each in PCCW in order to vote for the privatization offer.

Under the Hong Kong Companies Ordinance, such an offer would need the approval of either 75 percent by number of shares or 50 percent by number of shareholders to be passed. At the offer

Corporate governance (vote manipulation)—*cont'd*

price of HK$4.50 a share, Webb noted that 500 shareholders with 1,000 votes each would cost about HK$2 million, which would seem a relatively cheap way to garner a sufficient number of shareholders to effect the desired outcome, given that the deal was a multi-billion dollar one.

Webb said: "It is incredibly unlikely that several hundred people, most of whom happen to work for the same company, would separately, simultaneously and independently decide to transfer the same number of shares into their own name." However, he stated that there was at that stage no evidence of any involvement by any persons connected to PCCW.

Webb posted the findings of his investigations onto his Web site, cunningly called webb-site.com, and alerted the Securities and Futures Commission (SFC) as well as the Independent Commission Against Corruption (ICAC). He also called for the government to amend the ordinance, and follow the one-share-one-vote principle.

Following much heated debate at the shareholders' meeting on February 4, the vote for privatization was passed. However, the SFC was on the case, and a couple of months later three appeal court judges unanimously disapproved the deal. They declared that the privatization vote was "clear manipulation" that was against the interests of minority shareholders.

Another important element of good corporate governance with respect to the protection of minority interests is the fair appointment of independent non-executive directors to the boards of listed companies. Independent non-executive directors need to be able to act independently not just from management but also from controlling shareholders. Minority shareholders depend on these directors to make sure that their interests are not prejudiced.

In their comprehensive report on independent non-executive directors entitled *A Search for True Independence in Asia*, published in January 2010, Lee Kha Loon and Angela Pica of the CFA Institute examine a few examples, including one involving Swissco International.

EXAMPLE

Corporate governance (independent non-executive directors)

Details: Two independent non-executive directors of Swissco International, a Singapore-listed marine service provider, resigned in March 2008 after the executive chairman (who was also the majority shareholder) said that he wanted all independent non-executive directors to serve one-year terms with renewal only at the chairman's discretion. The two directors rightly felt that their independence would be compromised since their re-election would be subject to the chairman's decision. Independent non-executive directors should after all be accountable not to management or to the majority shareholder but to all the shareholders.

Conclusions: Analysts should look closely at the reasons given for an independent director's (or indeed an auditor's) resignation. If it's because they feel they have been compromised and cannot fulfill their independent functions, then alarm bells should ring. Of course compromised directors aren't always guided by their conscience and don't always resign, so analysts will need to judge for themselves whether the independent directors are able to perform their duties truly independently.

National interest

Of course, when it comes to making an investment in a company, all bets are off when antitrust and monopoly issues are at stake, and most states will defer to national interest as the final backstop.

EXAMPLE

Corporate governance (national interest)

Background: The prime minister of Australia, Kevin Rudd, proclaimed in February 2008 that the application by Aluminum Corp. of China (Chinalco) to increase its stake in Australian-listed Rio Tinto would be assessed on the basis of national interest. Government representatives later insisted that it was "agnostic" about the nationality of foreign bidders, and that it did not want to deter Chinese or other foreign investment. How was it going to turn out for Chinalco?

Corporate governance (national interest)—*cont'd*

Details: Rio Tinto was at the time the subject of an acquisition bid by BHP Billiton. Chinalco claimed that its purchase of Rio shares was purely for commercial and diversification reasons, a stance supported by the Chinese government, according to a *WSJ* report on February 6, 2008. However, many suspected that China might have wanted to block a BHP-Rio merger on the basis that the combined entity could force up prices of raw commodities such as iron ore, on which China depends heavily for its economic growth.

The decision was given to allow Chinalco to go through with its purchase. Memories of the unsuccessful bid by CNOOC of China for Unocal of the U.S. in 2005 on the grounds of national interest come to mind to serve as a comparison. The Chinalco bid was evidently undertaken in a more transparent way and at a time when Chinese companies (as well as sovereign wealth funds from China, the Middle-East and elsewhere) were riding to the rescue of banks rocked by the subprime crisis.

However, things didn't go so well for Chinalco the following year when it tried to double its stake in Rio. The latter rejected the bid, opting instead for a rights issue and an iron ore joint venture with BHP. The economics of the situation had by then changed, with renewed optimism in global stock and commodity markets. Chinalco must have wondered whether it wasn't just CNOOC all over again. (Shortly afterward, four Rio Tinto executives including an Australian national were arrested in China on charges of espionage. These were later changed to the less serious charges of bribery and stealing commercial secrets. All four pleaded guilty to bribery and one pleaded guilty to stealing commercial secrets. The Australian national was sentenced to 10 years in prison and the other three received prison terms of between 7 and 14 years. Chinalco had earlier denied that the arrests had been connected with the failed bid.)

Japan also provides some interesting stories on similar themes.

EXAMPLE

Corporate governance (national interest)

Details: "Keep clear of Japan, warns TCI chief" was a headline on the cover of the *FT Weekend* edition on April 19/20, 2008. This was the

---

Corporate governance (national interest)—*cont'd*

reaction by a managing partner of the Children's Investment Fund, an activist hedge fund, to the blocking by the Japanese government of the fund's attempts to increase its 9.9 percent stake in J-Power, an electric power wholesaler, on national security grounds. This was quickly followed by another front-page headline in the *FT*, on April 22, "Japan 'closed' to investors", with a story about Peter Mandelson, the European Union trade commissioner, rounding on Japan for exploiting the openness of other economies while erecting barriers to trade and investment at home.

Then on May 15, the Asian Corporate Governance Association (ACGA) published a policy document pressing for corporate governance reform in Japan. This was endorsed by leading global pension funds and fund managers including: Aberdeen Asset Management, Singapore; the California Public Employees' Retirement System (CalPERS), U.S.; Hermes Fund Managers, U.K.; and other large institutional investors. Areas for improvement which the document focused on include: the rights of shareholders as owners; using capital efficiently; the independent supervision of management; pre-emption rights; poison pills and takeover defenses; and shareholder meetings and voting.

Conclusions: There's often a gray area between what's legally or morally right and wrong, and there's no universally accepted definition anyway of "national interest". Both analysts and investors would be wise not to look at these issues in strictly black and white terms. "National interest" is the political joker in the pack that might be played whenever the stakes are high enough.

When the national interest card is used, the reputation (and hence sovereign rating and cost of capital) of the whole country may be at stake, not just of specific companies. Furthermore, poor corporate governance on a national scale is bad enough for foreign investors, but local investors themselves are also victims of corporate practices that can sometimes and in some places seem almost feudalistic.

Even where governments are held to account and where a degree of openness and transparency is taken for granted, it may still be difficult for analysts to predict the outcome of controversial national interest debates.

SIDEBAR

Corporate governance (national interest)

Details: The U.K. government approved the sale of British Energy to Électricité de France (EDF) in September 2008. British Energy controls the U.K.'s nuclear reactors and EDF is controlled by the French government. As you can imagine, some eyebrows were raised. The British government, however, defended the sale by arguing that the greater national interest for the country was to secure its long-term energy supply needs.

Another controversial situation that springs to mind, albeit one that involved a trade deal rather than a stock investment, was when in 2007 the U.K.'s Serious Fraud Office abruptly stopped its investigation into corruption charges related to an arms deal between BAE Systems and Saudi Arabia. As reported by the international press, Tony Blair, the then prime minister of the U.K., said that if the investigation into BAE had not been dropped, it would have led to "the complete wreckage of a vital strategic relationship and the loss of thousands of British jobs". Senior judges later criticized the government for "failing to recognize the rule of law" and accused it of allowing a foreign nation to "pervert the course of justice", as reported by the *FT* on April 11, 2008. BAE Systems denied any wrongdoing, but agreed to implement new ethical guidelines following the scandal. Eventually, the House of Lords ruled that the Serious Fraud Office had acted lawfully when it stopped its investigations,[23] thereby fueling speculation that more deals between BAE Systems and Saudi Arabia were in the pipeline.

In September 2009, the British government had to backpedal after initially denying that future oil exploration and trade deals with Libya were behind the freeing of the Lockerbie bomber.

By the way, when we talk about strategic industries we're not just talking about oil, iron ore, nuclear energy or contracts for fighter jets, as the following sidebar demonstrates.

SIDEBAR

Corporate governance (national interest—strategic industries)

When Pepsi wanted to buy Danone in 2005, France was ridiculed for declaring yogurt a strategic industry. China's blocking in March

Corporate governance (national interest—strategic industries)—*cont'd*

2009 of Coca-Cola's attempt to take over China Huiyuan Juice Group, China's largest producer of fruit juices, also attracted criticism for being protectionist and politically-motivated.

Perhaps it's not so funny after all for a country to regard food and drink as national concerns. Countries will make every effort to defend their own food resources and some would seek to expand their borders to increase their food supply. Hitler used *Lebensraum* as an excuse for Germany to invade neighboring countries. Empire-builders have colonized countries for centuries using military might to help enforce economic cooperation.

Following the Second World War the trend among companies in the developed world seems to have been to achieve similar ends in a more socially acceptable way, that is through capital investment. For example, the major international food and drink companies like Nestlé and Coca-Cola have been busy buying companies and entering into joint ventures with companies all around the world to secure their food and drink production lines.

The *WSJ* reported on August 26, 2008, that the United Arab Emirates and Saudi Arabia were seeking agricultural-investment opportunities in developing countries such as Sudan, Egypt, Turkey and Pakistan, in an effort to meet rising food demand. A couple of months later, Daewoo Logistics entered into a deal to grow crops in Madagascar to ship back to South Korea, and Cambodia was offering agricultural land concessions. The chairman of New York-based Jarch Capital, who is a former Wall Street banker, even secured a deal from a notorious warlord for 400,000 hectares of land in south Sudan, where land rights remain vague, as reported by the *FT* in January 2009. This breaks one of my personal rules for real estate investment, which is never to buy land from a notorious warlord in a market where land rights remain vague.

Efforts will no doubt be stepped up to secure supplies of the most precious commodity of all—water. Corporates will need to play fair. The Cochabamba water wars in Bolivia in 2000 serve as a reminder of how easily civil disturbance can erupt when municipal water supplies are privatized or controlled.

A discussion on national interests would not be complete without a few words on sovereign wealth funds, that is the funds set up by sovereign states to invest in markets around the world.

SIDEBAR

Corporate governance (national interest—sovereign wealth funds)

Before the financial crisis suspicions had been raised as to whether sovereign wealth funds (SWFs) had a political agenda as an ulterior motive, or whether their investments were being made purely for commercial reasons.

At the 2008 World Economic Forum in Davos, Switzerland, Lawrence Summers, the former U.S. Treasury Secretary, advocated for more transparency within SWFs and the introduction of a code of conduct whereby SWFs should disavow any political agenda. Consequently, in September the International Working Group (IWG) of Sovereign Wealth Funds announced a draft set of voluntary principles and practices, dubbed the "Santiago Principles". It must have been a challenge to get so many SWFs to reach an agreement. For example, Sultan bin Sulayem, the head of Dubai World, made it clear in an interview with the *FT* in April 2008 that moves in Europe to make SWFs more transparent would deter him from investing there.

On the receiving end, each nation would need to determine how rigid they would need to be in screening investments by SWFs, which would no doubt depend on the relative need for the investment. During financial crises, as the world experienced in 2007–2009, it may be the case that beggars can't be choosers, although it took a while before SWFs returned to the headlines having had their fingers burnt relatively early on in the crisis.

The Australian government issued a set of principles in February 2008 in an effort to enhance the transparency of its foreign investment screening regime. Going forward the Australian Foreign Investment Review Board would consider whether an investor's operations are "independent from the relevant foreign government". In the U.S., the Treasury increased the investigation powers of the Committee on Foreign Investment in the U.S. (CFIUS) to cover investments of below the previous threshold of 10 percent. Meanwhile, in August 2008, the Chinese government announced that it would establish a "joint ministerial meeting" system to look into any security issues that might apply when foreign companies make acquisitions in China.

Risk management

A company's willingness and ability to manage risk is another aspect of corporate governance that analysts should consider. They should also be aware that the company's managers and professionals themselves might be less than honest.

I'm sure Dan Reingold, a top-ranked telecoms analyst from 1989 to 2003, speaks for a generation of analysts when he reveals in his candid exposé of the rivalry between him and Jack Grubman entitled *Confessions of a Wall Street Analyst*:

> "The news of WorldCom's massive accounting fraud had shocked me to the core. How could I have missed it?" He goes on to say: "I was far too mired in my detailed models to truly grasp the looming disaster. They beautifully quantified different share prices in different situations but did not show how WorldCom had been using a series of ever-larger acquisitions to hide a slowing core business. The company was already beginning to spiral out of control. Though I wasn't mesmerized by the hype that had attracted many others to this stock, if I had been less analytical and more intuitive . . . I might have better understood WorldCom's addiction to acquisitions and, perhaps, aggressive accounting methods to fuel its continued growth. My lower rating was still too bullish. It did not capture what lay ahead for WorldCom and its investors."

Companies are on a slippery slope when they start making false statements to shareholders. The Enron and WorldCom cases have been well documented. Let's have a look at Vivendi, where investors claimed they'd lost money due to false statements made by the company.

CASE STUDY

Corporate governance (false statements by issuers)

Details: Investors sued Vivendi, a French company, in a class action suit in New York, after they'd lost billions of dollars between October 31, 2000, and August 16, 2002, when the share price fell from €84.70 to €9.30. The investors claimed that the company had made false statements about its true financial position, especially with respect to debt that it had accumulated during a US$77 billion acquisition spree in the 1990s.

It was apparently the largest securities class action going to verdict, according to a lawyer for the investors cited by Bloomberg on January 30, 2010. "We had 57 statements that we claimed were false, and the jury found that 57 statements were false." By one estimate, a million investors could

Corporate governance (false statements by issuers)—*cont'd*

claim up to US$9.3 billion.[24] Vivendi said it would appeal. The case may take a while longer to play out. (Note that earlier, in 2003, Vivendi agreed to pay US$50 million to settle civil fraud charges brought by the SEC, and the ex-CEO agreed to pay a fine of US$1 million.)

Conclusion: What can I say? Analysts can't take anything for granted. They need to question and cross-check information. If they suspect the company's management in any way, that is through the way they might be mistreating any class of stakeholder, then they need to probe more deeply. They need to highlight any corporate governance risks that they perceive, but still need to take care not to say anything defamatory about the company or its management, unless they are really sure of their facts.

Risk analysts try to identify the common denominators involved when firms fail or fall from grace. Often this is due to unauthorized trades or excessive risk-taking.

CASE STUDY

Corporate governance (risk management and rogue traders)

Summary: Investigators commissioned by the Singapore Exchange to examine the China Aviation Oil (CAO) collapse in 2004 noted "serious failures of corporate governance", according to Alan Waring and Steve Tunstall of *Asia Risk* in a letter published in the *SCMP* on June 29, 2006. The two risk analysts found a number of contributing failures that were uncannily reminiscent of the Barings collapse in 1995.

Separately, the *FT* compared the way £827 million in trading losses were incurred at Barings with the way about €5 billion was lost at Société Générale (SocGen) in January 2008. *Plus ça change, plus c'est la même chose* and all that.

Details: By the end of 2004 CAO had accumulated losses of over US$500 million related to petroleum derivatives trading. The Monetary Authority of Singapore announced in August 2005 that CAOHC, the

Corporate governance (risk management and rogue traders)—*cont'd*

holding company of CAO, had settled insider trading charges. To raise funds, CAOHC had evidently placed CAO shares with Deutsche Bank, while in possession of material, price-sensitive information regarding the trading losses. Both the CEO and the ex-head of finance were sentenced to jail.

Comparing the trading losses at Barings and SocGen, John Gapper noted in the *FT* of January 25, 2008, that both involved young male traders who had accumulated large positions in exchange-traded equity futures, and who had used their knowledge of procedures in the back office, where they had previously worked, to conceal the extent of their losses. Similarly, Waring and Tunstall of *Asia Risk* noted that the corporate governance failures identified in the Singapore Exchange investigation included the lack of effective systems at all levels, the absence of back-office safeguards and the concealment of trading losses.

Conclusions: One of the major jobs of securities-research analysts is to try to anticipate any problems in companies that may affect an investment in the shares of those companies, and draw these risks to the attention of investors. Analyzing a collapse or disaster after the event is too late for investors; so knowing these common denominators and watching out for them may help securities analysts identify the companies most at risk.

Yes, this is easier said than done, especially in extreme situations when you've got so-called "rogue traders" fraudulently trying to conceal their positions and cover their tracks. Nevertheless, analysts should at least make sure they understand the level of investment and resources that a subject company puts into its risk management procedures, and whether or not the efforts are sufficient for the type of company and the levels of risks that they tend to assume.

In addition to making every effort themselves to understand the true nature of any investments or contracts that the company has entered into, including any involving complicated derivative products, analysts should also assess the risk manager's own level of understanding. Analysts should also determine what eventualities would be covered or not covered by the company's insurance policies.

Various other studies around the world provide useful conclusions for analysts to consider.

EXAMPLE

Corporate governance (risk management and rogue traders)

FINRA, the U.S. regulator, published in April 2008 its Regulatory Notice 08-18, which gives guidance on the best practices for detecting and preventing "rogue trading". Sound practices include:

- heightened firm scrutiny of red flags such as trading limit breaches, unrealized profit and loss on unsettled transactions, unusual patterns of cancellations and corrections and a pattern of aged fails to deliver;
- increased password security and other protections of firm systems and risk management information; and
- creating a strong compliance culture within the firm.

Although not involving alleged "rogue-trader" fraud, UBS's 50-page explanation to its shareholders for nearly US$19 billion subprime-related writedowns in 2007 also provides lessons for risk managers anywhere. Key findings reported in the *FT* on April 22, 2008, were that senior management:

- was too distracted and spread too thinly, especially with the creation and winding down of Dillon Read Capital Management, its in-house hedge fund;
- was too focused on profit without paying enough attention to the risks; and
- relied too heavily on industry ratings of subprime assets.

Steve Vickers of FTI-International Risk has undertaken a study of multinational companies in Asia and has found that the structure and organization of some firms is a factor in making them more vulnerable to risk. He found that firms are subject to high risk of fraud where three or more of the following factors apply:

- A matrix management system, that is one without clear reporting lines, is used.
- The corporation has recently been through a business process re-engineering exercise or significant restructuring.
- Expatriate managers are rotated every two years or so.
- Local staff turnover is high.
- Internal controls are insufficient or not appropriate to the regional environment.

Corporate Governance (risk management and rogue traders)—*cont'd*

- Sophisticated controls or "firewalls" in practice fail to allow for collusion among staff in different departments.
- There is insufficient pre-employment screening and recently hired executives are permitted to recruit personnel from their previous companies.
- Anti-money-laundering programs are "wooden" or not relevant to local circumstances.
- External accounting procedures are weak and internal auditors are reluctant to confront local management.
- Warnings or minor fraud incidents tend to be covered up for internal corporate or political reasons.
- Morale is low.

Those wanting to read a systematic examination of the 2007–08 credit crisis and recommendations for reform should read the Corrigan report entitled "Containing Systemic Risk: The Road to Reform", published by Counterparty Risk Management Policy Group III on August 6, 2008.[25]

In order to appreciate more fully their buy-side clients' risk-management-related needs, analysts would also be advised to read "Risk Principles for Asset Managers", published by Buy Side Risk Managers Forum[26] and Capital Market Risk Advisors on February 25, 2008.

Analysts should also be aware that rogue-trading events are not once-in-a-generation events.

SIDEBAR

Corporate governance (risk management and rogue traders)

Rogue trading is going on all the time, to some degree. It's just that only the largest scandals hit the press.

- The U.K. branch of Toronto Dominion was fined £490,000 in 2007 after a fixed income trader attributed false values to his trading positions and created fictitious trades to hide losses on his book. As reported by Megan Murphy of the *FT* on December 18, 2009,

Corporate governance (risk management and rogue traders)—*cont'd*

this was followed by a £7 million fine for the company's repeated failure to control its traders.

- The *FT* of June 19, 2008, reported how Morgan Stanley had revealed that a London-based credit derivatives trader had incorrectly valued his positions, forcing the company to take a US$120 million revenue hit. (Repercussions from this included a fine of £1.4 million meted out to the firm by the FSA for weak controls and a fine of £105,000 to the individual involved. The individual was also banned from the industry.)
- The same *FT* report also referred to Credit Suisse's confirmation in March that US$2.8 billion of mis-markings was due to misconduct. (The FSA fined the company £5.6 million over this issue.)
- The suspension by Lehman Brothers of two traders from its exotic equity derivatives desk in London was pending a review of positions that could result in markdowns of up to US$150 million.
- One of the possible catalysts that sparked the bank run on Bank of East Asia in Hong Kong in September 2008 was the bank's restatement of its first-half results to take account of a loss of HK$93 million that a derivatives trader had apparently hidden.
- The next month, Caisse d'Epargne hit the headlines when it revealed that it had made a €600 million loss on equity derivatives trading.
- CITIC Pacific reported that losses from currency trades could hit US$2 billion (see earlier case study).
- A Merrill Lynch currency trader was suspended after running up losses of US$400 million on Norwegian and Swedish currency trades, according to the *New York Times* of March 6, 2009.

So the list goes on.

Perhaps the biggest "roguering" story of them all is the Madoff scandal. More like the biggest "rogering" story, if you ask me.

CASE STUDY

Corporate governance (transparency of operations)

Details: Warnings submitted by Harry Markopolos to the SEC years ahead of the Madoff blowup, which came to light in December 2008, claimed that there were two possible explanations for the fund manager's exceptional returns: i) that they were the result of illegal front-running of customer order flows; or ii) more likely, that the whole thing was one big Ponzi scheme. It transpired to be one big Ponzi scheme. I'll leave others to determine why the regulators failed to act on whatever warnings that they had received in the preceding years. Suffice it to say that the 70-year-old Madoff pleaded guilty to 11 criminal charges, and received the maximum sentence of 150 years. (Cue Woody Allen's line, in *Take the Money and Run*, that with good behavior he can cut the time in half.)

This case bears remarkable resemblance to a case that surfaced at more or less the same time involving Sir Allen Stanford and his Stanford International Bank:

- Each organization was dominated by an evidently self-centered individual (with both organizations being named after the respective individual).
- There was limited transparency with respect to their operations and investments.
- Each organization was not a clearly defined entity from a regulator's perspective, and therefore each could avoid focused regulatory scrutiny.
- In each case the firm of auditors was surprisingly small for such a large client.
- In each case there was a certain cachet to being a client, like being a member of an exclusive club.
- Returns were above-average and consistent.

Conclusions: These cases may be more relevant to financial advisers determining which fund or bank to invest clients' money in, rather than to securities analysts. Nevertheless, the conclusions would also be applicable to analysts who analyze companies and their securities.

Advisers who undertake due diligence on a fund to invest in should be suspicious if returns are too good to be true, and if the company is

Corporate governance (transparency of operations)—*cont'd*

secretive in the way it generates those returns. As Erin Arvedlund, the author of a *Barron's* article on Madoff that was published back in May 2001, said: "The lessons of Long-Term Capital Management's collapse are that investors need, or should want, transparency in their money manager's investment strategy."

Alarm bells should also ring when members of the major shareholder's family hold senior positions.[27]

The financial crisis also uncovered many other Ponzi schemes.

SIDEBAR

Ponzi schemes

Details: One bizarre case involved the so-called "Lebanese Bernie Madoff". Many Shiite investors put their faith and their money into the scheme, given the operator's apparent links with Hezbollah, according to the *New York Times* of September 15, 2009. A judicial official cited by the paper estimated that the amount lost by investors could be over US$1 billion.

Another case involved a self-proclaimed "Chinese Warren Buffett" who was arrested in Canada in January 2010. He was reported in the *SCMP* to have admitted to having operated a Ponzi scheme from 2004 to at least 2006, and to have raised up to US$75 million from more than 200 investors for his hedge fund, Oversea Chinese Fund. Members of the Chinese American community were specifically targeted.

Meanwhile, Kay Services was served with a US$3.8 million judgment (including a civil penalty of US$450,000) for operating a Ponzi scheme that targeted members of the Reverend Sun Myung Moon's Family Federation for World Peace, formerly known as the Unification Church (a.k.a. the Moonies). According to the SEC, the mastermind (the sole owner of Kay Services) promised investors a guaranteed return of 50–100 percent in one year. She was sentenced to 70 months in prison.

Ponzi schemes—*cont'd*

Then there was the New Zealand banker who was jailed for six years in March 2010 after defrauding clients of NZ$17.8 million to fund his lavish lifestyle of prostitutes, luxury property, cars and wine. This reminds me of George Best's answer when asked what had happened to all the money he'd earned from playing soccer. He said he'd spent a lot of money on booze, birds and fast cars, and the rest he just squandered.

Incidentally, in March 2010, the SEC charged a nationally recognized psychic—who billed himself as "America's prophet"—with fraudulently enticing more than 100 investors to invest more than US$6 million in the Delphi Associates Investment Group. He apparently claimed he would use his psychic expertise to provide investment guidance to his investing team. (There are some analysts I know who, I'm sure, use the same technique!) While perhaps not a Ponzi scheme in the strictest sense, one of the allegations was that funds were improperly used. Some money was diverted to the non-profit religious organization run by the psychic and his wife. No doubt he'll already have foreseen the outcome of his case.

Conclusion: With Muslims being the main victims in the Lebanese case, Chinese Americans in the Canadian case, Moonies in the Kay case and with the Jewish community being Madoff's main victims, at least we know that financial fraud is not prejudiced along racial or religious lines.

Another aspect of risk management, which is especially relevant for banks and financial institutions, is money-laundering (and its related cousin, terrorist-financing). I'll also include international-scale bribery and corruption here.

Banking regulators around the developed world have instituted anti-money-laundering (AML) measures, which reflect rules established by international organizations such as the Basel Committee on Banking Supervision and the Financial Action Task Force. These organizations identify countries that are deemed to be high-risk and categories of clients that need special attention. In the U.S. the responsibility falls to the Treasury Department's Office of Foreign Assets Control.

As the following case studies demonstrate, companies can fall foul of these international rules. Analysts need to determine that their covered companies have appropriate systems and procedures in place to mitigate the risks, that is that staff know their clients sufficiently well and conduct sufficient due diligence when opening new accounts.

CASE STUDY

Corporate governance (risk management and money-laundering, bribery and corruption)

Details: ABN AMRO was fined a total of US$80 million in December 2005 by U.S. federal and state regulators for failing to identify and report suspicious transactions where funds that originated in black-listed Iran and Libya were funneled via Dubai to the U.S. and onward. A month earlier Bank of New York had agreed to pay US$26 million dollars in fines and US$12 million as restitution. The charge was one of conspiracy for allowing a vice president of the bank and her husband, both Russian émigrés living in New York, to use the bank as a conduit to transfer about US$7 million of money that originated in Russia to third parties around the world.

According to *American Banker* (January 10, 2007), these fines were notable not just for their size but also for where the shell companies were located. In the past criminals had used offshore shells to conceal asset ownership. But as banks began to scrutinize offshore accounts, criminals increasingly opened shell companies in the U.S. and received the same anonymity.

If those cases involved large amounts of money, what about Credit Suisse which agreed in December 2009 to pay US$536 million to U.S. authorities to settle charges that it had handled payments to Iran and other blacklisted countries between 1995 and 2007, in defiance of U.S. sanctions. Lloyds TSB agreed in January 2009 to pay US$350 million in fines and restitution for conducting illegal transactions on behalf of customers from Iran, Sudan and other sanctioned countries. According to the U.S. Justice Department, the bank falsified wire transfers over a period of 12 years by deliberately removing material information—such as customer names, bank names and addresses—from payment messages, so that the wire transfers would pass undetected through filters at U.S. financial institutions. Lloyds commonly referred to this process as "repairing" or "stripping".

In the same month, the FSA in the U.K. fined Aon £5.25 million for failing to take reasonable care to establish and maintain effective systems and controls to counter the risks of bribery and corruption. The firm made various suspicious payments, amounting to approximately US$7 million, to a number of overseas firms and individuals in order to win or retain business. Payments were made to third parties in Bahrain, Bangladesh, Bulgaria, Burma (Myanmar), Indonesia and Vietnam. The firm settled early, otherwise the fine would have been £7.5 million. The FSA praised the company for blowing the whistle on itself.

Corporate governance (risk management and money-laundering, bribery and corruption)—*cont'd*

The month before, Siemens settled with the SEC in the U.S. by agreeing to pay a record US$800 million for making bribe payments totaling US$1.4 billion to various government officials around the world between 2001 and 2007. In connection with this fine, here's a revealing statement, as quoted in the *WSJ* on May 27, 2009: "A spokesman at Siemens . . . said the cost of addressing its own corruption allegations was nearly as much as its total fine of €1.22 billion (US$1.7 billion), including fines to the German government". Siemens managed, however, to secure individual settlements with some former board members as damages for breaching their organizational and supervisory responsibilities.

Daimler, the maker of Mercedes-Benz cars and trucks, agreed in March 2010 to pay fines amounting to US$185 million (US$93.6 million to settle the U.S. Justice Department's criminal charges and US$91.4m to settle the SEC's civil case). The company allegedly had made hundreds of improper payments to government officials in at least 22 countries to win contracts to sell hundreds of millions of dollars worth of vehicles, according to Bloomberg. Two Daimler subsidiaries, based in Russia and Germany, pleaded guilty as part of the settlement.

Conclusions: Talk about being caught between Iraq and a hard place.[28] In some places, it may be difficult to do business without greasing someone's palm. However, as we see from these cases, companies do risk being caught and having to pay large fines and suffer reputational harm. They also have to divert resources to deal with cases when they arise. As usual, analysts need to gauge the risk that their covered companies may be involved in illegal activities. It's an auditor's job to follow the money, but an analyst should still be alert to any warning signs or suspicious activity.

The Siemens comment about the costs of addressing the allegations reminds us of the old saying: "A stitch in time saves nine." In other words, it's usually cheaper to pre-empt a problem than to address it after the event. As with other corporate governance and risk management issues, analysts need to understand whether a company's management is devoting sufficient resources to pre-empt money-laundering or other illegal transactions, and to identify where the weak links might be. Again, this will enable analysts either to assign a premium or discount to valuations, or at least enable them to flag to clients any perceived risks.

Fines have increased dramatically in size in recent years, and look set to keep rising. However, fines aren't the only weapons in a regulator's armory. As we saw in Chapter 1, the Japanese regulator often prefers to ban a company from doing business for a period. They did this

Corporate governance (risk management and money-laundering, bribery and corruption)—*cont'd*

with Citigroup in both 2004 and 2009 for failing to develop adequate controls to detect suspicious transactions such as money laundering.

Analysts should not presume that a country's political agenda is black and white. The *New York Times* identified various international companies doing business in Iran, contrary to U.S. sanctions, that collectively received over US$100 billion in contract payments, grants and other benefits between 2000 and 2009. These included Royal Dutch Shell, Petrobras, Honeywell, Mazda and Daelim Industrial. As the British foreign minister said to M in the Bond film *Quantum of Solace*, "If we refuse to do business with villains, we'd have almost no one to trade with." Whether or not such companies have explicit or implied "get out of jail free" cards, changing political winds might affect their status going forward.

Aside: Of special interest to managers and compliance officers of securities firms is the FINRA case involving Scottrade, a brokerage that offers customers an online securities-trading platform. We see from FINRA's December 2009 list of disciplinary actions that the firm, without admitting or denying the charges, agreed to a fine of US$600,000 for failing to establish an anti-money-laundering program that was adequate for its business model.

Credit rating risks

It's not just equity analysts who can miss the signs. Credit rating agencies have also been criticized for failing to identify crises, such as the Enron collapse and later the subprime debt crisis. They have also been criticized for the inherent conflicts of interest that exist in the way they get paid for their services. (See Chapter 3 for more discussion on the issue regarding conflicts of interest, specifically the example entitled "Paying for credit ratings" at the end of the chapter.)

EXAMPLE

Analyzing risk (credit rating agencies)

Background: During the financial crisis, the three major international rating agencies—Standard & Poor's, Moody's and Fitch—suffered

Analyzing risk (credit rating agencies)—*cont'd*

widespread criticism that their ratings for structured products were too high. The *FT* of November 14, 2008, quoted James Simons, president of Renaissance Technologies, a hedge fund, as saying that the credit rating agencies facilitated the sale of "sows' ears as silk purses" because of their fanciful ratings, and that this lay at the heart of the meltdown. Francesco Guerrera, the *FT*'s U.S. business editor, remarked in the same newspaper on August 20, 2007, how the agencies had collectively been pronounced guilty by some in the financial community:

- guilty of not having warned investors of the impending disaster;
- guilty of failing to police the exotic financing devices being dreamed up by banks and hedge funds; and
- guilty of not acting fast enough once the rout set in.

Details: In July 2009, the U.S.'s largest public pension fund—the California Public Employees' Retirement System (CalPERS)—filed a suit alleging that Standard & Poor's, Moody's and Fitch "made negligent misrepresentation" to the fund, according to the *New York Times*. The suit claimed that the AAA ratings given by the agencies "proved to be wildly inaccurate and unreasonably high" and that the methods used were "seriously flawed in conception and incompetently applied".

Moody's and S&P's were also named as defendants in the Abu Dhabi Commercial Bank versus Morgan Stanley case in New York. The bank, based in the United Arab Emirates, alleged that the rating agencies had issued misleading "investment grade" ratings to a US$5.86 billion structured investment vehicle, previously known as Cheyne Finance, according to the *WSJ* on September 7, 2009. Interestingly, the judge ruled that the agencies could not rely on a constitutional freedom-of-speech defense "where a rating agency has disseminated their ratings to a select group of investors rather than to the public at large".

Earlier in the mispricing risks case study, we also saw how Paramax Capital came unstuck when the CDOs on which they had sold credit defaults swaps to UBS as protection proved to be not as low-risk as their triple-A ratings had suggested.

The problems don't just apply to the U.S. James Rose of Corporate Governance Asia drew to my attention a discussion aired by the Australian Broadcasting Corporation in Australia on July 23, 2007, about investors questioning the value of credit rating agencies that continued to issue relatively high investment-grade ratings on New Zealand's Bridgewater property group, failing to warn investors of its demise. One comment was that Bridgewater highlighted the positive ratings in the selling of its products right up to its collapse. New Zealand

Analyzing risk (credit rating agencies)—*cont'd*

investment analyst Brian Gaynor ended the discussion by arguing generally that companies can highlight to investors one positive credit rating while conveniently ignoring that other agencies might have refused to issue an investment grade rating on the company. He said: "If credit rating organizations aren't prepared to publish negative as well as positive (ratings), then the public can be misled to quite a large extent."

Aside I: My former colleague, Paul Bayliss, drew to my attention an interesting article published in Portfolio.com on November 11, 2008, written by Michael Lewis, author of *Liar's Poker*. In it he describes how an analyst-turned-hedge-fund-manager, Steve Eisman of FrontPoint Partners, was ahead of the curve in identifying underlying problems in the financial system. In attempting to understand how the rating agencies justified turning BBB loans into AAA-rated bonds, he asked a Standard & Poor's representative what would happen to default rates if real estate prices were to fall. The response, that S&P's model for home prices had no ability to accept a negative number, demonstrated the rating agency's assumption that home prices would only keep rising.

Aside II: As if the above conflicts weren't enough, the *FT* exposed on May 21, 2008, how senior executives of Moody's had known early in 2007 that certain triple-A-rated products called "constant proportion debt obligations" (CPDOs) should have been rated up to four notches lower after a coding error was corrected. However, they were downgraded only in January 2008 amid the general market decline. Moody's said they were conducting a thorough review of the matter, and within a couple of months its head of global structured finance had left the firm.

Conclusions: This particular section concerns the identifying by analysts of risks associated with investments. Ultimately, that's down to the skill and judgment of the analyst. The inherent conflicts of interest in the way credit rating agencies have traditionally been paid may have clouded some credit rating analysts' judgment. There have been various developments, at least in the U.S., to address these issues, and these are discussed at the end of Chapter 3 in the example headed "Paying for credit ratings".

Due diligence by investment bankers

It's probably useful also to look at the level of due diligence required by investment bankers who bring companies to market or advise their clients on M&A transactions. The term "due diligence" might generally apply to the process that any analyst undergoes in determining the truth about a company's financial wherewithal and the integrity of its management, and would include all the valuation and risk aspects covered above.

Specifically however, bankers need to undertake their own research or "due diligence" in deal-related situations. (Please also see Chapter 3 for a discussion on sell-side analysts undertaking so-called "pre-deal research" for the banks that are acting as sponsors, underwriters or advisers on the deal.)

CASE STUDY

Due diligence (failures)

Summary: Recent cases in Hong Kong demonstrate how seriously local regulators take the due diligence process that investment banks need to undertake when sponsoring new listings or advising on M&A deals. These involved Deloitte Touche Tohmatsu, ICEA Capital, Core Pacific-Yamaichi Capital, and CSC Asia. We'll look at a couple of these cases below.

Note that Hong Kong operates a dual regulatory system. Listing companies and applicants need to file prospectuses and disclosure documents both with the Hong Kong Stock Exchange (HKEx) and the Securities and Futures Commission (SFC).

Details: Deloitte Touche Tohmatsu, a global accounting firm that also has an investment banking arm, was banned by the HKEx in June 2006 from sponsoring new listings for nine months for its due diligence failures in respect to Codebank, an e-commerce firm that eventually collapsed—not to be confused with *Agent Cody Banks*, a film about a teenage secret agent. Deloitte settled with both the HKEx and the SFC without admitting liability. According to HKEx, as reported in the *SCMP* of June 28, 2006, Deloitte failed to disclose certain overdue and unpaid obligations in Codebank's listing document when it sponsored the firm's public offering in 2001. Eugene Goyne, director of enforcement for the SFC in Hong Kong, said: "The SFC will continue to take tough action against sponsors who fail to meet the required standards and seek to exclude them from the industry for lengthy periods."

In a separate earlier case, ICEA Capital—also without admitting liability—agreed to pay a record HK$30 million to the SFC as settlement for its due diligence failure in the listing of Euro-Asia Agricultural (Holdings), a horticultural firm, in July 2001.[29] According to an article by Enoch Yiu in the *SCMP* of January 28, 2005, this amount was believed to represent ICEA Capital's profit from the deal. Euro-Asia had allegedly

Due diligence (failures)—*cont'd*

inflated its revenue 20 times in the four years before the listing, which the investment bank had evidently failed to disclose. The chairman and founder of Euro-Asia, who in 2001 was judged by *Forbes* to be the second richest man in China, was jailed for 18 years for fraud.

Development: New guidelines for sponsors and compliance advisers became effective in Hong Kong on January 1, 2007, when they were added as an appendix to the SFC's "Fit and Proper Guidelines", which were issued in April 2006.

Conclusions: These cases specifically refer to the due diligence that investment banks have to undertake with respect to the deals they are involved in, whether as sponsors, underwriters or advisers. In situations where the company has not been listed before, the bank's analysts need to be extra diligent in unearthing information. The same principle applies to all types of research analysts. All need to make their best efforts to establish the truth about companies and managements, and then to disclose their findings to their client or clients.

Aside: The reference above to Cody Banks was not as flippant as you might think. Seriously, due diligence on any company, especially one that's not yet listed, may require real detective work. This is the kind of work that risk specialists such as Steve Vickers at FTI-International Risk in Asia and Frank Holder at FTI Consulting in Latin America get involved in. These investigators look beyond what a company officially reports and documents, and try to uncover who really pulls the strings at companies, what the company's reputation is like in the industry, where the company's managers have come from, how well regarded they are, and what political connections and influence they may have. They try to determine the full extent of a company's off-balance-sheet liabilities, and whether there are any regulatory, environmental or social issues that may pose risks in future.

Endnotes

1. From What Portfolio Managers Want from Security Analysts, April 26, 1993.
2. There is some debate as to what extent analysts owe a fiduciary duty to their firms' clients. The standard may not be as high as that which financial advisers are expected to be held to, for example, in terms of having to act in their individual clients' best interests. I would note the argument by the SEC's Elisse B. Walter, as reported in *InvestmentNews* in May 2009, that retail investors at least should not have to distinguish between different types of financial professionals and that they should all be held to a fiduciary standard.

3. Okay, since you ask, they were: TC Pipelines, Minrad International, IPC Holdings, Axsys Technologies, Randgold Resources, Fiberstars, Pharmaxis, Lifetime Brands, American Capital Strategies, Axesstel, TGC Industries, Brigham Exploration, Gasco Energy and Extra Storage Space.

4. Note that auction-rate securities are long-term debt securities, but because the interest rates are periodically reset at auctions, they are often traded as short-term securities.

5. The banks included the usual suspects such as UBS, Citigroup, Merrill Lynch, Wachovia, Bank of America, JP Morgan, Morgan Stanley, Goldman Sachs, Credit Suisse and Deutsche Bank, as well as RBC Capital Markets. RBC Capital Markets is part of Royal Bank of Canada, which is a big global financial institution in its own right. However, so far it seems to have gotten away relatively lightly, at least in this book.

6. The interest on U.S. treasury bills is commonly referred to as the "risk-free rate". However, even this is only risk-free insofar as the risk of default is concerned. Theoretically, the U.S. government can always print more money to pay off its debts, but this itself represents a devaluation risk. Also note that there's always the liquidity risk that there may not be a market for the securities until maturity, and of course the current interest rate will fluctuate with the market. The fact that the life of treasury bills is relatively short-term mitigates these risks to a certain extent, but does not remove them altogether. Following the Greek debt crisis in early 2010, investors will no doubt review their assumptions about sovereign creditworthiness.

7. The Corrigan report was a concerted effort by major players within the global financial industry to identify and address their own problems internally, without the need for overly burdensome regulatory supervision. It recognizes that individual institutions might need to make sacrifices, for example, in terms of increased investment in people and technology and changes to practices, for the sake of the common good and the stability of the markets. See www.crmpolicygroup.org.

8. The banks in the minibond settlement, reached with the HKSFC in July 2009, were: ABN AMRO, Bank of China (Hong Kong), Bank of Communications, Bank of East Asia, Chiyu Banking Corp., Chong Hing Bank, Citic Ka Wah Bank, Dah Sing Bank, Fubon Bank (Hong Kong), Industrial and Commercial Bank of China (Asia), Mevas Bank, Nanyang Commercial Bank, Public Bank (Hong Kong), Shanghai Commercial Bank, Wing Hang Bank and Wing Lung Bank. Note that the SFC had already reached agreements with Sun Hung Kai Financial and KGI Asia, and would later reach an agreement with Grand Cathay Securities.

9. International Risk later became part of FTI Consulting, and was renamed FTI-International Risk.

10. At issue in the Stoneridge versus Scientific Atlanta case in the U.S. was whether investors in companies that have been found guilty of fraud could also sue third-party business partners who had aided and abetted in the fraud, such as suppliers and advisers to those firms. In a close 5-3 vote in January 2008 the Supreme Court decided that investors could not sue third-party business partners. If the vote had gone the other way, the case could have deterred international firms from doing business in the U.S. This prompted some commentators to suspect that the outcome was at least partly motivated by political considerations.

11. For details of the BAE Systems arms scandal, see the national interest sidebar in the corporate governance section later in this chapter.
12. Tobin's q ratio is named after the late James Tobin, a Yale University professor and winner of a Nobel Prize for Economics. The concept of the Tobin tax on forex transactions was also named after him.
13. See *Quarterly Journal of Economics*, Vol. 118, No. 1, pp. 107–155, February 2003, available at http://ssrn.com/abstract=278920.
14. See www.ifc.org.
15. Toyota announced the main recall on January 21, 2010. The president of Toyota issued the public apology on January 31. The company then announced on February 9 a further recall of 437,000 hybrid cars due to faulty brake systems.
16. By Toyota's own estimate its global recall of cars in early 2010 would cost about US$2 billion in warranty costs and lost sales, not taking into account individual and class action lawsuits. By comparison, JP Morgan estimated that the company's one-time recall-related costs could total ¥400 billion (about US$4 billion in round numbers) plus an additional ¥100 billion for settling litigation costs, as reported by the *WSJ* on March 10, 2010. Toyota's share price declined about 20 percent in the two weeks following the announcement of the recall on January 21, 2010, representing about a US$30 billion decline in market value. Meanwhile, comparable auto stocks like Honda and Ford were down only about 5 percent (although Honda had another round of its own recall problems ahead of it, over defective airbags). Transport safety regulators in the U.S. fined Toyota the statutory limit of US$16.4 million in April 2010 for being too slow in disclosing details about its pedal defects. Given that there were two separate defects involving the pedals, a second fine was also being considered.
17. Lee Kha Loon is now Asia Pacific Head of Standards and Financial Market Integrity for the CFA Institute.
18. See www.crmpolicygroup.org.
19. For full details, see www.icahnreport.com.
20. See *Related-Party Transactions: Cautionary Tales for Investors in Asia*, published in January 2009 by Lee Kha Loon of the CFA Institute and a colleague of his at the time, Abe de Ramos.
21. See also the section in Chapter 1 entitled "Catering to socially responsible investors", where we see that Lazard Korea seeks to invest in companies which they think are poorly run, so that they can encourage change and thereby add value.
22. Fortis Insurance (Asia) was formerly known as Pacific Century Insurance (PCI). The newswires reported that in 2007 Pacific Century Regional Development, controlled by PCCW's chairman, sold its controlling stake in PCI to Fortis Insurance (Asia).
23. BAE Systems agreed in February 2010 to pay £30 million in the U.K. for not keeping proper records of payments in respect to a sale of a radar system to Tanzania. At the same time, it agreed to pay US$400 million in the U.S. to settle wider bribery and fraud allegations. The fact that the British settlement did not cover the Saudi Arabian scandal, whereas the American settlement did, prompted a British politician to say that it was "a damning indictment of the political interference by the British government", as cited by Bloomberg.

24. Vivendi included a €550 million provision for the lawsuit in its fourth quarter of 2009, but said the amount of damages it might have to pay "could differ significantly" from this amount, as reported by the *WSJ* on March 2, 2010.

25. The Corrigan report was a concerted effort by major players within the global financial industry to identify and address their own problems internally, without the need for overly burdensome regulatory supervision. It recognized that individual institutions might need to make sacrifices, for example in terms of increased investment in people and technology and changes to practices, for the sake of the common good and the stability of the markets. See www.crmpolicygroup.org.

26. See www.buysiderisk.org.

27. My former colleague, Paul Bayliss, drew to my attention reports suggesting that Madoff's brother was simultaneously both the head of compliance and trading for the firm, which would seem a little conflicting.

28. A senior official in the Coalition Provisional Authority in Iraq and a U.S. contractor pleaded guilty in 2006 to conspiracy, bribery and money laundering. Court papers detail how the contractor bribed officials with cash, cars, watches and plane tickets to secure reconstruction contracts, and arranged for women to provide sexual favors at his Baghdad villa. (Hey, I've got to sell this book somehow!) According to Bloomberg, payments associated with the deals were traced to bank accounts in Iraq, Romania, Switzerland and Amsterdam.

29. This record was broken in June 2008 when the ICEA group was fined an additional HK$38 million by the SFC for breaching compliance rules between 2002 and 2004. Among the charges, the regulator specifically noted a failure to separate ICEA Securities' proprietary trading and ICEA Capital's corporate finance activities on a couple of occasions.

Chapter 3

Independence of Research and Conflicts of Interest

Key points ⫸

- Potential conflicts of interest can occur in many ways. These include potential conflicts between sell-side research analysts and: i) their banking or corporate finance colleagues; ii) the clients for whom they provide research; and iii) the issuers whose securities they recommend.
- Traditionally, there has also been a perceived conflict of interest in the way credit rating agencies have been paid for their services.
- Sell-side research analysts should undertake research coverage for the benefit of their buy-side brokerage clients, and should be independent and unbiased.
- Analysts on the public side of "the Chinese wall" must base their views and conclusions on publicly available information.
- By receiving private or deal-related information or by giving overly favorable views on companies that are banking clients of the bank, an analyst's independence and integrity would be compromised. Bankers should not ask for, and analysts should not promise to deliver, any favorable research on any company.
- Analysts should not help in bankers' solicitations for business. Trilateral meetings between analysts, bankers and current or prospective corporate clients give rise to the appearance of a conflict of interest, and should be avoided. Meetings between corporate clients and analysts may be acceptable if they have been requested by the client, not the banker.
- Apparent or potential conflicts of interest should be managed appropriately. To avoid even the appearance of impropriety, any contact between analysts and bankers or their corporate clients should be managed through the compliance department or a gatekeeper, with records maintained.
- In published research, analysts should certify that their views are independent, and should disclose any interests in or relationships with the subject company.
- Regulators and courts don't even need to understand the complexities in the arguments of analysts' research or in the products being sold; they merely need to catch inconsistencies in the way they are being brokered or promoted.

Summary

The independence of research is an important enough subject to warrant its own chapter. Research analysts are potentially very influential—a good research analyst or a particularly good research report might have the power to move the market. As such, various players might be tempted to apply pressure on analysts to write research that suits their own agenda. These might include banking and corporate finance colleagues (at least for the sell-side research analysts of the so-called bulge bracket firms, that is the major investment banks), sell-side clients, sales/brokers, proprietary traders and the subjects of research reports.

Analysts owe a duty to their client(s). As such, any decision to initiate coverage on a security should be driven by client demand, rather than by the requests of say banking or corporate finance colleagues.

The evident lack of independence was at the crux of the Global Research Analyst Settlements in 2003/04—the result of a campaign originally spearheaded by Eliot Spitzer, attorney general of New York, to uncover and address conflict-of-interest issues in the major investment banks operating in the U.S. In the first round in 2003, a total fine of US$1.4 billion, made up of penalties, disgorgements and other payments, was meted out by the U.S. authorities to 10 major U.S. and global investment banks. The banks also made commitments to change the way they conduct business.

Furthermore, renewed accusations during the subprime-driven credit crisis in 2007 regarding the way credit rating agencies get paid may also have prompted, or at least accelerated, the SEC's approval of NRSRO (nationally recognized statistical rating organizations)[1] status for the first time to an agency that does not get paid by the issuer whose bonds it rates, as well as a review of regulations in both the U.S. and Europe, and even in markets like India (where, incidentally, issuers have had to obtain a credit rating as part of the IPO process).[2]

Separating research and banking

Sell-side securities-research analysts are on the "public" side of the so-called Chinese wall, and cater to their buy-side brokerage clients, for example mutual funds and hedge funds. Investment bankers are on the "private" side, and may be privy to non-public information about their corporate clients. While on the public side of this wall, analysts must base their views and conclusions on publicly available information; they should not let their independence be compromised by receiving private or deal-related information from their colleagues in the banking department.

Buy-side clients, whether institutional or retail, expect sell-side analysts and brokers to act in their (the clients') best interests, rather than in the interests of the investment bank. Apart from any consequences arising from regulatory breaches, it is surely also a matter of commercial common sense—if clients think they are being treated unfairly, they'll take their business elsewhere.

CASE STUDY

Conflicts of interest (global settlements)

Summary: The Global Research Analyst Settlements in 2003 and 2004 proved to be a turning point for the major global investment banks. Settlements were reached between the U.S. Securities and Exchange Commission (SEC), 12 Wall Street firms and two individual analysts. Specific charges brought against the settling firms varied but generally included one or more of the following:

- Inappropriate influence by investment banking over research analysts.
- Inadequate supervision of research and banking departments.
- Issuing research reports that were misleading, exaggerated or unwarranted, and/or that contained opinions for which there was no reasonable basis, and/or that omitted material facts, and/or that omitted warnings about investment risks, and/or that included insufficient disclosure of interests.
- Receiving payments for research without disclosing them.
- Failing to produce all e-mail communications promptly when requested (see the case study in Chapter 4).

In the first and main round in 2003, the institutional parties to the settlement agreed, without admitting or denying the charges, to pay a collective fine totaling US$1.4 billion and to change the way they run their business, promising in effect that any actual or perceived conflicts of interest would be avoided or managed appropriately. Part of the fine was allocated as a distribution to customers, part for investor education and part for the procurement of independent research.

Details: The settling banks were: Bear Stearns; Citigroup (including Salomon Smith Barney); Credit Suisse First Boston; Goldman Sachs; J.P. Morgan; Lehman Brothers; Merrill Lynch; Morgan Stanley; UBS Warburg; Piper Jaffray; Deutsche Bank; and Thomas Weisel Partners. (The first 10 settlements were made in April 2003, with the other two being made in August 2004.) The individual analysts, who also settled in the first round, were Henry Blodget, then head Internet analyst at Merrill Lynch, and Jack Grubman, then head telecom analyst at Citigroup/SSB. Note that since these settlements, Wachovia has also agreed to a settlement with state regulators[3] in respect to conflict-of-interest issues. As with the other banks, Wachovia neither admitted nor denied the allegations.

There's little need to examine all the cases individually, especially since they have been so well documented. Let's just take the employers of the two censured individuals as examples. Citigroup/SSB consented to censure, a total payment of US$400 million and an undertaking to

Conflicts of interest (global settlements)—*cont'd*

ensure future compliance. Merrill Lynch also consented to censure, a total payment of US$200 million and the same undertaking. They had been charged with issuing fraudulent and misleading research, and conflict-of-interest offenses.

The cases of the two individuals, Jack Grubman and Henry Blodget, have also been well documented. In April 2003, following NYSE hearings and related SEC actions, both consented to censure, were barred permanently from the industry and fined: US$15 million and US$4 million, respectively. The charges against them were that they issued fraudulent and misleading research, including views on investment banking clients that were contrary to their privately held views (for example, the infamous "piece of shit" comment in an e-mail from Blodget).

It was a couple of years later, in May 2005, that the NYSE took action against Grubman's supervisors at SSB during the period in question: JH, director of global equity research, and KM, director of US equity research. They both consented to censure, a penalty of US$120,001 each and a 15-month supervisory suspension for failing to supervise Mr. Grubman and preventing him from publishing fraudulent and misleading research. And, as we saw in the case study on co-authorship liability toward the end of Chapter 1, co-authors of research are not immune either. In that case, it was Grubman's co-author of a research report on Winstar Communications who was fined.

Aside I: Separately, the *New York Post* reported on December 22, 2004, that, although UBS had a "buy" on HealthSouth while it provided them with investment-banking services, the analyst covering the stock told institutional investors privately in an e-mail that he "would not own a share" of the company. The analyst resigned from UBS. HealthSouth and its management have been the subject of their own fraud scandals.

Aside II: In addition to the settlements with the regulators, class action lawsuits have also been brought by investors in relation to alleged false and/or misleading research. These can take years to process. For example, a U.S. federal judge awarded class certification in August 2009 to investors who were suing Lehman Brothers, Morgan Stanley and Goldman Sachs for allegedly issuing misleading research on RSL Communications that artificially inflated the stock price in the hope of securing business. All investors who bought RSL common shares between April 30, 1999, and December 29, 2000, would qualify to join the class action.

Conclusions: Analysts must not lose sight of their independent role, and in whose interests they should be acting. Furthermore, it's not just the brokerage firms and lead analysts who risk being censured and fined

Conflicts of interest (global settlements)—*cont'd*

over conflict-of-interest issues; colleagues, team members and supervisors are also personally accountable. The penalties now being meted out to offenders are much more significant than previously.

There's no such thing as a private or an internal e-mail. Any e-mail can find its way to clients, regulators, the courts and the press. If clients learn they are being treated unfairly, they'll take their business elsewhere; if the regulators, the courts and the press find evidence of wrongdoing or immoral behavior, they'll be keen to investigate further to see what other, perhaps more serious, skeletons they can find.

Incidentally, the concept of an analyst privately buying or not buying shares in a company he recommends, as raised by the UBS case, poses its own moral dilemma. Should an analyst practice what he preaches and own the shares he recommends? Some might argue that that's the best endorsement an analyst can give to support a recommendation. However, the counter argument is that an analyst who promotes shares that he owns may be putting his own interests ahead of those of his clients. Ultimately, regulations now invariably demand that analysts disclose whether they have material stakes in the companies covered (see the section on disclosures below).

The subprime-driven credit crisis of 2007–08 also generated conflict issues. The first criminal charges against Wall Street professionals during this period were made against the fund managers of the two Bear Stearns funds that collapsed early on in the crisis. These were similar to those made against Blodget and Grubman after the dotcom crisis, as detailed above.

CASE STUDY

Conflicts of interest (collateralized debt obligations)

Summary: The allegations against the two Bear Stearns managers, RC and MT, were that they had been touting their funds as an "awesome opportunity" at the same time as they were privately telling colleagues about their concerns. Allegedly, one of the fund managers had switched about US$2 million from the fund he was running into another one without disclosing this to investors. They were acquitted in respect to the criminal charges in November 2009, although the SEC said that it would continue with its civil case.

Conflicts of interest (collateralized debt obligations)—*cont'd*

Details: The *American Criminal Law Review* juxtaposes these two paragraphs, taken from the indictments against the two individuals:

- "The subprime market looks pretty damn ugly. If we believe the CDO report is anywhere close to accurate I think we should close the funds now. The reason for this is that if the CDO report is correct then the entire subprime market is toast. If AAA bonds are systematically downgraded then there is simply no way for us to make money—ever."
- "So, from a structural point of view, from an asset point of view, from a surveillance point of view, we're very comfortable with exactly where we are. The structure of the Fund has performed exactly the way it was designed to perform. It is really a matter of whether one believes that careful credit analysis makes a difference, or whether you think this is just one big disaster. And there's no basis for thinking this is one big disaster."

The first paragraph is a cleaned-up version of an e-mail allegedly sent by MT to RC's wife, using his personal e-mail, on April 22, 2007. The second paragraph represents alleged statements made by the two managers to senior Bear Stearns executives two days later.

Separately, a hedge fund in Connecticut called Pursuit Partners sued UBS over their selling of CDO products while allegedly knowing that they were about to be downgraded. According to Reuters commentary on September 10, 2009, the judge heard evidence that Moody's gave UBS a sneak peek into its decision-making process and that UBS used the information to its advantage. The judge cited an e-mail from a UBS employee saying he had "sold more crap to Pursuit", according to the *Wall Street Journal* of September 11–13, 2009. "OK still have this vomit?" was another e-mail quote cited by Bloomberg. Hadn't they learned anything from Henry Blodget? By way of a prejudgment remedy, the judge ordered UBS to set aside a bond of US$35.5 million to cover likely potential damages.

Conclusions: MT and RC were declared not guilty in the criminal case. However, whenever a case goes to trial it really can go either way. The arguments presented still demonstrate that regulators and courts don't necessarily need to understand the complexities of products such as CDOs to ascertain whether fraud is going on; they could just need to catch inconsistencies in the way fund managers, brokers or analysts promote their ideas.

Yet again we see that e-mails, even personal e-mails, can find their way into the public domain.

Please also see the "managing conflicts of interest" case study about Goldman Sachs later in this chapter.

We looked at cases of mis-selling of auction-rate securities (ARS) in Chapter 2. Below we look at allegations regarding research-specific conflicts of interest arising from these cases. At the end of this chapter we also look at conflicts with respect to credit rating agencies (see the example entitled "Paying for credit ratings").

CASE STUDY

Conflicts of interest (auction-rate securities)

Summary: The auction-rate securities settlements in the autumn of 2008 also took into account evidence of conflicted research, according to Andrew Cuomo, the New York attorney general, as quoted in a Reuters article on August 22, 2008.

Details: Merrill Lynch had been accused by the Massachusetts secretary of state, William Galvin, of co-opting its research department to help place the securities with customers. In his testimony to Congress, Galvin spoke about "particularly egregious" actions at Merrill Lynch, which "co-opted its supposedly independent research department to assist in sales efforts geared toward reducing its inventory of ARS", as reported by Securities Industry News on September 29, 2008. Galvin said that Merrill Lynch permitted its sales and trading department, including the ARS desk, to "unduly influence and pressure the research department in a number of ways".

These included an instance in which a managing director in charge of the auction-rate securities desk e-mailed a research analyst stating that "research focusing on the high quality of . . . ALL tax status, auction municipal bonds and student loan-backed bonds . . . would be extremely helpful".

Galvin added that Merrill Lynch sales executives also attempted to manipulate the way analysts responded to questions during sales calls, resulting in misrepresentations. Galvin continued: "Research analysts routinely soft-pedaled significant negative events, and omitted material information which a reasonable investor would need to form an objective opinion as to the suitability of an investment."

In another instance quoted, the research department apparently agreed to retract and rewrite a note after the managing director of the auction desk had complained in an e-mail to the Financial Products Group that the research note may singlehandedly undermine the auction market. The e-mail was apparently written in capital letters.

Conclusions: The previous global settlements case study showed the potential conflicts of interests between analysts on the public side of the Chinese wall and their banking colleagues on the private side.

Conflicts of interest (auction-rate securities)—*cont'd*

This case shows how analysts also need to maintain their independence from other colleagues who are also on the public side, that is the product-origination desks and the sales and traders who deal in those products.

The case also demonstrates, as mentioned frequently elsewhere in this book, how there's no such thing as an internal e-mail; any e-mail can find its way into the public domain.

Inevitably, there will be some clients who are not fazed by conflict-of-interest issues; they are sophisticated enough to understand the issues involved, and to take them into consideration when sifting through brokers' recommendations. Such clients get to know which analysts they trust and which they don't. As mentioned at the beginning of the book, trust has to be earned.

In *The Super Analysts* by Andrew Leeming, Murdoch Murchison of Templeton says: "I think as responsible adults, we have to recognize the way the sell-side makes their money and make sure that as fund managers we fully understand that." The book was published before the Blodget and Grubman cases and it's unclear, to me anyway, whether Murdoch Murchison was referring to the potential conflicts arising from banking relationships or to some brokers' instincts to "churn and burn" to make money, or perhaps both. It doesn't really matter since, either way, the point is that some sophisticated fund managers are prepared to see through all that.

Furthermore, in their research, as reported in the *Financial Times* on May 26, 2006, Lily Fang of INSEAD and Ayako Yasuda of the Wharton School conclude that "the best way to prevent analysts from skewing their research is not by tying their hands with regulation but by linking their rewards to personal reputation".

Managing contacts between analysts and bankers

After the first round of global settlements the then chairman and CEO of the NYSE, Dick Grasso, famously remarked: "This historic settlement establishes a clear bright line—a banker is a banker and an analyst is an analyst. The two shall never cross." Some houses, especially those involved in the global settlements, have tried to bar any communication between analysts in the research departments and bankers in the investment banking, underwriting or corporate finance departments—at least not without an accompanying compliance gatekeeper as a chaperone. However, it seems impractical to do this completely—at least for companies not involved in the global settlements, and a more reasonable approach might be to determine to what extent any meetings are appropriate, to manage them appropriately and to maintain records as an audit trail. After all, if the meetings are deemed appropriate, then there's nothing to hide. Regularly educating the analysts and bankers about these measures also helps in the understanding of the issues involved.

While not suggesting that this next scene would necessarily be an appropriate setting for a meeting, it helps to demonstrate the potential conflicts involved. . . .

Bilateral meetings between analysts and bankers and trilateral meetings between analysts, bankers and corporate clients must inevitably raise at least the appearance of conflicts of interest. However, there should still be some leeway for analysts to meet with banking clients, at the clients' request, provided that the motivation for the meeting is honest. For example, the corporate client may want to discuss with the analyst, strategist or economist their independent views on the sector, market or economy. Provided analysts discuss their already-published views, rather than provide new analyses and recommendations, then their own brokerage clients should not be disadvantaged or prejudiced.

Note that if a bilateral meeting between an analyst and a corporate client is convened at the request of the banker, rather than the client, then this might give rise to at least the appearance of conflict of interest. For example, it could be argued that the banker was merely enrolling the services of the analyst to help the bank solicit new business or to boost the bank's standing in front of the corporate client (with regard to the extent of services they can provide, for example).

There may also be occasions, such as widely attended industry conferences or gala events, which may be of interest to all parties independently. It's difficult to argue that, given the purposes of the gathering, individuals should be barred from attending merely because someone on the other side of the wall had accepted the invitation first.

Gatekeeper approval: It makes sense, however, for any exceptions to be approved by someone within the organization, such as a compliance officer or a gatekeeper, who can be seen to be independent and who has no particular axe to grind. Such intermediaries should be trained to distinguish between what would constitute an appropriate meeting and what wouldn't, and then keep a record of the approvals given. Ultimately, a bad call on their part in approving a meeting that might border on the inappropriate can at least be put down to the poor judgment of a disinterested party, and the independence and integrity of the analyst can be kept intact.

Notwithstanding the above possible exceptions, analysts should remember the golden principle that, while they are on the "public" side of the wall, they should only discuss public information.

Disclosures of interests and relationships

Following the global settlements, regulators around the world have started to review and improve their regulations, specifically with regard to the disclosures that analysts must give in their research reports (and in other research communications, such as those made through television and radio). New regulations were introduced in the U.S. following the Sarbanes–Oxley Act, and since then new consolidated FINRA rules have been put in motion; the European Commission introduced its Market Abuse Directive and Hong Kong's SFC added new research-disclosure requirements to its code of conduct.

Different regulatory regimes around the world may have slightly different requirements, and those involved in the preparation and distribution of research need to ensure that specific regulatory requirements are addressed for the markets in which they publish and market their research. Usually, its legal and compliance department or external legal advisers will help a brokerage firm in drawing up disclosures to suit the requirements. As mentioned in Chapter 1, such advice may be needed to determine the extent to which disclosures are needed for credit research in specific markets. In general, regulations demand that research reports disclose whether the entity producing the research:

- has had an investment banking relationship with the subject company over the recent past (say, the past 12 months);
- expects to receive, or intends to seek, compensation for investment banking services in the near future (say, the next three months);
- has a financial interest in the subject company (say, over 1 percent);
- makes a market in the company's securities;

And whether the analyst writing the research and giving the recommendations:

- received compensation from the subject company in the recent past;
- has a financial interest in the company; or
- is an officer or director of the company.

Normally these disclosures would encompass members of the analyst's household and associates as well. Further disclosures required may include, as in the U.S., histories of recommendations.

CASE STUDY

Conflicts of interest (private trading contrary to recommendations)

Summary: The NASD announced on February 8, 2006, that it had imposed a fine of US$350,000 against Sanford C. Bernstein & Co. LLC of New York and a fine of US$200,000 against CBH, one of the firm's research analysts, for selling shares in Morgan Stanley and Lehman Brothers contrary to his recommendations, thereby violating NASD rules on conflict of interest.

Sanford Bernstein and CBH neither admitted nor denied the charges, but consented to the entry of NASD's findings.

Details: The press release stated that in 2004 Sanford Bernstein—at CBH's request—sought, unsuccessfully, an exemption from the rule prohibiting the sales, arguing that CBH's circumstances constituted a "hardship" and that he should be allowed to sell his holdings.

Thereafter, Sanford Bernstein developed a plan—approved by the firm's legal and compliance department and senior management—which it believed would allow CBH to sell his holdings in Morgan Stanley and Lehman Brothers without violating NASD rules. Under this plan, CBH issued what were purported to be his "final" reports on Morgan Stanley and Lehman on December 23, 2004. Those reports rated the two companies "outperform" (the firm's highest rating) and "market-perform", respectively, and purportedly "terminated" coverage, while indicating that CBH intended to resume coverage in February 2005 (after selling all of his holdings in both companies).

Separately, we see from FINRA's list of actions taken in June 2008 that PK, without admitting or denying the findings, consented to a fine of US$200,000 (although much of this represented the disgorgement of unlawful profits). He was also barred from association with any FINRA member. The charges were that he'd executed securities transactions in a manner inconsistent with his research recommendations and that he'd opened a trading account at another firm without telling either that firm or his own employer about his relationship with the other.

Conclusions: Analysts should obtain research-management and compliance approval for any securities transactions, let alone those for companies

Conflicts of interest (private trading contrary to recommendations)—*cont'd*

they cover. (Some companies may have rules prohibiting analysts from undertaking personal transactions in the securities of companies they cover or that are in a relevant sector.) However, even if individuals believe they have the protection of the company and compliance approval, they can still be held liable if it can be demonstrated that their motivations were not sound or if they were trying to circumvent the rules.

When writing research on companies in their sector, analysts should ensure that full disclosure is made in their research reports.

Analysts terminating coverage need to be confident that they really do wish to terminate coverage and are not using termination as an excuse to side-step potential conflict-of-interest issues.

This case serves once again to remind analysts that it's not just the company that gets penalized for conflict-of-interest breaches—individuals do, too. At US$200,000, personal fines are not token gestures, not to mention the risks to job security and reputation.

Analyst certification: U.S. regulations also demand that analysts certify that the research they have written accurately reflects their own personal views, and that their compensation does not or will not depend on how favorable their recommendations or views are.

CASE STUDY

Analyst certification

Details: In FINRA's round-up of disciplinary actions for July 2009, we see that Wedge Securities in Colorado was fined US$20,000 for failing to include the required analyst certification regarding the analyst's compensation in a research report. Furthermore, the firm also failed to state "in a clear and prominent manner" that the views expressed in the report reflected the analyst's personal views. The firm neither admitted nor denied the findings.

Conclusions: Analysts in the U.S. don't just need to make these statements in their research reports, as required by Regulation Analyst Certification, but they need to make them clearly and prominently. This means that reference should be made on the front cover of the report.

Over-disclosing: The question sometimes arises as to whether it's possible to over-disclose in research. The point that over-disclosing (disclosing more information than is necessary) might mean that the disclosures that really should be highlighted get lost among the red herrings seems reasonable. However, disclosures in themselves are matters of fact (for example, "the analyst holds securities of this company"). Provided of course that the disclosures are factually correct and up-to-date, it's difficult to see how regulators can outlaw over-disclosing.

An analyst needs to be judicious in determining what disclosures really need to be made, paying regard to regulations and common sense (that is, readers' expectations). Ultimately, disclosures are required for securities or investment research, so again it goes back to the definition of "research" (see "The realm of research" in Chapter 1). In other words, disclosures are only really required where an investment implication is made for a security, rather than for mere passing references to a company. Furthermore, the NYSE/NASD joint memo of September 2003 that discusses and interprets rules says: "If a research report does not contain any rating—express or implied—of the subject company's stock, the report is not required to include the ratings distribution information required by the SRO Rules. In addition, if the report does not include either a rating or a price target for the company's stock, the report is not required to include a price chart."

CASE STUDY

Conflicts of interest (disclosures)

Summary: The *Financial Times* reported on July 1, 2006, that the French Court of Appeal had upheld a lower court finding that Morgan Stanley did not disclose its corporate relationships properly, although it overturned the finding that the bank's research was biased. This was in relation to a suit brought against the bank by LVMH, a luxury-goods maker. Both sides evidently claimed victory.

Details: LVMH had contended that a research report written by a Morgan Stanley analyst, CK, was biased against LVMH in favor of Gucci, a rival to LVMH and an investment banking client of Morgan Stanley. Although the bank was cleared of the charge of biased research, it was still found to have caused "moral and material" damage to LVMH.

The *Times* of November 27, 2002, gave some details of the allegedly misleading disclosures in Morgan Stanley's research report, particularly that the bank and LVMH shared a common director and that the bank could become an adviser to LVMH in future. LVMH disputed the validity

Conflicts of interest (disclosures)—*cont'd*

of these disclosures, and claimed that they gave the impression of a closer relationship between the two parties than actually existed.

Separately, various cases in the U.S. demonstrate the importance of providing accurate disclosures. Citigroup was found by the NASD in July 2006 to have failed to include numerous disclosures in technical and quantitative research, and was fined US$350,000. Credit Suisse was found to have used unclear language in its disclosures to describe price-target valuation methods and the risks to those price targets. The firm was fined US$225,000. Morgan Stanley was fined US$200,000 for failing to disclose clearly and prominently the percentage of buy, hold and sell ratings as well as analyst-performance ratings. Deutsche was fined US$950,000 by the NYSE in December 2006 for failing to include disclosures in research reports and for public appearances. This much larger fine was not just for inaccurate and inadequate disclosures but also for supervisory deficiencies—the publishing department had evidently repeatedly warned the research managers that their manual system of data collection was inadequate, but the supervisors failed to address the deficiencies. By November 2007, it was Wachovia's turn to incur the wrath of the U.S. regulators and it consented to a fine of US$300,000 for deficient disclosures. None of these firms either admitted or denied the charges.

Conclusion: Although it is difficult to argue that one can over-disclose, these cases demonstrate that analysts, data managers, research managers and compliance officers need to ensure that disclosures are accurate, up-to-date and not misleading.

By the way, the wider issue of the capture and retrieval of data is a growing concern for many banks and brokerages, as they struggle to keep up with new regulations. Many regulators not only require all these relationships and cross-holdings to be disclosed, but now also require that best execution is achieved for clients (and demonstrated to them) when trades are made.

Writing research on banking clients

Investment banks tend to keep two lists of deal-related names. The first is a list of companies on which the bank imposes research restrictions (often called the "restricted list") and would include names of companies where the bank is currently involved in a deal which has already been made public. Generally, to avoid conflict of interest, new research would not be permitted for such names.

The second, often called the "watch", "gray" or "quiet" list, is a sensitive list of potential deals or new deals pending public announcement, which would represent "private" information. Only personnel who are "over the wall", or at least on the wall, would be privy to this information, including compliance officers, gatekeepers and supervisory analysts.

Analysts who are not over the wall should be able to continue writing their independent research, notwithstanding that their banking colleagues may be in the process of pitching to the subject company in respect to a banking deal. In other words, the integrity of the Chinese walls should be presumed to be intact, at least until there is real risk of conflict of interest (see the Citi case study below).

Where one risk lies, from an appearance perspective at least, is where, for example, an analyst publishes a research report on a company more or less at the same time that the bank announces a financing or advisory arrangement with that company. If the analyst is, for example, initiating coverage with a buy recommendation or upgrading a recommendation to a buy, clients' eyebrows might be raised if, lo and behold, the bank has just won a mandate to act for the company. The analyst could be accused of attempting to "condition the market" prejudicially ahead of the deal with a bullish report on the subject company. Local regulators and takeover panels may also have specific requirements whereby they need to give approval or at least be alerted when a firm wishes to publish research on a company that it is doing or trying to do business with. As such, it's important for all research to be checked before publication to ensure that actual or perceived conflicts of interest are avoided or managed, as appropriate.

Compliance departments should also check these watch lists whenever employees wish to conduct their own personal trading.

CASE STUDY

Conflicts of interest (watch lists)

Details: Morgan Stanley, without admitting or denying the charges, agreed with the SEC to pay a US$10 million settlement in June 2006 for failing to maintain proper procedures to prevent the misuse of insider information. One of the charges, detailed on the SEC's Web site, was that the bank "failed to conduct any Watch List surveillance on hundreds of thousands of employee and employee-related accounts".

Morgan Stanley's list-checking procedures were again in the limelight in 2009, this time in Hong Kong. A former managing director in Morgan Stanley's fixed-income division, DJ, was charged with insider dealing in the shares of CITIC Resources, at a time when he was advising the company about financing for its acquisition of some oilfields in Kazakhstan. During the trial, it was revealed that a compliance officer had indeed approved DJ's purchase of HK$87 million of shares in CITIC Resources. However, as reported by the *FT*, when she looked up the company on the internal watch list she had mistaken the company for its sister, CITIC Pacific. Furthermore, she had asked DJ whether he was working on anything in particular on the company, to which he apparently replied that it was not his daily job and that it was just a "relationship thingy". DJ was convicted of insider trading in September 2009, and jailed for seven years. While not accusing Morgan Stanley of any wrongdoing, the judge did criticize the firm for not having adequate staffing levels in compliance and for poor communications between the compliance department and the fixed-income team.

Conclusions: Irrespective of any potential liability on the part of an employee wanting to make a trade, compliance officers need to check lists carefully and need to ascertain the full extent of the prospective trader's knowledge or involvement in any business activity being undertaken by another part of the group.

A compliance officer might also want to query any instances of trading that seem inconsistent with the employee's normal trading habits.

Aside: The SEC in the U.S. had to tighten its own trading rules for staff following a probe into the stock dealings of two of its own enforcement lawyers. The lawyers allegedly made trades into companies that were, or

Conflicts of interest (watch lists)—*cont'd*

that became, the subjects of SEC investigations. The changes, introduced in May 2009, brought the SEC's procedures up to at least the standard that they expect banks and brokerages to adhere to. These include: a ban for all staff, whatever their position and level of inside knowledge, from trading in the shares of companies under investigation; pre-clearance for all their securities transactions; an authorization by staff for their brokers to supply the SEC with copies of trading statements; and confirmation by staff that they don't have any nonpublic information about the companies they're trading in.

Here's an interesting case to demonstrate various apparent conflicts at work.

CASE STUDY

Conflicts of interest (managing apparent conflicts)

Summary: The principle that apparent conflicts between the public and private sides of investment banks can exist and can be managed was demonstrated clearly in June 2007 when the Australian Federal Court cleared Citigroup of the conflict of interest and insider trading charges brought against the firm more than a year earlier by the local regulator, the Australian Securities and Investments Commission (ASIC).

Details: The *WSJ* of June 29-July 1, 2007, summarized that ASIC had claimed that Citigroup failed in its fiduciary duty when it traded on its own account in the shares of Patrick Corp. while advising Toll Holdings Ltd. on a hostile takeover bid for Patrick. ASIC had also focused on a cigarette break during which a Citi prop trader had been instructed by his boss to cease buying Patrick shares just before the takeover bid was announced. The federal court judge ruled that there hadn't been any insider trading or conflict of interest: i) the contract between Toll and Citigroup specifically excluded a fiduciary duty on the part of Citigroup; and ii) Citigroup had "effective measures" to insulate traders from sensitive information known to the banking division.

Conclusions: The integrity of the Chinese wall can be relied on, provided appropriate measures have been installed. However, the exclusion of a fiduciary

Conflicts of interest (managing apparent conflicts)—*cont'd*

duty in this particular case is a crucial element. With such exclusion, the arrangement between two parties could be deemed to constitute a normal commercial contract where the parties could be presumed to be free to pursue their own interests. Without such exclusion, however, a bank involved in a deal could be held to owe its corporate client a fiduciary duty to act in the client's interests and to achieve the best price for the client.

Banks also always have to be mindful of any potential conflicts of interest with their own brokerage clients. As such, anything that a bank does that might affect the price of a transaction in which it is involved— from trading on its own account or encouraging brokerage clients to trade (including, for example, the publishing of research on the companies) could be deemed to be a conflict of interest between the bank and either its corporate client or its brokerage clients, or both. With all these forces at play, I would again reiterate how important it is for all research to be checked and approved before publication.

The case also again demonstrates that regulators are not omnipotent or infallible, and that they merely seek to stake out the parameters of their powers as widely as possible, just as any political, bureaucratic or commercial organization tries to do.

Aside: Separately, in the January 14, 2008, issue of *The Wall Street Journal*, Mark Maremont and Susanne Craig describe how J.P. Morgan had been accumulating shares in Rural Cellular Corp. at the same time as the bank had been advising Verizon Wireless on its takeover of Rural. A spokesman for J.P. Morgan said that the purchases were on behalf of clients and were totally appropriate. By reviewing stock-ownership and deal records the *WSJ* also identified dozens of other similar situations where investment banks including Citigroup, Credit Suisse, Goldman Sachs, Merrill Lynch and Morgan Stanley appeared to be buying shares in target companies at the same time that their bankers were advising the acquirers. These firms either declined to comment or said they found no problems with the trading. The article also cited the example of the takeover of Centura Banks by Royal Bank of Canada in January 2001. Credit Suisse was apparently the adviser to both firms, and apparently traded in the shares of the target company as well. Credit Suisse declined to comment.

In *Asiamoney's* Brokers Poll 2007, Goldman Sachs was voted as having the least independent research, for the sixth year running. Paul Bernard, managing director of Asia-Pacific investment research for Goldman, commented that the perception that the firm is the region's least independent brokerage was unfair. Goldman analysts around the world adhere to the standards set under the Global Research Analyst Settlements; they personally confirm that their research is independent; they need to convince the investment research committee of their views; and their published research makes clear the distribution of buy, hold and sell ratings, and how many buys, holds and sells have been assigned to companies with which the firm does investment banking business or in which it has investments. Having worked for many years in the same type of environment myself, I appreciate the regime that analysts need to follow.

But the perceptions continued to plague Goldman. On the one hand the company was widely praised in December 2007 for having bucked the trend among global investment banks by generating profits out of the subprime crisis through short-selling collateralized mortgage/debt obligations (CMOs/CDOs). On the other hand the firm was criticized for selling such toxic paper to its clients.

This leads us on a slight detour from the subject of conflicts between research and bankers to look at Goldman's specific conflict issues, which involve alleged misstatements and omissions to clients.

CASE STUDY

Conflicts of interest (managing apparent conflicts)

Background: Lloyd Blankfein, the CEO of Goldman Sachs, conceded that the industry had "let the growth and complexity in new instruments outstrip their economic and social utility as well as the operational capacity to manage them", as reported by the *FT* on September 10, 2009. This echoed a comment by Lord Adair Turner, the chairman of the U.K.'s FSA, that many investment bankers perform a "socially useless activity".

The infamous quote made by Matt Taibbi in *Rolling Stone* magazine in July 2009 that Goldman Sachs is "a great vampire squid wrapped around the face of humanity" graphically represented one prevailing view about the company. (Taibbi apparently went on to apologize for defaming such a beautiful creature as the Vampyroteuthis infernalis.)

Details: Even so, the market was not prepared for what happened on April 16, 2010. The SEC formally charged Goldman Sachs and one of the firm's vice presidents with fraud. The SEC alleged that Goldman Sachs did not disclose to investors that it had allowed one of its major hedge fund clients, Paulson & Co., to heavily influence which mortgage securities to

Conflicts of interest (managing apparent conflicts)—*cont'd*

include in a CDO investment portfolio being marketed to clients, and that Paulson & Co. was shorting the CDOs in a bet that their value would fall. The SEC's enforcement chief, Robert Khuzami, issued this statement: "The product was new and complex but the deception and conflicts are old and simple." Goldman denied the accusations. The firm's share price fell over 12 percent on the day, dragging down other banks with it.

Conclusions: As we saw with the CDO case earlier involving the Bear Stearns fund managers, regulators don't even need to get to the bottom of the complexities involved in the products being sold; they can bring charges for the way they are being sold or presented to clients. The same principle must also apply to research analysts' output, however complicated the research arguments might be. I reiterate again how important it is to make sure disclosures are accurate and up-to-date.

It remains to be seen whether Goldman is successful with its defense and whether the firm has indeed been able to manage these apparent conflicts of interest. It also remains to be seen which other firms are yet to face the music. Ultimately, lawmakers need to determine how useful to society side bets using such derivatives really are and how transparent the information about the trade needs to be, not just to both sides of the trade but also to the wider market.

Aside: Meanwhile, J.P. Morgan and HSBC were the targets of a *New York Post* scoop in April 2010 that also had the potential to disrupt markets, albeit involving commodities rather than securities. A whistleblower named Andrew Maguire, as it happens an ex-Goldman commodities trader, had come forward to spill the beans on how these two banks were able to manipulate the gold and silver markets. Would these allegations have enough weight to tarnish these banks' reputations or would the story be just a conspiracy theory?

Note that regulators have only recently started clamping down on commodities markets. In its first commodities-related market abuse case against an individual, the FSA fined a former broker with Sucden Financial £100,000 in June 2010 for manipulating coffee futures prices. In April 2010, Moore Capital agreed to pay the Commodity Futures Trading Commission (CFTC) US$25 million for attempting to manipulate the platinum and palladium markets, and Morgan Stanley and UBS agreed to pay US$14 million and US$200,000 respectively to settle charges that they had concealed block trades of crude oil. (Interestingly, Morgan Stanley paid US$4.4 million dollars in 2007 to settle allegations that it had charged clients storage fees for metals that they didn't physically own. Nice one.)

Being "over the wall": Sometimes, if allowed, an analyst with specialist knowledge might be asked to be brought over the Chinese wall to help bankers in a particular project. In such situations, the analyst might be exposed to private information and cannot therefore hold himself out to clients as an independent research analyst. He would thus be restricted from writing independent research until the information to which he is privy becomes publicly available or is no longer relevant or price-sensitive.

"Pre-deal" research

In some regulatory regimes the research departments of syndicate banks that are helping a company to raise capital by selling new shares in the market may be able to publish research on those companies ahead of the offering, subject to conditions. Whereas U.S. regulators regard this practice as being unacceptable on the grounds of conflict, some regulators have taken the more relaxed view that any information on a hitherto privately held company can be useful to the market, even if prepared by someone closely associated with the transaction.

In deciding whether to issue so-called pre-deal research, research management needs to be satisfied that the motivation for doing so is to help their buy-side clients in their information-gathering exercise before they make their investment decisions. The research department's motivation in being involved in pre-deal research should not be to help the bankers in their business. Any pre-deal research report should not be regarded as a marketing document for the deal; it should be independent and unbiased. When bankers are soliciting for new business, neither they nor research personnel should make any promises regarding the publishing of research, and should certainly not promise that any such research will be favorable.

By the way, bankers also have to undertake their own due diligence in bringing companies to market or advising their corporate clients in M&A situations. For an example of what can go wrong in this regard, see the case study on ICEA Capital and Deloitte Touche Tohmatsu in Chapter 2.

EXAMPLE

Conflicts of interest (pre-deal research)

Summary: A *Financial Times* article of January 3, 2006, looking at initial public offerings (IPOs) in the U.K. quotes the FSA as saying: "The process in which a company chose its bank only after it had seen some research might encourage issuers to exert pressure on competing banks to produce analysis that was favorable or that justified a higher valuation price."

Details: Specifically, on November 8, 2005, Reuters had reported that the U.K.'s Financial Services Authority (FSA) was looking into the way Inmarsat handled its initial public offering. The article suggested that the company had asked banks to compete for roles in the IPO by coming up with valuations and research before bookrunners were chosen. A later Reuters article, however, of November 22, 2005, reported that Inmarsat was not being investigated.

The *Sunday Times* reported on May 28, 2006, that Permira, Europe's largest private equity group at the time, was preparing a flotation of business-travel firm Hogg Robinson, employing a controversial technique that has been scrutinized by the FSA. The newspaper continued that the firm had hired Lazard and Merrill Lynch to advise on the timing of the float, and planned to appoint several other banks to "prepare research on Hogg Robinson before deciding on the bookrunners".

Conclusion: I would make no prejudgment about any research prepared in these examples. However, I would say that, generally speaking, the so-called beauty-parade bidding process—where allowed—could put pressure on analysts to produce favorable reports on the companies to which their bank was pitching, thereby exposing the analysts and their firms to potential charges of conflict of interest. Analysts need to take care that their independence is not compromised.

Securities of non-U.S. companies can only be offered in the U.S. by being registered under the Securities Act of 1933 (which involves jumping through hoops of fire) or by being exempted from registration. The main exemption mechanism is Rule 144A, a safe harbor permitting the resale of certain restricted securities within the U.S. to qualified institutional buyers (QIBs), sophisticated institutional investors who don't need the same level of protection as retail investors. As resale, these would constitute private placements, that is in the form of global depositary receipts (GDRs), rather than public offerings of new shares from issuers. As such, they represent an indirect way that foreign companies can raise capital in the U.S. The QIBs can usually trade the securities between themselves.

(Rule 144A issues are not to be confused with "Private Investments in Public Equity", or PIPEs, which are private placements targeted more at a smaller number of "accredited", that is high-net-worth, investors through a Regulation D registration exemption mechanism. Investors are restricted from selling the securities on until the securities are registered or the lock-up period has ended.)

Regulation S of the 1933 Act is a safe harbor provision in respect to offers or sales of foreign securities not being listed in the U.S. or being registered under U.S. laws. Under this provision and in the jurisdictions where the practice is allowed, pre-deal (IPO) research can be published for restricted distribution, with distribution specifically restricted from the U.S. and U.S. persons (with similar exclusions normally applying for Canada and Japan at least). As such, capital is not raised at all in the U.S.

Given the potential liability for the company and analysts producing the research, legal guidance should be followed in each case. A special disclaimer and disclosure page should be added upfront, stating the bank's involvement in the deal and which safe harbor provision is being invoked. Restrictions and provisions invariably apply, especially with regard to the distribution of the reports, with the location and level of sophistication of the clients being factors for consideration, as mentioned above. Normally a footer would be added at the bottom of each page stating which markets the report cannot be distributed to. Furthermore, pre-deal research reports would normally be individually numbered as an extra distribution control measure.

As for the content, the analyst should appreciate that he should be looking only at the company and its business, not its securities. Recommendations, valuations and forecasts by the analyst should normally be avoided. However, exceptions could perhaps be made for limited valuations and forecasts, provided they are given for indicative purposes only, and are not presented as implied recommendations for the securities. For example, valuations could be expressed as a range for the whole company, and any forecasts limited to two years. As usual for any independent research, the analysis should be balanced, with risks drawn to readers' attention. As mentioned in Chapter 1, more thorough due diligence than normal would be required because the analyst would not have a history of public records such as stock exchange filings to rely on.

One question I've been asked is to what extent an analyst can have access to the draft prospectus when preparing his pre-deal research report. For regular IPOs the analyst is formerly brought over the wall and made an insider for the time being. Whatever information he receives from the company is usually private information anyway, because the company hasn't been listed and hasn't therefore needed to make any information public. Note that technically speaking it's not really "price-sensitive" information at that stage anyway, since the shares aren't being traded. As such, there shouldn't be any problem whatever information analysts are made privy to, including the draft prospectus. However, steps have to be taken to ensure that the analyst's published research does not contradict anything in the prospectus when that document is eventually published and when the security is priced, because henceforth any material information not published by the company would constitute "price-sensitive" information. It's at that point that the regulator gets concerned, and that's a reason why external lawyers get involved—they vet the research to make sure there is nothing that contradicts the prospectus.

My former colleague, Paul Hedley, cautions though that there may be a higher risk for spinoff situations where the already-listed parent company spins off a subsidiary. Because the parent is already trading, any private information gleaned before the stock is priced and starts trading might actually be "price-sensitive". Nevertheless the same principles still apply.

So, either way, there shouldn't be any problem with the analyst getting access to the draft prospectus (and any other hitherto non-publicly available information), as long as the eventual research is not based on any information that is inconsistent with information contained in the prospectus.

Incidentally, I would also remind readers of the insider trading case in Chapter 1 involving Mark Cuban. We concluded from that case that if you bring someone "over the wall" by sharing inside information with them, you should ensure that they not only agree to keep the information confidential but also agree not to trade on the information. Also, as we saw from the Moore Europe and Dresdner Kleinwort bond-trading cases, traders can no longer rely on the historic practice of trading after being "sounded out" on a potential new deal.

When the blackout period starts ahead of the sale of the securities, and the company fully enters the regulators' purview, then the analyst should not publish anything more on the name. Even passing on factual press commentary on the name could prompt some critics to argue that the analyst was trying to offer biased support for the transaction by, for example, only passing on positive press commentary.

When the blackout is over, up to 40 days after the closing of the offering/settlement date,[4] then regular research can be distributed to clients. This would be billed as a regular initiation, and can include a formal recommendation or rating, a target price and per-share numbers. As a formal initiation there would be no reference to the pre-deal version or to any changes of earnings estimates from that version. The special restricted distribution disclaimer and footer would be replaced by regular disclaimer and research disclosures.

Note that pre-deal research reports are not to be confused with "pump-and-dump" spam e-mails that circulate, often ahead of IPOs. These schemes might promise huge or guaranteed returns, perhaps based on some rumor or information that isn't yet known to the market. Invariably the spammer exhorts the reader to act immediately, otherwise they'll miss this once-in-a-lifetime chance! Such e-mails have no legitimacy, and invariably break securities laws and regulations on multiple counts (that is circulating rumors to manipulate the market prices of securities, trading on inside information, using promissory or exaggerated language, not drawing risks to investors' attention or not having a reasonable basis for views).

Influencing of analysts by issuers

In maintaining their independence, research analysts have to guard against the persuasive influences not only of their banking colleagues but also of the companies they write about. To this end, most developed markets have rules to deter issuers from bribing analysts with cash payments or excessive gifts or entertainment.

CASE STUDY

Conflicts of interest (bribes)

Summary: As widely reported in the press in May and June 2005, an analyst at UBS at the time of the offense was sentenced to two years in prison for accepting a bribe of HK$1 million to publish a favorable stock report on a Hong Kong-listed textile-manufacturing company. The analyst had denied the charge. Three other defendants, including a director of the textile company who had offered the bribe and an ING fund manager who had been bribed to buy and hold the shares, were also sentenced.

However, in September 2006 the analyst's conviction was overturned when the court of appeal determined that recorded evidence from meetings at which he was not present should not have been used against him, and should merely have been regarded as hearsay.

Conclusions: In this case the analyst was eventually cleared. Irrespective of any monetary thresholds for gifts that may be prescribed by regulations and company policies, analysts should be able to detect when they are being compromised. Indeed, the more lavish the gifts offered, the more the analyst should question the reasons why a company would feel the need to present such gifts.

By accepting bribes, analysts risk not only being caught by the regulatory and legal system but, in extreme cases, exposing themselves to blackmail and extortion at the hands of the bribers.

Here's a slightly different situation, but you get the picture.

EXAMPLE

Conflicts of interest (favors)

Summary: In the July 27, 2007, issue of the *FT*, Francesco Guerrera and David Wighton reported interesting findings of research undertaken by James Westphal of University of Michigan and Michael Clement of University of Texas. Between 2001 and 2003 the researchers carried out a study on 1,800 equity analysts and hundreds of company executives in the U.S. They found that executives significantly reduced the chances of analysts downgrading a rating on their company's stock by offering them favors. These favors included introductions to executives at rival firms, career advice, and agreeing to meet with the analysts' clients. In the same issue of the *FT*, Guerrera also noted that Wall Street observers say there is anecdotal evidence that some CEOs and CFOs have begun using coded hand movements to pass on additional financial information to particular analysts.

Conclusion: The Spitzer investigations and the global settlements focused primarily on conflicts between analysts and their banking colleagues. The foregoing case study on bribery demonstrates that there are also serious conflicts of interest between analysts and the companies they write about, and that analysts can still be found liable for giving in to such temptations. This research on favors granted to analysts demonstrates that these conflicts can manifest themselves in more subtle ways as well.

Another subtle form of influence that analysts need to be mindful of is when company executives try to steer them to focus on or ignore particular businesses or particular line items of the P&L, for example during a results presentation. The investor relations officer might try to persuade analysts to ignore the net earnings result this year when valuing the company because of certain unusual factors, and instead concentrate on operating profit or other recurring earnings measures.

EXAMPLE

Conflicts of interest (issuers guiding analysts)

Details: My former colleague Diego Marconato, founder of Asia Technicals, remembers Cisco Systems trying to explain to analysts in April 2001 how the group had to write off US$2.5 billion of excess inventories (in the form of new Internet switching components) as an unlucky once-in-a-hundred-year occurrence, when the company reported its first quarterly loss in its 11 years of trading as a listed company. Diego couldn't help but be amazed that the company was trying to couch the exceptional item in terms other than what it really was—just a bad loss-making business decision that directly affected the bottom line, not an exceptional item to be conveniently explained away as a one-off. According to the *FT* of April 18, 2001, Nikos Theodosopoulos, networking analyst at UBS Warburg, felt the same way: "They made a big bet on continuing high demand, and it didn't pay off."

Separately, Barclays had a tough time convincing the market about its on-going profitability when it reported pre-tax profit of £6.1 billion for 2008, a year when international bank profitability had gone out of style. Simon Nixon of the *WSJ* noted that without one-offs such as a £2.2 billion gain from the Lehman acquisition and gains on the value of its own debt the bank would have reported a loss.

Conclusion: Analysts need to be satisfied in their own minds that whatever earnings measures they focus on are appropriate for that particular company at that particular time. In any case they owe it to their clients to explain their choice of valuation methodology and also to provide valuations based on alternative or more standard methodologies anyway for their consideration.

Another interesting situation is where an analyst covers an issuer and is then hired by that company. At what point during the recruitment process should the analyst put his or her hands up and say, "Sorry, I can no longer cover this company objectively"? It seems reasonable enough to me that a securities firm should not be blamed for something outside its knowledge or control. The onus must surely lie on analysts to recuse themselves once they are in a situation of conflict. The personal challenge for an analyst, of course, is how to tell his current employer that he can't write objectively on an issuer while he's still in negotiations with that company over a job. Perhaps a simple "I am in possession of some confidential information that precludes me from writing about this company at this time" might keep the less-inquisitive among management, compliance and sales at bay. Clearly, once an employee gives his termination notice, to leave either for a competing securities firm or for a covered company, he is conflicted and can no longer write independent securities research. As always, let's see how regulators deal with the problem in practice.

CASE STUDY

Conflicts of interest (employment)

Details: The NASD issued a news release on June 27, 2007, to the effect that it had fined Wells Fargo Securities US$250,000 for failing to disclose an analyst's employment with a covered company, that it had fined its former director of research, DvD, US$40,000 and imposed a supervisory suspension against him for 60 days, and that it had filed a complaint against the analyst involved, JJ. Wells Fargo and DvD consented and settled without either admitting or denying the findings. The complaint concerns the issuing of positive research reports by JJ on Cadence Design Systems while she was in negotiation to join the company and after she had agreed to join the company as vice president of investor relations, but without any disclosure as to her conflicting position. At least one of the reports was published after JJ had already told the director of research and others at Wells Fargo.

Two years earlier, on June 23, 2005, the *Wall Street Journal* reported the timeline of events surrounding JO, a research analyst at HSBC Securities, and his subsequent employment by a covered company, Mittal Steel, as their head of investor relations. JO tells a news service on April 26, 2005, that the company's first quarter was "a very good result in line with expectations". Three days later he finalized plans to join the company, and on May 5 the company announced that it had hired him. The *WSJ* quoted an HSBC spokesman that the bank can't address such possible conflicts of interest "until and unless an employee informs us of his intention to resign".

Separately, entries on the SEC's Web site dated July 16, 2004, and April 26, 2006, give details of a research analyst employed by Connecticut Capital who wrote research on a company, CyberCare, while simultaneously being employed by CyberCare's PR firm. The extremely bullish research report—the rating was "strong buy" with a 12-month target

Conflicts of interest (employment)—*cont'd*

price at US$52 per share, more than four times the price at the time of US$11.25—did not disclose this relationship. Both Connecticut Capital and the analyst consented to the SEC's findings without admitting or denying the allegations. CyberCare entered into its own settlement with the SEC, again without admitting or denying the findings, with respect to charges that it had issued false and misleading press releases regarding non-existent or grossly exaggerated agreements.

Here's an interesting one: From FINRA's round-up of disciplinary actions for April 2009, we see that an analyst was fined US$10,000 and suspended for 12 months for making false, exaggerated, unwarranted or misleading statements. The findings stated that she was also in a "romantic relationship" with an executive of one of her covered companies, without disclosing this fact, thereby creating a conflict of interest. The lady consented to the findings, without admitting or denying them. (I can think of a couple of ways a romantic relationship disclosure could be worded, but I doubt the editors would accept them.)

Conclusions: It may be unreasonable to expect an analyst to disclose every time he or she has a job interview. What does seem clear is that as soon as an analyst has decided to take a job with a covered company, or has any other ongoing relationship with that company (or with an executive of that company), then the analyst needs to make full disclosure in any research report on that company.

Independent research firms

As part of the global settlement in 2003, the research departments of the settling organizations have to be separated from the investment banking departments. In addition, in respect to each security they covered and rated, they had to offer a recommendation or rating from an independent research house. For example, of the US$400 million penalty imposed on Citigroup, US$75 million was designated to be used for the procurement of independent research. This idea was evidently greeted with mixed enthusiasm.

Over the next few years not all the firms managed to comply with the terms of the settlement. For example, Credit Suisse agreed in August 2009 to pay a fine of US$275,000 to FINRA to settle charges that it had failed to make all the required current independent research available to its customers, and then for failing to implement measures to prevent additional failures.

With some relaxation in July 2009 to the terms of the agreement imposed on the settling banks (those that survived the financial crisis at any rate), independent research firms will need to look to their laurels to stay competitive.

Even independent research houses cannot escape charges of conflict of interest, as separate lawsuits in the U.S. brought by Biovail, Overstock and Fairfax Financial against hedge funds and independent research analysts demonstrate. These were initiated even before the stories of abusive short-selling by hedge funds hit the headlines during the subprime crisis in 2007–08, which are detailed in Chapters 1 and 2.

CASE STUDY

Alleged conflicts of interest (independent research firms)

Summary: The *New York Times* of March 26, 2006, reported: "At the heart of Biovail's racketeering lawsuit . . . is an audacious claim: that some of the nation's biggest hedge funds colluded with independent research firms and analysts at big banks to produce purposely misleading research with the sole object of driving down a company's stock price." Similar charges have been made separately by Overstock.com and Fairfax Financial against hedge funds and independent research analysts.

Details: Biovail alleged that Gradient Analytics, an independent research firm, published in June 2003 a negative report on the Canadian pharmaceutical company to its clients, but only after it had given enough time for SAC Capital Advisors, who had originally requested the research, to build up a short position in the company. Biovail contested, by my interpretation, that the issue was not a sour-grapes reaction on their part to a negative recommendation by a research firm and to the short-selling of the stock, but, rather, argued that it was a case of market misconduct

Alleged conflicts of interest (independent research firms)—*cont'd*

whereby the client had persuaded the research firm to write negative research, and that the research firm held up publishing the research more widely to give the client time to build up a short position.

Both Gradient and SAC denied the allegations. Herb Greenberg noted in the Dow Jones News Service on March 30, 2006, that Gradient's research is private and subscription-based, and pointed out that "Gradient discloses clearly to its clients that its reports may have been the result of custom reports that were done for another client".

Both this case and the similar Overstock case took on wider implications when the SEC issued subpoenas to journalists, requesting related communications. The SEC admitted that this request had been extraordinary, and proceeded instead to issue subpoenas directly to Gradient, requesting their communications with reporters. It was then reported by the press on February 15, 2007, that the SEC had declined to bring charges against Gradient, without giving reasons for the decision. However, Biovail said it would not drop its lawsuit against Gradient and SAC.

Then it was the turn of Biovail to be on the receiving end of the SEC's investigations, and this culminated in a March 2008 settlement by Biovail, without admission of guilt, to the tune of US$10 million. The accusations by the SEC and the Ontario Securities Commission against Biovail and four executives related to accounting fraud, specifically that the executives "overstated earnings and hid losses in order to deceive investors and create the appearance of achieving earnings goals". This seemed to vindicate the analysts, and on April 24, 2009, Dow Jones reported that, with little fanfare, Biovail had pared down its claims against SAC Capital and Gradient. Indeed the boot was now on the other foot, with SAC Capital and Gradient filing their separate complaints against Biovail in February 2010 for malicious prosecution.

Separately, an investigative report by Bethany McLean published by *Fortune* on March 19, 2007, and one by Anthony Effinger in the October 2007 issue of *Bloomberg Markets* examine the case of Fairfax Financial, which had accused hedge funds and independent research analysts of attempting to drive its stock price down to benefit short positions. SAC Capital is also a defendant in this case. The defendants denied the accusations.

Aside I: The twists and turns of these cases provide interesting reading, what with Fairfax effectively admitting its own accounting irregularities when it restated earnings to correct five years of errors, and with one of the analysts, SC of MI4 Reconnaissance, being arrested on separate

Alleged conflicts of interest (independent research firms)—*cont'd*

federal charges of embezzling money from a former employer (which SC denied). Another analyst, JG, was dismissed by his employer, Morgan Keegan for "violation of a firm policy relating to his apparent advanced disclosure of his initial research report on Fairfax", as reported by Dow Jones Newswires on September 11, 2008.

Furthermore, Biovail's lawsuit against Gradient and SAC for racketeering was originally filed as a response to its own shareholder lawsuit, in which shareholders claimed they lost money from the share price decline as a result of fraudulent statements made by Biovail. In December 2007, without admitting guilt, Biovail settled this action by agreeing to pay US$138 million. Biovail's woes continued with the firm agreeing to pay US$24.6 million to settle a case involving its heart drug, Cardizem LA.

Aside II: In a similar vein, *Barron's* reported on May 26, 2008, how Lehman Brothers had reacted to criticisms raised by David Einhorn, the founder of Greenlight Capital, a hedge fund, regarding the valuations that Lehman had assigned to the CDOs on its own balance sheet. In a statement, Lehman said that Einhorn "cherry-picks certain specific items from our 10-Q (its quarterly filing to the SEC) and takes them out of context and distorts them to relay a false impression of the firm's financial condition". Greenlight was short Lehman stock at the time. For more on Greenlight and the controversies surrounding short-selling, please see Chapter 2.

Conclusions: In 2006, the *New York Times* said that the Biovail case would either open another chapter of corruption and greed on Wall Street or it would just be a case of another company resorting to lawsuits to silence its critics. Gradient believes they have been vindicated by Biovail's 2008 settlement with U.S. and Canadian regulators, hence their countersuit. One conclusion on this basis would be that companies should think twice about suing analysts or complaining about analysts who criticize them or who have sell ratings on their stocks. (Also see the example in Chapter 2 where a Morgan Stanley analyst was barred by OCBC from attending their analyst briefings.)

Of course there may be times when the company may be justly grieved. As reported by the *WSJ* on March 29, 2008, Andrew Calamari, associate director of the New York office of the SEC, said: "They (short-sellers) are not . . . just shorting a stock to bring it down, but they're shorting because they think it's a bad company. Sometimes they're right;

Alleged conflicts of interest (independent research firms)—*cont'd*

sometimes they're wrong." Analysts need to make sure they have valid reasons whenever they criticize a company or assign a sell rating to their securities.

It remains to be seen how the Overstock and Fairfax cases turn out, and it will be interesting to see who, if anyone, comes out smelling of roses.

Paying for sell-side research

As mentioned in the Introduction, it's not really my place to foresee how the world of securities research will evolve, from a business perspective. However, I have included some comments arguing the case for and against fundamental research in the section on Analyst Surveys in Chapter 1. Furthermore, it may be appropriate to end the chapter on conflicts of interest by looking at developments in the way sell-side research is actually paid for by buy-side clients.

The traditional way of rewarding brokers for their research is the so-called soft-dollar practice of bundling together fees for advice (that is, for the research) with the commissions generated for transactions. The major concerns of these methods include conflict of interest and lack of transparency. Justin Schack, in his comprehensive article entitled "Sins of commissions", published by *Institutional Investor* on December 14, 2005, succinctly describes soft dollars as the "use of customers' money to pay brokers for buying and selling stocks in funds and then using what amount to kickbacks from those commissions to buy everything from analyst reports to data feeds to office furniture".

However, some might think that the use of soft dollars is the most practical compromise despite the drawbacks. As Winston Churchill said about democracy, that it's the worst form of government except for all the others, so too some might describe the use of soft dollars as a form of compensation for brokerage services. After more than a year of consultations and assessment of soft dollar practices, the International Organization of Securities Commissions (IOSCO) concluded in its final report on the subject published in November 2007: "Soft commission arrangements present a challenge to regulators. The arrangements can provide useful benefits to CIS (collective investment scheme) investors, but can be subject to abuses. SC5 (IOSCO's standing committee on collective investments) will continue to monitor regulatory developments related to soft commission arrangements to determine whether general principles can be developed." So there you have it.

During its consultations, IOSCO ascertained that most regulatory regimes permit soft commission arrangements so long as they follow either specific regulations, or, if there are no specific regulations, so long as the arrangements generally follow fiduciary principles (including best execution) and that conflicts are disclosed. For example, the European Commission recommends member states "to identify as soft commissions any economic benefit, other than clearing and execution services, that an asset manager receives in connection with the fund's payment of commissions on transactions that involve the fund's portfolio securities".

In terms of what can be included in soft commission arrangements, most jurisdictions allow the inclusion of goods and services that benefit the client in the investment process. These would include execution as well as research and analysis, but not salaries, travel expenses and office equipment.

Of course the disclosure requirements represent major conditions in themselves. The need to make detailed disclosures means that permitted costs relating to execution and research should be separately identified anyway, and these costs would therefore in effect be unbundled.

Ultimately, the market itself may be the best arbiter. One example to demonstrate this is Japan. Although there is no regulation of soft commission arrangements in this jurisdiction, IOSCO noted that it is common practice that securities companies provide institutional investors with their internal research material free of charge. The following example also shows that, whatever may or may not be happening in the regulatory world, market participants are finding their own commercially-driven solutions.

EXAMPLE

Transparency in paying for research

Summary: As we saw at the beginning of Chapter 1, Anthony Bolton, the famed fund manager from Fidelity, stated in his book that he has always been a proponent of using the best outside research to complement Fidelity's in-house research. So how does Fidelity pay for this outside research?

First we must understand that Fidelity comprises two major companies: Fidelity Management & Research (FMR), which services the US market; and Fidelity International (FIL), which services international clients.

Details: The *Wall Street Journal* of May 19, 2006, reports how Thomas Weisel Partners has agreed with Fidelity (FMR) to separate the fees it

Transparency in paying for research—*cont'd*

charges for research and stock trading, following similar agreements to unbundle fees already made between Fidelity and both Deutsche Bank and Lehman Brothers. Thomas Weisel said Fidelity "will separate payments for research products or services from trading commissions for brokerage services and will pay for research directly in cash, instead of compensating these firms through trading commissions as under soft-dollar practices".

This may have been an attempt on behalf of the parties concerned to keep pace with anticipated changes in the regulatory environment. However, as seems likely from a Greenwich Associates study, as reported by the *FT* on August 9, 2007, the pendulum may now have swung the other way, with some big investors lifting their use of soft dollars as the expected crackdown by regulators failed to materialize. (Following the financial crisis the regulators have had their hands full anyway with other issues, such as bank capital adequacy, securitization, credit rating agencies and executive remuneration.)

Meanwhile, another development involves commission-sharing arrangements (CSAs), whereby a fund manager pays a commission for the execution of a trade, but part of the commission is passed on to the research house (such as an independent or boutique research firm), which provided the investment or trade idea. Fidelity International adopts the CSA route.

Conclusions: The *WSJ* article goes on to report that Thomas Weisel said that if the unbundling trend continues within the industry, it could force commission prices lower, although the firm was unable to predict whether the arrangement would affect future trading volume with Fidelity.

It remains to be seen what changes in regulations may ensue, but evidently Thomas Weisel and Deutsche Bank see practical benefits in agreeing to adapt to the wishes of such an important buy-side client as Fidelity.

There will no doubt always be a demand for good investment ideas, whether these come from bulge-bracket firms or independent research houses, but how these ideas are monetized will continue to be a challenge going forward.

Aside: I just can't resist including a reference to the US$8 million fine that Fidelity in the U.S. paid to the SEC in March 2008 to settle claims that employees accepted lavish gifts and entertainment from brokers in exchange for business. One particular event allegedly included a dwarf-tossing competition. I'm not making this up.

Managers at firms that employ a soft dollar policy need to determine what expenses can be covered by the arrangement and what should not be. As we see from the following case study, it's important for the policy to be clearly disclosed and managed.

CASE STUDY

Transparency in paying for research (inappropriate payments)

Summary: Terra Nova Financial was fined US$400,000 by FINRA in November 2009 for "making more than US$1 million in improper soft dollar payments to or on behalf of five hedge fund managers, without following its own policies to ensure the payments were proper". Three officers of the company, including the chief compliance officer, were suspended and fined a total of US$45,000.

Details: FINRA's press release stated that Terra Nova made the payments without receiving adequate documentation or conducting an adequate review to determine that the payments were for expenses authorized by fund documents. The bulk of the payments were for ill-defined consulting fees and expenses. However, specific items included meals, clothing, auto repairs, parking tickets, limousines, airline tickets and hotel stays, often paid for by credit card. The most notable item was US$13,700 for seven trips by a hedge fund manager to a "gentlemen's club" over a two-week period.

Conclusion: There's too much of this going on, and I'm not having any of it. Seriously, as FINRA's chief of enforcement, Susan Merrill, said in the context of this case: "Broker-dealers that collect soft dollars and make payments for their hedge fund clients must possess and implement adequate procedures that govern their soft dollar practices." Transparency is key.

A similar tug-of-war to that discussed above for equity research is being played out in the world of credit rating agencies. Apart from perhaps some sort of government control or subsidy, the two free-market ways of paying for credit rating agencies' services boil down to either the "issuer pays" or the "investor pays" model. In recent times at least, it has been the issuer who has paid, and as we saw at the end of the risk section in Chapter 2 (see the example on Bridgewater property group), there has been an evident conflict of interest in this method. However, an "investor pays" model is not without its flaws either since this might result in an elitist system where only institutional investors might be able to afford the research. At least with the "issuer pays" model, all investors can get access to the ratings for free. New developments and measures at least look like they will increase competition and disclosure, which can only be good for investors.

EXAMPLE

Paying for credit ratings

Background: *Barron's* in the U.S. published a comprehensive article about credit rating agencies on December 24, 2007, written by Jonathan R. Laing and entitled "Failing Grade". The article identified the various issues involved and suggested solutions. One of the ideas offered was that the way agencies get paid should change. Traditionally agencies get paid by the issuers, and one complaint has been that the issuers will only commission the agencies to start with if the rating will be positive. Barron's cites former Clinton secretary of labor, Robert Reich, who wrote in his blog that the system is tantamount to movie studios hiring critics to review their films and paying them only "if their reviews are positive enough to get lots of people to see the movie". The article also referred to a certain rating service called Egan-Jones that had been trying for a decade to win official agency status. The interesting point to note about this firm is that it does not get paid by the issuer whose bonds it rates, but by institutional investors.

The *WSJ* of June 4, 2008, quoted the former president and chief operating officer of Moody's who acknowledged that "what the market doesn't know is who's seen certain transactions but wasn't allowed to rate those deals". In another startling revelation, Elliot Blair Smith in his Bloomberg article of September 24, 2008, quotes a former Standard & Poor's managing director saying that S&P's executive committee had ordered him to grade a real estate investment that he'd never reviewed. The rater stated that relying on a competitor's analysis was one of a series of shortcuts that undermined credit grades issued by both S&P's and Moody's.

The *WSJ* of October 24–26, 2008, reported how internal documents and e-mails released at a House of Representatives hearing showed

Paying for credit ratings—*cont'd*

how far Moody's and Standard & Poor's went to accommodate bond issuers that generated giant fees for the two firms. Executives were torn between maintaining the integrity of the ratings and easing standards in an effort to win more business. The infamous comment by one Standard & Poor's analyst that a deal could be structured by cows and they would still rate it says it all.

In Europe too, regulators evidently appreciated the need for change, as noted by Gillian Tett reporting for the *FT* from the World Economic Forum in Davos, Switzerland, in January 2008. Charlie McCreevy, European Union financial commissioner, said, ". . . we have put them [credit rating agencies] on watch that things cannot stay the same". Similarly, Malcolm Knight, the head of the Bank for International Settlements, remarked: "The whole question of the role of ratings in the regulatory system does have to be looked at."

The example relating to New Zealand's Bridgewater property group, detailed in Chapter 2, also demonstrates how global the problem had become.

Developments: In May 2008, IOSCO published various amendments to its Code of Conduct for Credit Rating Agencies. Note that IOSCO does not have statutory authority in any one market or over any particular credit rating agency. However, it does exert an influence on all its members, which include the main securities regulators around the world. Among the amendments were recommendations to:

- Encourage the differentiation between ratings for structured products and those of regular bonds.
- Discourage "ratings shopping" by issuers for credit ratings.
- Ensure appropriateness and transparency in methodology.

In the U.S., Egan-Jones was approved as a nationally recognized statistical rating organization (NRSRO) at the end of 2007. It was the first agency to be approved by the SEC as an NRSRO in the U.S. that does not get paid by the issuer whose bonds it rates, but by investors who subscribe to its services.

The SEC announced in July 2008 the findings of their investigation into Fitch, Moody's and Standard & Poor's. As reported by Paul Davies, Joanna Chung and Gillian Tett in the *FT*, the SEC chairman, Christopher Cox, said: "We've uncovered serious shortcomings at these firms, including a lack of disclosure to investors and the

Paying for credit ratings—*cont'd*

public, a lack of policies and procedures to manage the rating process and insufficient attention to conflicts of interest." Note that a month earlier the New York attorney general, Andrew Cuomo, had reached a settlement with these three firms under which they would get paid for their review even if their ratings weren't eventually used by the issuers. They would also need to disclose the fees that they are paid for nonprime-mortgage-backed securities. The SEC announced measures in December 2008 that would "ensure that firms provide more meaningful ratings and greater disclosure to investors". However, one criticism that was not addressed was the fact that the need to use credit ratings is hard-wired into, that is mandated by, securities regulations. The SEC went some way to address this concern when it announced in September 2009 that it would eliminate references in "certain SEC rules and forms".

Meanwhile in Europe, German Chancellor Angela Merkel called for the creation of a European credit rating agency to challenge the dominance of the U.S. agencies. The European Commission announced in November 2008 that it would be formally regulating credit rating agencies. The commission's aims, as reported by *Newsweek*, were to:

- Ensure that credit rating agencies avoid conflicts of interest in the rating process or at least manage them adequately.
- Improve the quality of the methodologies used by credit rating agencies and the quality of ratings.
- Increase transparency by setting disclosure obligations for credit rating agencies.
- Ensure an efficient registration and surveillance framework, avoiding 'forum shopping' and regulatory arbitrage between EU jurisdictions.

Conclusions: The issue is evidently a global one, and as such really needs a globally applicable solution, perhaps resulting in more involvement with IOSCO.

The new measures and new competition will hopefully go some way to address the concerns regarding conflicts of interest, at least in the U.S. and Europe. It remains to be seen what measures are adopted elsewhere in the world, and whether the markets are happy with the arrangements.

In defense of rating agencies, Vickie Tillman, executive vice-president of Standard & Poor's in New York, says in her letter to the

---

Paying for credit ratings—*cont'd*

FT of June 20, 2008: "The acid test of how effectively a ratings firm manages potential conflicts, of course, remains its track record—that is, the historic correlation between ratings and defaults." S&P's later introduced 27 internal practical steps to strengthen its rating process, including the in-house credit analyst certification program mentioned in the continuing education section in Chapter 1 and the setting up of a risk assessment oversight committee, as reported by Rebecca Knight in the *FT* on January 4, 2010.

Endnotes

1. Following the passing of the Credit Agency Reform Act in the U.S. in 2006, the SEC introduced in June 2007 an oversight system for credit rating agencies. These now need to be formally registered as "nationally recognized statistical rating organizations" rather than being passively recognized as such through so-called "No-Action Letters" issued by the SEC, as had been the case since 1975.
2. See Securities and Exchange Board of India (Disclosure and Investor Protection) Guidelines, 2000.
3. See NASAA.org press release of July 5, 2006.
4. In the U.S., where pre-deal research is not permitted, FINRA proposed in October 2008 that the post-IPO blackout period for FINRA-registered broker-dealers involved in a deal should be reduced from 40 days to 10 days, and that for secondary offerings the blackout period, previously 10 days, should be eliminated altogether.

Chapter 4

Non-research: E-mails, Blogs and Internal Communications

Key points ⫸

- If an analyst's motivation for selectively distributing a supposed "non-research" e-mail on a rated or unrated stock is to encourage trading in the name, then the communication could be deemed to be new research, and the analyst could be accused of treating clients unfairly. If the firm's prop traders use the information to trade in the counter ahead of the client base, charges of front-running could be made.
- Thus, the distribution of supposed non-research e-mails represents a risk for analysts and the research firm, and should therefore also be subject to an approval process. It need not be as rigorous a process as for research, provided that the professionals involved are trained to distinguish between research and non-research.
- Research is generally defined by its content rather than by the person who prepares or distributes it. So sales and traders also need to ensure that their own communications do not constitute new research.
- In practice, there's no such thing as an "internal-use-only" e-mail; any private or confidential e-mail can find its way to clients, the regulators, the courts or the press.

To recap, it is best practice that material that is classified as "research" should be subjected to an approval process before being made available to all clients simultaneously (that is, by being published through the firm's formal publishing system). Indeed, research that is published by a member of FINRA, the U.S. self-regulatory organization, must be approved by a qualified research principal or supervisory analyst. This means that it must be published before being presented at an internal sales/traders meeting, to avoid potential risks of front-running.

Analysts can come to their own conclusion as to whether or not their words constitute "research" by asking themselves: "Is what I am writing commercial or value-added, and do I expect sales to be able to use the information to encourage clients to trade in the name? Is this the kind of information that would be useful to all clients who may be interested in this company, not just my focus clients?" If the answer to either question is "Yes", then the analyst should really publish the note as a research report with a formal investment conclusion, rather than merely distribute the material by e-mail to a limited number of recipients.

Non-research communications, including market letters, sales literature, media appearances and e-mail commentaries, must still be subject to an approval process, but not necessarily by a research principal or supervisory analyst. This is a bit of a catch-22 since if the supposed "non-research" is distributed but is then found to have research characteristics, it should probably have been reviewed by a research principal. This is why it's important for analysts (and sales and traders for that matter) to appreciate what constitutes "research". Understanding the distinction between research and non-research has repercussions for analysts in the way they communicate—whether with external clients or internal clients (including cash sales, prop traders and the structured products team) and by whatever method (whether through formal publications, e-mail correspondence, faxes, blogs, postings on networking sites,[1] morning sales meetings, phone calls, one-on-one meetings, road shows, conferences or mass-media appearances).

CASE STUDY

Approval of e-mail and media appearances

Summary: A NYSE Hearing Board decision in July 2006 gives details of violations by Daiwa Securities America Inc. The charges included failing to review or approve employees' radio or television appearances; failing to review or approve market-research letters sent to customers by e-mail and facsimile; and failing to retain electronic communications. Without admitting or denying guilt, the company consented to censure and a US$250,000 fine.

Background: Although the NYSE requires all research to be approved by a supervisory analyst, other communications with the public need merely be approved by a "member, allied member, supervisory analyst or qualified person". A NYSE memo of January 1998 introduced rules regarding supervision and review of communications with the public, with specific reference to e-mail and facsimiles. In it, the NYSE expressed its belief that "each member and member organization should have the flexibility to adopt and implement its own supervisory procedures relating to communications with the public based on the firm's structure, the nature and size of its business, and its customer base, rather than having a mandated pre-review requirement of all communications". The memo also made clear that procedures for review of communications (other than research) need only provide for "reasonable supervision for each registered person", and that, in conducting reviews, members and member organizations may use "reasonable sampling techniques". Furthermore, as we saw from endnote 1, FINRA has also now introduced guidelines on blogs and postings to networking sites.

Conclusion: Non-research communication with customers or the public, including via e-mail, fax and networking sites, is still subject to an approval process, albeit one that is not as onerous as for research.

Approval of e-mail and media appearances—*cont'd*

Note that media appearances should also be treated with care. An analyst who gives recommendations on TV may still be regarded as airing "research", and would still therefore be obliged to disclose shareholdings and relationships.

Aside: It's not just the person giving the interview who needs to be careful, but also colleagues in the background. The Seven TV Network in Australia received complaints about a TV broadcast in February 2010 that showed a Macquarie Private Wealth representative giving an interview about interest rates, while in the background a colleague was viewing pictures of a topless model. He was keeping abreast of latest developments, don't tell me—just like the SEC officials in the U.S. who were caught viewing porn on their government computers, as reported by the *Washington Times* in February 2010.

Objective commentary on non-rated companies

There is wide scope, in my view, for both analysts and sales/traders to write objective commentary or reportage on unrated (or, of course, rated) companies that do not fall under "research" definitions and restrictions. To what extent analysts should spend resources writing objective commentary on a company that they don't officially rate or cover, and whether the commentary is published formally to all clients or distributed selectively via e-mail (see below), would be a matter for research management to decide, bearing in mind the usefulness to clients and the rules on "research".

Where analysts submit for e-mail distribution material on unrated companies which they regard as "non-research" commentary, it is important to determine what their motivation is for doing this. There may be a good reason for commenting on non-rated companies such as competitors, suppliers and customers of covered companies or within the covered sector; for example, for comparison purposes or to provide data points during the results-reporting season. However, if the motivation is to steer traders and sales to trade in the specific name, then this could give rise to accusations of front-running or unfair treatment of clients. These charges might have even more substance if the analyst were subsequently to publish the comment as a formal research report for general distribution.

To avoid triggering research criteria (the need for disclosures, fair distribution and so on), commentary on non-rated companies should reflect publicly available information, with sources given, and should be objective and factual. If the analyst covers the industry anyway, he would be able to include his published views on the industry when providing commentary on non-rated stocks.

I believe that such "non-research" commentary on non-rated companies can include facts, news, earnings results and even rumors, provided that analysts source the rumor as being publicly available information and give the respective parties a chance to represent themselves (using such phrases as "Mr. X declined to comment/was not available for comment", for example). A broad and brief objective comment about the news or results should also be acceptable, provided the analyst doesn't indicate any new investment view or recommendations. In other words, any knee-jerk reactions or broad-brush conclusions the analyst may reach when commenting on the news should relate to the company, its business and the industry it's in, rather than to the security and its valuation.

Price and valuation: I would argue that sales targets published by the subject company itself and consensus earnings forecasts can be given, provided they are publicly available. (Analysts should have permission from the data vendor to provide the forecasts, and acknowledge them as the source of the information.) I would further suggest that valuations can be shown based on these forecasts, and that these can be set against other publicly available valuations, such as those of other comparable companies in the market or sector. Again, it should be made clear what prices and whose published estimates the comparative valuations are based on (and these can include the brokerage's own for any of the companies being compared that they formally rate or cover). Investors can see for themselves whether the valuations are comparatively low or high, so the writer need not say explicitly that the stock is comparatively "cheap" or "expensive". It could be argued that saying something is "cheap" does not necessarily mean "good value", but there seems little point in debating semantics with the regulators if they suspect you're steering investors toward an investment decision. It may be better not to arouse the regulators' interest to start with.

One of the general rules for "research" is that analysts should always identify whose views, estimates and forecasts are being used, including their own, but for non-rated companies the commentary should be seen to be objective and factual. So the analyst should attribute the information (to management or the press, for example) or make clear what measurable assumptions are being used (for example, a P/E assuming annualization of first-half results). For non-rated or non-covered companies, analysts should avoid subjective indicators such as "we believe", "we expect" and "in our view", at least with respect to comments relating to the security's price or value as an investment, if not in respect to the company's business or general industry trends.

It is especially important to avoid giving opinions as to what extent a non-covered stock's current price or valuation or discount to peers' or its own historic valuations is justified or appropriate, or to what extent any company or consensus targets are achievable. There may be positive and negative factors to a company's business, but it's the assessment as to what extent all these factors and risks are priced into the security that, in my mind, is the crucial step that takes objective/factual/measurable commentary or reportage over into the realm of research. As with any purchase, whatever the pros and cons of the item, it's the extent to which you think the price is worth paying that will ultimately determine your purchasing or investment decision. After all, as we saw in the example on media commentators in the "Realm of research" section in Chapter 1, newspaper and wire reporters and commentators are generally not subject to securities regulations, provided they don't offer investment advice on specific securities. (Thomson Financial demonstrates how factual and objective the whole results-reporting exercise can be by using computers to generate results stories.)[2]

I would add that the risk that the communication might constitute research inevitably increases when reference is made to the security's price and valuation. Some might argue, for example, that by not referring to the price or value at all, one cannot be seen to be giving sufficient information on which to base an investment decision: after all, you wouldn't buy a car without knowing the price. So, whereas analysts always need to give the price of securities on which any recommendations or valuations are based, I would suggest the price does not need to be quoted in the case of non-research commentary when not giving recommendations or valuations.

Analysts should be able to alert readers to volatile activity in the market or possible short-term trading opportunities provided they do so in an objective way (saying, for example, "Short-term traders might be interested in the recent trading activity of XYZ Ltd.", rather than "We think XYZ Ltd. should be bought/sold").

E-mails

Again I would reiterate that analysts need to appreciate fully the difference between what needs to be published to clients fairly ("research", subject to appropriate approval processes) and what can be distributed selectively by e-mail, for example ("non-research"). Material that is deemed not to be research, whether on rated or non-rated companies, need not be published fairly to all clients, and could perhaps be distributed selectively to individual clients.

I would argue that in selective-distribution, non-research e-mails (whether on rated or unrated companies), analysts can again include facts and earnings results; price alerts; reminders of their already-published views for the industry and for rated securities, including recommendations, target prices, estimates and valuations; and unconfirmed reports (provided they give the publicly available source of the rumor and make clear that it is unconfirmed information), as well as broad and brief commentary on the news or results. Analysts should not, of course, include unpublished, price-sensitive information in any commentary (whether the material is classified as research or non-research, and whether it is on rated or non-rated securities).

The following case again demonstrates the dangers of distributing research as e-mail commentary, and again demonstrates that it is the content that is important in determining whether or not material constitutes research, rather than the official title of the person preparing and distributing the material.

CASE STUDY

E-mails as research

Summary: On the NYSE Web site, we see that in January 2005 PCH, a sales representative with Smith Barney (which became part of Citigroup before being handed on to Morgan Stanley), consented to censure, a nine-week suspension and a US$40,000 fine for sending out an e-mail containing inaccurate and misleading information on a company under the title "Short ideas in Apparel Names". PCH sent the e-mail to two clients and other salesmen, one of whom forwarded the e-mail to about 13 other clients.

There was evidently a misperception in the market that the analyst covering the sector had downgraded the stock, although the analyst didn't even cover the stock. The stock price declined as a consequence, thereby attracting the regulator's attention.

Citigroup also consented to a censure and a fine (US$350,000) for failing to train and supervise its employees in the management of appropriate e-mail communication.

Conclusion: As was also evident from the Jack Grubman and Henry Blodget cases, there's no such thing as an internal or restricted-distribution e-mail. Any e-mail can find its way to the press, to regulators and to the courts, as well as to clients.

So analysts, sales and traders must follow the same standards whenever they communicate, whether externally or internally, in print, by e-mail or on air. It is also important that appropriate approval is secured before publishing or distributing any comments, whether internally or externally.

Also, see again the example in Chapter 1 where a semiconductor equipment analyst resigned from Morgan Stanley after letting a select group of clients know by e-mail that he had picked up some information on a stock and thus had "greater conviction" on his overweight position.

There doesn't necessarily even have to be an active investment or trade recommendation for an e-mail to constitute "research".

An analyst once asked me for approval for an e-mail commentary on an Indian oil company in his coverage universe. His draft e-mail showed detailed analysis of his new estimates of the subsidy-sharing burden that the company would have to bear. However, he argued that these would be offset by refining margins that were higher than previously expected following a major hurricane in the Gulf of Mexico. As a result, he concluded that he would not be changing his earnings forecasts for the company, and therefore presumed this could be distributed by e-mail as "non-research". However, I concluded that even though the net result of his analysis was neutral, his analysis still constituted "research" and, as such, should be published to all clients fairly. After all, following his analysis, it was only coincidental that the net impact on his forecasts was neutral; it could have been positive or negative, thereby prompting changes of forecasts. And even if there were no changes to the formal recommendation or estimates, there may still have been a shift in perceived risk, prompting some clients at the margin to buy or sell who might otherwise not have done so. Ultimately, if investors ask an analyst what they should do on the back of some information, and the analyst gives reasons why they should do nothing, this would still likely constitute "analysis and sufficient information on which to base an investment decision".

Following this logic, analysts should always avoid ending a non-research communication by saying that they maintain or reiterate their rating, lest a regulator regards this as some kind of investment conclusion to the foregoing analysis—which may take the comment into the realm of research. If analysts do feel obliged to refer to the latest published rating or recommendation in a non-research note, then they should include it for reference at the beginning of the note rather than as a conclusion at the end.

If analysts send e-mails to a limited number of recipients as "non-research" commentary, they should not then publish it later to clients as a "research" report, unless it has been substantively built-on, otherwise they might be conceding that the original e-mail was "research" after all and should have been published first.

The long and short of it is that it's safer from a compliance perspective for analysts to publish their comments and views formally to all clients fairly (that is, simultaneously) through the publishing system than to send e-mails to selected clients.[3] From a commercial perspective, however, research management might prefer to try to limit formal publishing to proper value-added "research", so as not to dilute the value of the product with lower-value market commentary.

Retention of electronic communications: Research firms should also be aware of any local requirements to retain their electronic communications. For example, firms subject to U.S. regulations are required to keep both internal and external electronic communications, whether classified as research or non-research, for three years. As the following case study clearly illustrates, substantial fines have been meted out for failing to retain electronic communications. Note that, although in practice it would probably fall to the operations and IT departments to make sure the firm's obligations are met, analysts must remember that their own communications are recorded and retained for future access by internal compliance/auditors and external regulators.

CASE STUDY

Retention of e-mails

Summary: In Chapter 1, we saw how Banc of America Securities was fined US$10 million by the SEC in 2004 for failing to produce documents and e-mails promptly with respect to investigations about improper securities trading (and then was fined US$26 million in 2007 for the actual trading offenses). Then we see the newswires reporting on September 28, 2007, that Morgan Stanley had agreed to pay US$12.5 million to settle charges that it had erroneously told arbitration claimants and regulators that e-mails they sought were lost in the September 11, 2001, terrorist attacks. The payment comprised a US$3 million fine and US$9.5 fund to pay arbitration claims. It was just over a year earlier, on May 10, 2006, that Morgan Stanley had consented to operational deficiencies and supervisory violations concerning the production of e-mail records in connection with the NYSE's research-analyst conflict-of-interest investigation. On that occasion the firm consented to censure and a payment of US$2.5 million. This was part of a wider payment of US$15 million, including payments for related SEC and NASD actions. In neither the 2006 nor 2007 cases did Morgan Stanley admit or deny guilt.

Retention of e-mails—*cont'd*

Details: In the 2007 case, Morgan Stanley had claimed that the destruction of e-mail servers at the World Trade Center had resulted in the loss of all pre-9/11 e-mail. Apparently the firm had subsequently managed to restore millions of messages from back-up tapes stored elsewhere, but then Morgan Stanley Dean Witter destroyed many of these messages by overwriting tapes and allowing employees to permanently delete e-mails. According to Dow Jones, Morgan Stanley had even told one Kansas City investor that her files had been destroyed in the attacks, even though she hadn't opened her account until October 2001. The firm blamed a "simple and honest mistake" in that particular situation, apologized and agreed to settle. In the 2006 case Morgan Stanley failed to produce tens of thousands of e-mails. It also failed to produce e-mails promptly because it delayed loading millions of e-mails into its searchable archive database, and destroyed thousands of e-mails by overwriting them.

Separately, HSBC Securities consented to censure by the NYSE and a US$500,000 fine in December 2004 for failing to preserve electronic communications, and for not promptly reporting the violation. Piper Jaffray agreed to pay FINRA a fine of US$700,000 in May 2010 for similar offenses.

Conclusion: With fines of this magnitude being levied, I'm sure firms will be keen to ensure their e-mails are retained, and that they are retained in an easily retrievable and searchable format. Analysts therefore need to know that their e-mail communications are on record and can be used as evidence against them. Moreover, with modern technology, needles can be found in haystacks—a specific e-mail can be searched for and found in a batch of millions.

"Internal Use Only"

Note that marking an e-mail to sales as "Internal Use Only" does not really provide any protection for analysts (or for economists for that matter, as AX of Morgan Stanley found out after the leaking of an internal e-mail, in which he expressed personal views about Singapore, which, he conceded, were not appropriate for public consumption, according to the *WSJ* of October 5, 2006). Not only do regulators and other authorities have far-reaching powers to gain access to internal correspondence, but saying that something should not be sent to clients could arouse a degree of interest that may not be warranted, rather like saying, "Do not peep through this hole!"

If an analyst's e-mail provides sufficient information for the recipient to make an investment decision, then it would probably be deemed to constitute "research" and, as such, should be published to all clients through the formal publishing system. If it's not deemed to be "research", then it should be able to be distributed to anyone, and not be withheld from clients. As a general rule, anything from an analyst that is too sensitive for clients is probably also too sensitive for the sales department, which after all represents the client base.

Endnotes

1. FINRA in the U.S. introduced guidelines in January 2010 to help broker-dealers deal with blogs and communications on social networking sites such as Facebook, Twitter and LinkedIn. Ultimately, if the comments constitute research, then disclosures, supervision, record-keeping and so on would be required.
2. See the *Financial Times* of August 18 and 19, 2006.
3. As mentioned in Chapter 1, it may be acceptable for firms to provide different research products and services to clients of different classes, provided all clients within each class are treated equally and provided the firm discloses its research distribution policy to all clients.

Chapter 5

General Writing, Editing and Publishing Considerations

Key points IIII➡

- Analysts need to stand out from the crowd by grabbing readers' attention. Summarizing their messages in titles, key points, bullets and/or executive summaries, and having key forecasts and data consistently positioned, must surely help readers: these may be the only comments some readers will have time to read.
- Actionable recommendations should be unambiguous and highly visible. Analysts should make clear why their comments are relevant to their covered companies, market or sector.
- Dedicated readers may understand industry jargon and abbreviations, but it will be difficult for analysts to expand their readership to a wider audience, unless their writing is clear and self-explanatory. They should not presume prior knowledge among readers.
- Analysts should not make false promises. They should distinguish whether a comment or view is attributable to the subject company or to a third party; whether it reflects their own view or analysis; or whether it is merely a suggestion of a natural consequence or likelihood.
- Analysts should be transparent in their communications. They should not be afraid to concede that they got a call wrong, and should not try to cover up their mistakes. If analysts give clients what they want, and earn their trust, they will surely be rewarded accordingly.
- Analysts do not operate under a free-speech environment. Not only are they subject to securities regulations and intellectual-property laws, they are also faced with social, political and religious sensitivities in the countries which they operate in and market to.
- That still leaves room for humor, provided the message is clear and not offensive. Analysts who can pull it off might make themselves stand out in the minds of clients.

Introduction

Previous chapters examined the importance of publishing research to clients fairly, and focused on principles of publishing securities research, especially with regard to common securities regulations.

The following thoughts do not necessarily concern securities regulations, but include some common-sense suggestions as to how to write for the reader, with specific reference to the securities industry. Some of the content, especially the comments on using the right words, may be more useful for non-native English speakers.

Getting the message across

Analysts need to stand out from the crowd, given the intense competition to win business from clients. In addition to getting a product to market on time and getting the market to know of the product, another major rule of commerce—from ancient trading posts along the Silk Road to Web sites on the Internet—is to have the most eye-catching and easily accessible items on display. An analyst's published research has to be presented in such a way as to grab the reader's attention as quickly as possible. This is not just beneficial to the analyst, but it helps the reader too. Readers (both internal sales/traders and external clients) need to be able to see instantly what the topic is, what the analyst's message or story is, and what his conclusions are.

Given the commercial aims of sell-side analysts, what they write should ideally have an investment conclusion, especially one that is immediately actionable, provided they are licensed to give such investment advice. This is one factor that differentiates securities-research analysts from academic analysts or newspaper reporters (see the example in Chapter 1 on media commentators). These conclusions should be upfront and highly visible in a report. Thus, if readers take nothing else away from a report, at least they will have the analyst's conclusions and actionable recommendation.

There's no harm in repetition, to reinforce the message. As the old PR/ marketing adage goes: "Tell your readers what you're going to tell them; tell them; then tell them what you told them." This forms the traditional structure of more or less any presentation or report (introduction, details and conclusion), and can be just as applicable for securities research reports. I trust I have repeated myself enough in this book that readers can't fail to have picked up on the key messages.

Headlines and covers

The headline should ideally be able to tell the whole story in one snapshot. It should at least immediately grab the readers' attention by, for example, showing how the news or analysis affects the analyst's views or recommendations on his covered security or sector. Analysts really should make apparent the extent to which the news is a surprise; that is, the extent to which it had already been factored into their estimates or into the stock's price by the market. For example, "Disappointing first-half result prompts earnings downgrade" may seem hackneyed, but it is still much more meaningful than just "First-half results". Detailed comparisons of the analyst's views with those of the consensus can then be given in the body of the report.

Some analysts use film, book or song titles effectively as catchy titles for their research, and I would refer readers to the section on copyright and plagiarism in Chapter 1 for an explanation as to why such use would not normally infringe copyright rules. If the analyst or editor can come up with a snappy or witty title, then all well and good. I remember one clever title that Andrew Leeming came up with for one of his Asian banking reports when we were both at ING Barings: "Shift Happens". This was at a time when there was widespread talk of a "paradigm shift" in global productivity. However, care is needed with humor, given the potential for misunderstanding. Similarly, care must be taken with the use of photos, cartoons and other images, as the following example illustrates.

EXAMPLE

Standards of taste

Summary: The *Financial Times* reported on January 15, 2005, that Bank of America's investment bank had fired AS as head of high-yield research for superimposing his head onto the body of a woman to illustrate the cover of a research report on the lodging industry. His colleague JK was also fired. The company did not comment on the matter and neither AS nor JK could be reached for comment.

Conclusion: The *FT* seemed to imply that the dismissals may have been part of Wall Street's efforts to clean up its "locker room" image. Whether this was the real reason or whether there were other underlying issues is not clear. AS was known for his comic covers, and some clients said they would miss him. Evidently his style did have some appeal. Nevertheless, the case helps to demonstrate that there's a thin line, or at least a gray area, between what one person might deem to be in good taste and what someone else might think is bad taste.

I trust the use of the Alex cartoons in this book is acceptable to readers. They bring a little light relief to otherwise serious subjects. Messrs. Peattie and Taylor, the creators of the cartoons, have kindly given me permission to include the cartoons.

The title is the first, and sometimes the only, thing readers see as they scroll down the screen to see the morning's offerings from brokers. I've seen examples of headlines showing "XYZ Ltd. (unrated) does such and such", only to find in the body of the text that XYZ is a subsidiary of one of the analyst's rated companies, and that its actions have had a direct impact on his view for that rated company. This should be drawn out in the title. In the body of the text, analysts can then give details of the news and explain why they have come to their conclusions.

Note: commentaries on unrated companies may happen to be of interest to sales and readers in their own right, although they would presumably not provide sufficient information for clients to make investment decisions (otherwise such commentary would constitute new "research"—see

Chapters 1 and 4). However, wherever possible analysts should try to make a connection between the unrated company and their rated companies (which may be, say, a competitor or parent) or at least the sector generally. As a matter of course, analysts should identify the listing and coverage status of companies they feature, although this may not be relevant for passing references.

Bullets, key points and executive summaries

Bullets and executive summaries may be the only pages that some readers read, or the only pages that readers pass on to their colleagues or stock-selection committees. It should be apparent upfront why the analyst is writing the report now. What event has happened to prompt the publication? And what effect does the analyst think the news will have on his covered company's earnings estimates and valuations?

Since securities analysts are in the valuation business, they should as a matter of course include in the bullets and executive summary what valuation their target price is based on, and why they think it's appropriate or achievable within the stated time-frame.

For changes of recommendation and target price especially, they should say what their old view was, what element of the valuation has changed (for example, the discount rate assumed, their estimates, the multiple or year of valuation) and why they think their new valuation/ multiple is more appropriate/achievable. Comparisons to the stock's historic valuations or to peers, for example, would add further support.

Analysts should also spare a line or two to summarize the main risks they see to their investment case, with details given in the text. The higher the upside potential afforded by their target price, the more clients would expect to read about associated risks.

Publishing and distribution

The principle of treating all clients fairly by making research available to them all simultaneously (or at least to all clients within the specified class or category of clients, provided the distribution policy has been disclosed to all clients) has been discussed at length in Chapter 1.

Burying new research, such as multiple changes of recommendations, in the middle of a published report, such as a sector or market compilation, might satisfy in principle regulators' requirements to make new research available to all clients simultaneously. However, it may not be the best marketing and distribution practice, since many readers might miss the individual changes. Readers not only include clients, but also database managers, both internal and external, who monitor analysts' recommendations.

It may therefore be prudent not only to publish the whole compilation report as one item, but also to separate out individual reports by company, showing the individual recommendation changes. This may be especially relevant for electronic versions of large compilation reports, which take time to download.

Writing the text

In this book, I have probably breached all of George Orwell's basic rules for writing, but more than half a century after they were first written they still provide a good set of examples for all English-language writers to follow. In my view, they could apply as well to writers of securities research as they do to novelists.

EXAMPLE

Writing rules

Firstly, here are George Orwell's rules for writing:

- Never use a metaphor, simile or other figure of speech which you are used to seeing in print.
- Never use a long word where a short one will do.
- If it is possible to cut out a word, always cut it out.
- Never use the passive where you can use the active.
- Never use a foreign phrase, a scientific word or a jargon if you can think of an everyday English equivalent.
- Break any of these rules sooner than say anything outright barbarous.

Here are some alternative rules for writers penned by the late William Safire, author and political columnist for the *New York Times*:

- Remember to never split an infinitive.
- The passive voice should never be used.
- Do not put statements in the negative form.
- Verbs has to agree with their subjects.
- Proofread carefully to see if you words out.
- And don't start a sentence with a conjunction.
- Don't overuse exclamation marks!!
- Also, avoid awkward or affected alliteration.
- Take the bull by the hand and avoid mixing metaphors.
- Last but not least, avoid clichés like the plague; seek viable alternatives.

Use the right word

The choice of words used gives the reader an impression of how the analyst thinks. It may be true that equity or credit analysis is part science and part art, but clients would probably be more easily convinced if it at least appears that the analyst has used scientific and measurable methods to reach his/her conclusion.

The late Nico Colchester saw the world in terms of crunchiness and sogginess. In his famous editorial for the *Economist* in 1988, he described crunchy systems as being "those in which small changes have big effects leaving those affected by them in no doubt whether they are up or down, rich or broke, winning or losing, dead or alive", whereas sogginess is "comfortable uncertainty". He concluded: "A crunchy policy is not necessarily right, only more certain than a soggy one to deliver the results that it deserves. Run your country, or your company, or your life as you think fit. But whatever you decide, keep things crunchy."

Following Colchester's advice, in the following paragraphs I have applied this distinction to the context of an analyst's choice of words, with "crunchy" signifying "measurable and decisive", and "soggy" signifying "doubtful and intangible".

The word "will": It is an offense, at least under U.S. securities regulations, to use promissory language. When using the word "will", as in "something will happen", analysts should distinguish whether the comment is attributable to: a) the company or a third party; b) their own views or analyses, using "crunchy" words with supporting evidence; or c) necessity, habit, natural consequence or likelihood.

EXAMPLE

Vocabulary for attributing forward-looking comments (using *"will"*)

A third party: For example, "management confirms/thinks/says/indicates/suggests/has planned/agreed/decided/scheduled"; or "according to the company/press reports/consensus estimates (including the name of the data-provider)/industry sources" and so on.

The analyst's own view or analysis using crunchy words: For example, "I think/analyze/calculate/gauge/measure/appraise/conclude/deduce/expect/anticipate/estimate/forecast/reason/reckon/evaluate/assess/confirm/rate/recommend/consider/ascertain"; or "in my view/opinion, by my analysis/calculation/investigation" and so on.

Vocabulary for attributing forward-looking comments (using "*will*")—*cont'd*

Necessity, habit, natural consequence or likelihood: For example, "necessarily, by necessity, by law, according to regulations, under the terms of the agreement/contract, as required by court order, no doubt, undoubtedly, seemingly, arguably, invariably, inevitably, presumably, effectively, naturally, surely, normally, probably, perhaps, likely". Alternatively, analysts can use words such as "would, could, should, might, may, can, must, needs to, has to, tends to", depending on the meaning desired.

Notes: Analysts do not necessarily need to disclose industry sources such as suppliers, customers and competitors in their published reports, but they should bear in mind that they may be called upon by a regulator or a court to substantiate their comments or claims. If the source is from within the company being discussed, it should be seen to be an official source; otherwise, the analyst might risk charges of trading on inside information.

Similarly, qualifying words such as "allegedly", "evidently" and "apparently" may be useful, but analysts should still be satisfied that they can provide supporting evidence if ever required.

For sensitive topics, especially prospective mergers or acquisitions, qualifying phrases such as "in our view" and "we think" are not enough; analysts need to explain what they base their views on (to avoid the appearance of impropriety). The NYSE specifically states: "Qualifying comparative claims with phrases such as 'we believe' or 'to the best of our knowledge' will not release the firm from its responsibility of being able to substantiate the underlying claim." (See Chapter 1, especially the case study on Jeffrey Putterman.)

Certain disclaimers are also useful for analysts to make clear that they are not implying that a certain outcome is definite. For example:

- Past performance is no guarantee of future performance.
- The prices of stocks can go down as well as up.

As discussed in Chapter 1, disclosing where their information comes from protects analysts from possible charges of spreading rumors to manipulate prices (if the information turns out to be false), trading on inside information (if the information turns out to be true) or defamation/ libel (if the accuracy of the statement can be challenged). Analysts also help their readers in risk-weighing that information when they make their investment decisions.

The words "relatively" or "comparatively": These words are useful, especially when it comes to references to stocks being cheap or expensive (they are only cheap or expensive compared with, for example, other stocks or their own history—in absolute terms they can still halve or double in price again). These words may also help provide some defense when criticizing management, for example. As mentioned in Chapter 1, there's usually a way of criticizing management constructively but, as a last resort, it would be easier to justify that management is, for example, relatively inept in some specific aspect(s), as opposed to being absolutely inept.

Measurements and direction/degree of movement

The direction and degree of movement (whether in terms of absolute or relative changes in actual or estimated sales, earnings or valuations) are common themes in analysts' work.

Identifying units and benchmarks: An analyst needs to make clear what is being measured and what benchmark any rate of change is being measured against. For example, the statement "The company's results rose by 20 percent" is meaningless. An analyst would need to make clear:

- what the results relate to (for example, sales, earnings before tax, net earnings as absolute results or perhaps as margins);
- the period to which they relate (for example, the month of December, the quarter/half/year ending December); and
- the period with which the results are being compared (for example, month-on-month, year-on-year).

Incidentally, if the percentage change in net earnings does not correlate to the percentage change on a per-share basis, the analyst would need to clarify what has happened to the number of shares during the year to explain the difference.

Percentage movements: I would encourage analysts to describe movements and directions in fraction or percentage terms rather than absolute terms. Words like "a quarter" or "25 percent" are more meaningful and easier for the readers or audience to remember than absolute numbers like 16,781,250 compared with 13,425,000, whatever the units being compared. The absolute numbers can be recorded in tables.

Analysts should take care to distinguish between percentage movements and percentage-point movements. For example, a move from 2 percent to 3 percent is either a 50 percent move or a one-percentage-point move. And what a difference a preposition makes—"falling 1 percent" is different from "falling to 1 percent".

When analysts talk about a percentage change (to net earnings numbers, for example), they should make clear whether the change represents earnings growth/decline from the previous period's numbers, or whether it perhaps represents a change in forecasts from the analyst's previously held forecasts.

Value and volume: If sales are being measured, then the analyst would need to make clear whether the numbers given are on a value or volume basis. If on a value basis, then it must be clear which currency is being used. Readers in the U.S. might assume that $ refers to U.S. dollars, whereas Asia Pacific readers might be thinking in terms of Hong Kong, Singapore, Australian, New Zealand or New Taiwan dollars.

Confusion may arise where, for example, an American or global depositary receipt is quoted in U.S. dollars, but earnings are reported in a different local currency. Similarly, some Singapore-listed companies that aren't national companies are quoted in U.S. dollars, and Chinese "H" shares are quoted in Hong Kong dollars, although earnings are generally reported in *renminbi* (RMB).

Rates and yields: When discussing rates and yields, it should be clear what the analyst is talking about—interest rates, exchange rates, dividend yields, passenger yields and so on. I often see analysts write that bonds have risen or fallen, without making clear that it is the yields they are talking about, not their prices.

Premiums and discounts: Similarly, when an analyst is talking about spreads or a security's premium or discount, it should be clear what the difference relates to. The statement "The stock's discount is 30 percent" is meaningless on its own. Premiums and discounts could, for example, represent the difference between the security's current price or valuation and that of:

- some other valuation of the security (say net asset value or discounted cash flow);
- other instruments or classes of shares of the same company (A shares, H shares, GDRs);
- benchmarks or comparable peers in the sector or market; or
- the security's own historical price or valuations.

As usual, the analyst should also make clear whose estimates any valuations, including those of any comparables used, are based on.

Choice of vocabulary: To avoid repetition, a variety of words to describe different changes may also be useful, as listed in the box below. Again, the

---

EXAMPLE

Vocabulary for describing movement and performance

Action (transitive/intransitive): change, revise, amend, tweak, raise, increase, upgrade, lift, climb, rise, inflate, improve, expand, enlarge,

---

Vocabulary for describing movement and performance—*cont'd*

add, gain, balloon, surge, blow out, escalate, accelerate, advance, appreciate, strengthen, creep up, speed up, race, spiral, trend, lower, decrease, reduce, downgrade, erode, dilute, slow down, recede, decelerate, deteriorate, depreciate, weaken, deflate, decline, diminish, discount, contract, subside, subtract, collapse, slip, slide, shrink, sink, fall, settle, pare, trim, shave, cut, prune.

Degree: very, greatly, considerably, extremely, excessively, increasingly, significantly, substantially, meaningfully, noticeably, materially, marginally, moderately, slightly, lightly, partially, fairly, reasonably, relatively, comparably, rather, quite, approximately, roughly, especially, incrementally, immediately, quickly, slowly, gradually, decreasingly, at a fast/slow clip/pace/rate, to an extent/degree.

---

above list may be more useful for analysts whose mother tongue is a language other than English.

Words to avoid or use carefully

Soggy words such as "feel", "believe", "bet", "gamble", "guess", "suppose", "speculate", "conjecture" and "suspect" are all good English words. When used properly they can be effective. However, so often the impression given is that the analyst is merely basing his views on hunches (or perhaps even inside information) rather than on solid facts and analysis.

Care should be taken with words such as "certainty" (there's no such thing, according to Benjamin Franklin, except for death and taxes), "actually", "in fact" and "obviously" (which sounds condescending; in any case, nothing is ever obvious in this business).

Sometimes words such as "concerns", "doubts", "worries", "expectation" or "anticipation" represent more accurately the market's feelings than the overused word "rumor". As we saw in Chapter 1, "rumor" could be a warning flag to a regulator. Analysts should always quote the source of unconfirmed reports, and give the respective parties a chance to represent themselves.

As George Orwell urges, writers should avoid the passive voice ("it is expected/estimated" and so on). Apart from being required under various securities regulations, readers want to know whose forecasts are being used—the fact that they are reading a certain analyst's research presumably means that they are interested in that analyst's views. If a client is taking the time to read an individual analyst's views, then the client may well value that view more than that of the consensus. If so, the analyst who uses the passive voice will have missed an opportunity, since the client would not necessarily know whose view is being expressed.

Bullshit Bingo: Of course, no discussion on using words judiciously would be complete without a comment on "Bullshit Bingo", the game played by bored professionals who count the number of times a presenter at a meeting uses business/executive jargon or clichés. The original source seems to be anonymous, and it seems to be an extension of "Buzzword Bingo", but hats off to whoever first coined these two terms anyway. Acknowledgments also to whoever first coined the words and phrases that make up this ever-evolving list!

EXAMPLE

Bullshit Bingo (vocabulary and phrases)

Examples: paradigm shift, strategic fit, technology platform, mind-set/mindshare, face time, client interface, integrated business plans/solutions, legacy systems, executive-empowerment, skills-set, multi-tasking, multi-user functionality, task-oriented, hard-wired, goal/objective-oriented, results-driven, client-focused, proactive, best in class, core competencies, low-hanging fruit, blue-sky thinking, think outside the box, leverage the franchise, leverage synergies, gain traction, add granularity, drill down, execute on key deliverables, get up to speed, hit the ground running, level the playing field, shift the goal posts, give someone a heads-up, take off-line, own the space, take ownership of, get someone's buy-in, reach out to someone, cascade information, team with someone, team player, take one for the team, step up to the plate, bring to the party, take risk off the table, circle the wagons, raise the bar, touch base, pass the baton/ball, keep your eye on the ball, ballpark figure, game plan, knowledge base/management/worker, bandwidth, workaround, reverse engineering, key takeaways, ahead of the game/pack, on the same page, behind the curve, out of the loop, where the rubber meets the road, at the coal face, in the trenches, 24/7. . . .

EXAMPLE

Clarity of communication

Summary: The Plain English Campaign awards its Golden Bull Awards annually. Its Web site, www.plainenglish.co.uk, provides hilarious reading. Just hope the campaigners don't find anything I've written that deserves a prize.

Details: One winner for 2007 was Virgin Trains, which answered a customer's query as to why its Web site did not include a particular ticket price with: "Moving forwards, we as Virgin Trains are looking to take ownership of the flow in question to apply our pricing structure, thus resulting in this journey search appearing in the new category-matrix format."

Another winner was Nestlé, which gave the following explanation for one of its problems: "'Green sauces' are an important product group for Buitoni Pesto Basilico. Their quality and flavor profile are enhanced by the basil used in production. However, Buitoni faced sensory profile reproducibility problems due to heterogeneous raw material, challenging the production of uniform quality." (Note though that Nestlé must have been doing something right because they came first in the "Food Producers" category of Institutional Investors' Best European Investor Relations ranking for 2008.)

Jonathan Guthrie, writing in the *FT* issue of December 13, 2007, gives an example of a bank trying to explain to shareholders in an upbeat way that bad investment decisions had resulted in a US$10 billion write-down. The headline was: "UBS strengthens capital base and adjusts valuations". The bank explained that it had "revised key input parameters of the models that are used to estimate lifetime default . . . for subprime mortgage pools". Guthrie quipped that in layman's terms, this meant that Billy-Ray in Redneck, Florida, was no more likely to repay his home loan than to sell his assault rifle and take up *tai chi*.

On the same theme of trying to explain billions of dollars in subprime-related writedowns, Henny Sender reported in the weekend *FT* of December 22–23, 2007, that Morgan Stanley was reviewing the position of its chief risk officer, Tom Daula. According to senior executives, the incumbent was too late to sound the alarm about the dangers stemming from the bank's exposure to subprime-related trades, or had used language that was "too technical or obscure". On February 22, David Wighton reported in the *FT* that Daula was stepping down, but added that Mr. Daula's supporters claimed that his repeated warnings were ignored.

Clarity of communication—*cont'd*

Conclusions: From these latter two *FT* stories I wonder if managements think it's not okay for employees to use obscure language when dealing with the board but that it is okay to use obscure language when dealing with shareholders?

In any case, from our perspective, analysts need to be suspicious of a company's motives if they can't immediately understand what the representative is saying (and I would refer back to the discussion on corporate governance in Chapter 2). They also need to make sure they communicate clearly themselves when writing research reports for clients, otherwise they might find themselves as winners in the next Global Bull Awards, or worse still, losing their clients' business.

Aside: I always chuckle to myself whenever I see analysts or the press using euphemisms like "near-prime" as a substitute for "subprime", "high-yield" for "junk", or "standstill" for "default". Who are we all kidding?

Here's another cartoon in the same vein as the Bullshit Bingo cartoon above, but it also seems quite appropriate following a discussion on plain English. I just hope my American friends and ex-colleagues won't mind another giggle at their expense.

Clarity, consistency, conformity and continuity

Analysts should remember that dedicated readers may understand industry jargon, abbreviations and acronyms, but it will be difficult for these analysts to expand their readership to a wider audience, including strategists and generalists, unless their writing is clear and self-explanatory. George Orwell's rules again hold true.

Be consistent or explain inconsistencies

Sometimes strategists or traders may make comments that seem to be at odds with the analyst's formal recommendation. Similarly, some forecasts may be based on different economic assumptions from those used by the economists. Strategists and analysts need to draw any apparent inconsistencies to their readers' attention to avoid any possible confusion, as discussed in Chapter 1.

Analysts' valuations in reports should be priced on the same date for consistency's sake and for ease of comparison (unless they're including in, say, a compilation report or already-published research, which need not be re-priced as long as the original publishing date is clearly shown). However, if they have made any significant changes to their investment view since the pricing date or since the date of the published research, they should make this clear to readers (in the form of asterisked footnotes, for example).

Editorial departments and style guides

Analysts in some research departments are required by company policy to follow a uniform editorial style. Such an approach provides consistency and helps in branding. However, whether or not the analyst follows a style guide, the most important thing is that the message is clear and not open to misinterpretation.

Many large research departments devote editorial resources to ensure that the analyst's language is clear, and that arguments are well structured and well presented. Editorial teams help to ensure not only that recommendations and views are consistent within each product and across all products, or that inconsistencies are explained, but also that the right amount of research is distributed to clients in the right way at the right time.

The importance of grammar and punctuation should not be underestimated. In her self-proclaimed zero-tolerance guide to punctuation entitled *Eats, Shoots & Leaves* (Profile Books, 2003), Lynne Truss gives many examples to demonstrate how meaning can be lost or changed by careless use of punctuation. She quotes a writer who tells us that punctuation marks are the traffic signals of language: they tell us to slow down, notice this, take a detour and stop. One example the author gives illustrates the point how meaning can be totally reversed with misuse of punctuation:

A woman, without her man, is nothing.

A woman: without her, man is nothing.

Then of course, there are apologists who defend the use of bad spelling, as long as the meaning is clear; as succinctly put in the text below, which circulated around the Internet in September 2003. The original source, as far as I can tell from a search of the Internet, is still unknown, but I acknowledge whoever first penned it.

"Aoccdrnig to a rscheearch at an Elingsh uinervtisy, it deosn't mttaer in waht oredr the ltteers in a wrod are, the olny iprmoetnt tihng is taht frist and lsat ltteer is at the rghit pclae. The rset can be a toatl mses and you can sitll raed it wouthit porbelm. Tihs is bcuseae we do not raed ervey lteter by itslef but the wrod as a wlohe."

Translations into different languages

The language in which a report is published should not really matter from a regulatory perspective.

Take, for example, a situation in which a report is published in a language which the majority of clients may not speak. This is surely not a regulatory problem, but merely a business problem: either the broker helps the clients by translating it for them, or clients help themselves by either learning the language or hiring their own translators.

One caveat would be that if the research report is to be distributed into a market such as the U.S., where there is a requirement that research reports are first approved by a supervisory analyst, then the approved version should be published first, or at least simultaneously with any translations.

The following example, though not securities-specific, demonstrates the risks of mistranslations.

EXAMPLE

Mistranslations

Summary: The *Wall Street Journal* of May 12, 2005, recounts the confusion in the global currency markets on May 11 caused by the mistranslation of an article in China News Service on the potential revaluation of the Chinese *yuan*.

Mistranslations—*cont'd*

Details: Whereas the original version apparently expressed views as to how an appreciation of the Chinese currency would play out, a translation in the People's Daily Online suggested that China had already decided to revalue the *yuan* by 1.26 percent within a month and 6.03 percent in 12 months (figures which turned out to be only the quoted forward market rates).

The translation soon got picked up and distributed by Bloomberg and Reuters, and resulted in the trading of an estimated US$2 billion within a few minutes, according to Claudio Piron, Asia currency strategist for J.P. Morgan.

The *People's Daily* realized the mistake, withdrew the article and published an apology.

Conclusion: While this is not specifically a securities issue, at least three principles are at play from our perspective: i) the need to ensure translations are accurate; ii) the appropriate attribution of sources; and iii) the acknowledgment of responsibility and the correcting of errors (see below).

Aside: The *SCMP* published a lovely story on December 13, 2008. The editors of the *Max Planck Institute Journal* were looking for some Chinese characters to use on the front cover of their next publication. A classical Chinese poem would be nice, they thought. What they got, and what they published, without realizing it, was an advert for "lusty, pretty-as-jade housewives with hot bodies to work as nightclub hostesses". Wonder how many replies they got, and who did the interviewing.

Publishing independent yet integrated reports

Reports and notes should be as stand-alone/independent as possible. In other words, a reader should be able to read the report without necessarily having prior knowledge of the subject matter.

However, an analyst's work may be part of a wider research effort from the brokerage firm. In order to avoid potential for confusion on the part of the reader, views therefore should still be consistent across the products, or any apparent inconsistencies should be explained.

It would help readers always to remind them what the relationship may be between group companies (they change frequently anyway) and/or what contribution each has made to the analyst's estimate of the parent's earnings or net asset value. If a company has changed its name, analysts should remind readers what the old name was or which old companies now comprise the new company.

Analysts should be encouraged to make cross-references to other research reports that they or their colleagues may have written on the same company or sector, which may be of interest to the firm's readers. They should give their readers a choice by flagging their colleagues' recommendations, including those for other types of securities or financial instruments recommended by the firm. If you don't give your clients what they want, someone else will.

Sensitivity to politics and religion

Securities-research analysts will find that, in practice, the concept of "free speech" is an elusive ideal. We have already discussed at length what analysts can and cannot say within the parameters of best practice and securities regulations. Regard also needs to be given to socio-political sensitivities and local laws and customs.

EXAMPLE

Sensitivity to politics and religion

Summary (politics): The *Shanghai Daily* reported on September 1, 2005, that a Fudan University professor had sued Deloitte Touche Tohmatsu for allegedly violating China's anti-secession law by listing China and Taiwan as separate countries. Deloitte consequently made efforts to redress the situation, and changed the country list of its simplified-character Chinese site to indicate countries and "regions".

There have also been examples in China of reporters and commentators being charged with espionage or for divulging "state secrets".

Summary (religion): The sensitivity in respect to religious beliefs has been well demonstrated by the global furor resulting from the publishing by the Danish newspaper *Jyllands-Posten* on September 30, 2005, of cartoons depicting the prophet Muhammad in a manner that proved to be insulting to large numbers of the Muslim community. Two years later the issue flared up again when a Swedish paper, *Nerikes Allehanda*, printed a cartoon showing the head of the prophet on the body of a dog. Then in mid-February 2008 there was rioting in the streets of Denmark and elsewhere (or, as the *New York Post* wittily put it, "Something's rioting in the state of Denmark"), after a plot to assassinate one of the original cartoonists led to reprints of the cartoons by national newspapers.

Lest any Christian readers get on their high horse over the use of language, I would draw their attention to Ireland's blasphemy laws, which were put in force in January 2010, and under which blasphemers can be fined up to €25,000.

Sensitivity to politics and religion—*cont'd*

The debate pits defenders of free speech against those who feel the press should have more of a moral responsibility not to publish anything that may be deemed insulting or blasphemous.

Conclusion: Securities publishers, of course, have different restrictions and agendas. There are securities regulations to consider (for example, U.S. regulations against communications that are inflammatory or in bad taste). There are also commercial consequences to consider; that is, of insulting potential investors who can just take their business elsewhere. Ultimately, research analysts should provide unbiased, analytical and intellectually rigorous evaluations of companies, without resorting to emotional appeal.

On a specific point of interest, analysts should not forget to source any maps they use. With disputed boundaries in both China and India, for example, an analyst might as well not provoke a potentially hostile reaction from authorities by representing any boundaries shown as their own assumptions.

Correcting errors

Analysts should never knowingly publish information that is wrong or misleading. This might range from information that may be out-of-date to views that may be exaggerated and unwarranted. Extreme cases may involve copyright and plagiarism, which we covered separately in Chapter 1. The issue of conflicts of interest and analysts embellishing their views on securities was also covered separately, in Chapter 3.

Under more normal circumstances, reports containing errors may be published accidentally. In the world of publishing securities research there is inevitably a trade-off between quality and speed to market, and thus the incidence of errors may be higher than in some other areas of publishing. There would seem to me to be five courses of action that can be taken in such circumstances, depending on how serious the errors are and considering the readers' interests and needs.

EXAMPLE

Courses of corrective action:

- Do nothing.
- Repost only the electronic version of the report, merely for the record and for future retrieval.

Courses of corrective action:—*cont'd*

- Repost the electronic version of the report, flagging it as "Revised".
- Repost the electronic version of the report and reprint/redistribute any hard copy, with a factual erratum or retraction message specifying what the errors are.
- Republish as per the previous option, and issue a public apology.

Materiality of the error

My underlying principle is that if the error is material and would affect an investor's decision to buy or sell, or not to buy or sell, then the publisher should at least flag the change as "Revised", if not issue an erratum notice. Such instances could include wrong/inconsistent investment recommendations, or material corrections to target prices, valuations and estimates.

In situations where there might be a complaint from a third party (for example, a company complaining about information published about it that is factually incorrect), the publisher should really be seen to be doing everything reasonable to amend the situation.

In any rare situation where the publisher agrees that the third party might have justifiable grounds to take legal action, the former should be seen to be taking all reasonable steps to rectify the situation and to alert readers. Thus, in addition to flagging the revised version, one could issue a retraction or publish an erratum message. An erratum message, with a factual description of the error, would normally suffice. However, on extreme occasions and in certain cultures, a public apology may be required, and no doubt the broker's lawyers would advise in such situations.

Let's look at some examples of publishing errors. The first one evidently involves the accidental publishing of an out-of-date news story. The consequences, although brief in terms of time, were serious in terms of financial loss.

EXAMPLE

Publishing of out-of-date story

Summary: In the space of an hour or so on September 8, 2008, the share price of United Airlines plunged from US$12 down to nearly US$3

Publishing of out-of-date story—*cont'd*

(representing US$1 billion in total), before shooting back to about US$11.00. What happened?

Details: As reported by the *New York Times*, a link to a *Chicago Tribune* article headlined "United Airlines Files for Bankruptcy" appeared in the "Most Viewed" box in the *Sun-Sentinel*, and was automatically picked up by Google. Apparently, someone from a financial information company searched on Google for recent bankruptcy stories, found the article, and published a summary of it on Bloomberg. This led to panic-selling of the shares of UAL by the market. The trouble was that the source *Chicago Tribune* article had been published six years earlier in 2002.

Conclusions: Publishing teams, including those working in securities research, need to take care that they do not publish news and views that are out-of-date.

    As a complete technophobe myself, this vindicates my sense that humans are relying too much on computers. The author Arthur C. Clarke and film director Stanley Kubrick highlighted the potential problem decades ago, in the film *2001: A Space Odyssey*, in which the rogue computer HAL 9000 mutinies against the crew of the spaceship Discovery.

Aside: Talking of space ships and news mix-ups, what about the two newspapers in Bangladesh, which had to issue an apology to their readers in September 2009 for passing on a story from the satirical U.S. Web site the *Onion* on the assumption that it was true. The *Onion* had reported that Neil Armstrong had confirmed that the Apollo 11 moon landing was an "elaborate hoax" and "one giant lie" for mankind. Notwithstanding that some conspiracy theorists really do think the landing was fake, the original story that Armstrong had confirmed this was merely a spoof.

    The next example directly relates to securities research, and concerns the sensitivities that analysts face when publishing research.

EXAMPLE

Retractions

Summary: In January 2004, an analyst at Citigroup Smith Barney retracted statements he had made in a research report about the

Retractions—*cont'd*

strength of Sodexho's balance sheet, apparently under pressure from Sodexho. According to the *Asian Wall Street Journal*, Sodexho "made a thinly veiled lawsuit threat against Citigroup".

Comment: Given that the retraction came two days after a fine was imposed by the French courts on Morgan Stanley for allegedly biased research against LVMH, the *AWSJ* queried whether European analysts at least would steer clear of making critical calls on companies for fear of being sued. (Incidentally, note that on June 30, 2006, as reported in the *Financial Times* on July 1, 2006, the French Court of Appeal overturned the lower court finding that Morgan Stanley's research was biased, although it upheld findings that MS did not disclose properly its corporate relationships. For further details, see the case study in Chapter 3.)

Conclusion: Analysts need to take care when publishing their views. They need to be able to substantiate any criticisms of the companies they cover, and may be called on to make public apologies or retractions for any factual errors made or perhaps even for any embarrassment caused.

The following case is also worth looking at since it straddles the issuing of apologies and political sensitivities, as well as internal review processes.

EXAMPLE

Retractions

Summary: The following apology from Ernst & Young, dated May 12, 2006, was widely reported in the press: "The NPL [non-performing loans] report did not go through our normal internal review and approval process before it was released to the public and, as it contains errors, we are withdrawing the report. We sincerely regret any misleading views that the report conveyed."

Comment: In his Monitor column in the *South China Morning Post* on May 16, Jake van der Kamp suggests that the author of the report was a victim of political sensitivity. The published apology talked of "errors"

Retractions—*cont'd*

and "misleading views", whereas the US$911 billion identified in the report as being the non-performing loan exposure for China's banks was clearly only a "potential future amount".

And the Lex column in the *Financial Times* that same day asks: "Has Ernst & Young forgotten the importance of being independent?" The *FT* raises the point that the retraction, ahead of the Bank of China listing, would please Beijing, but adds that suspicions that voices have been stifled would ultimately be detrimental to China itself.

Conclusion: Whatever the NPL figure really was, markets in any case are all about confidence. In extreme cases, a company that might otherwise have survived can be pushed over the edge into bankruptcy by overly or unduly negative press (see the references in Chapters 1 and 2 to Bear Stearns, Lehman Brothers and HBOS, and the suspicions aimed at hedge funds and their short-selling practices). Irrespective of any impact on a company's share price as a result of reduced investor confidence, the company's earnings and relationships with customers and suppliers may be affected to extent that may not otherwise have been the case. It is natural for the subject of the negative press to be defensive in such situations.

Nevertheless, analysts and consultants have a duty to their clients to give them their independent views, provided these views are based on good, sound facts and analysis. In some markets where facts may be relatively difficult to determine (perhaps due in part to the size of the market and level of transparency) and where political sensitivity may be high, analysts may need to take extra care and may need to make extra qualifications when publishing their conclusions. And they would be wise to secure the full backing of their employer by ensuring that all internal-review systems and approval processes have been adhered to.

Note that when an investment opinion is hold or neutral, I'd see even less reason to flag revisions unless the change might be sufficient to persuade some clients to consider actively buying/overweighting or selling/underweighting instead. My reasoning would be that if the analyst is not actively recommending clients to make an investment, they would have less opportunity to lose money on that investment. They could complain, of course, about missing an opportunity if the additional information was material enough to make them consider making an active investment, which makes it important for the publisher to determine if the change is material.

If there are just small typographical errors (typos), embarrassing spelling mistakes, or some additional or revised details regarding, say, divisional or quarterly results (which are sufficiently minor not to affect the investor's overall investment decision), the publisher might consider simply reposting the revised electronic version of the publication for the record, without drawing readers' attention to the fact.

It all boils down to a matter of judgment. Publishers and research supervisors should ask: "Would investors be misled, prejudiced or otherwise disadvantaged, and could the brokerage firm or the analyst be sued, either by the investors or by the subject of the report?" Mistakes happen, but appropriate handling of the situation goes a long way to mitigate these mistakes.

Helping the reader

Clients have plenty to read on a daily basis, and unless the publisher thinks it really is important for them to re-read something, they should probably be left alone to get on and read new material without having to re-read old material. By constantly flagging revisions, a publisher risks cheapening the currency of the product; investors will get tired of so many revisions and not re-read any of them. By determining for clients which revisions are important, publishers are, in effect, helping them.

In my view, a balance has to be drawn between encouraging the client to re-read all revised items by flagging revisions, and leaving the client to get on with life by not flagging all of them. Of course, the publisher should not risk being accused of trying to pull the wool over investors' eyes by not flagging something that could be deemed material; so if there's any doubt as to the materiality of a change, the prudent course would be to flag the change.

Of course, the best practice is not to publish any errors to start with, and for all claims, views and recommendations to be suitably sourced and supported. And on that note, I will end by apologizing in advance for any errors or oversights contained in this book.

Index